Loving Nature

Loving Nature

Ecological Integrity and Christian Responsibility

James A. Nash

ABINGDON PRESS
Nashville
in cooperation with
THE CHURCHES' CENTER FOR THEOLOGY
AND PUBLIC POLICY
Washington, D.C.

LOVING NATURE:
ECOLOGICAL INTEGRITY AND CHRISTIAN RESPONSIBILITY

Library of Congress Cataloging-in-Publication Data

Nash, James A., 1938–
    Loving nature: ecological integrity and Christian responsibility
/James A. Nash.
        p.   cm.—(Churches' Center for Theology and Public Policy)
    Includes bibliographical references and index.
    ISBN 0-687-22824-7 (pbk.: alk. paper)
    1. Human ecology—Religious aspects—Christianity. I. Title.
II. Series: Publications of the Churches' Center for Theology and
Public Policy.
BT695.5.N37   1991
241'.691—dc20   91-14240
                                                                              CIP

96 97 98 99 00 01 02—10 9 8 7 6 5

MANUFACTURED IN THE UNITED STATES OF AMERICA

PREFACE

No book really emerges in splendid isolation, despite the necessary withdrawal for research and writing. It is a product of human interdependence, reflecting even when reshaping the contributions of countless others, known and unknown, past and present. Consequently, I owe hefty debts of gratitude to many benefactors. A handful of them must be acknowledged here.

The influences of my prime mentors at Boston University, Professor Emeritus Paul K. Deats, Jr., and Dean Emeritus Walter G. Muelder, pervade these pages. The late Luther MacNair, civil libertarian and witness for environmental concern, often prodded me—with his inimitable gentility—to undertake this work; I remembered. Mark Burrows, Douglas Meeks, and Bruce Birch of Wesley Theological Seminary, Roy Enquist of Gettysburg Theological Seminary, Lisa Newton of Fairfield University, Freeman Sleeper of Roanoke College, Carol Franklin of the American Baptist Churches' Washington Office, and Ann Geer, Director of the Council of Churches of Greater Springfield, read one or more chapters. J. Philip Wogaman, Professor of Social Ethics at Wesley, and Larry Rasmussen, Reinhold Niebuhr Professor of Social Ethics at Union Theological Seminary, New York, read nearly the whole manuscript. In addition to reading portions of the manuscript, my former colleague and now my successor as Executive Director of the Massachusetts Council of Churches, Diane

Kessler, offered a patient ear and wise advice. The criticisms of these colleagues helped me avoid some errors and oversights; their kind and encouraging words served as a stimulant for continuing the task. Of course, I alone bear the blame for the remaining flaws—which, indeed, remain in some instances because I resisted good counsel.

Corrective insights came also from students in recent courses I taught on ecological ethics—in the Washington Theological Consortium, Wesley Seminary's Lay Resource Center, and the Christian Enrichment School in Fort Myers, Florida. Two Wesley students from my consortium course, Leo Maley III and Jenny Holmes, helped greatly by bombarding me with references for further reading. Paul Seaman, Office Manager for the Churches' Center for Theology and Public Policy, competently and patiently typed the drafts and abundant revisions. The Board of Directors of the Churches' Center generously gave me the time and the enthusiastic support for this project.

The editorial staff involved in this project at Abingdon Press—Rex Matthews, Ulrike Guthrie, and Donald Baker—have been uncommonly perceptive, sympathetic, and cooperative.

My wife, Mildred, read the whole manuscript twice and tried, gently and usually successfully, to save me from stylistic and substantive indiscretions. Even more important, she and our daughters, Noreen and Rebecca, have tolerated most of my peculiarities, often shared in my natural wanderings and wonderment, and honored my commitments even when they were skeptical. This book is justly and lovingly dedicated to them and a family friend.

This book is only an interim witness in an urgent and ongoing process of ethical extension. I hope, however, that in alliance with the corrective and creative initiatives of critics, it will be a contribution to the emergence of an adequate ecological ethic and ethos in our time.

—James A. Nash

CONTENTS

To Mill, Nor, Becca, and Marty

INTRODUCTION

S top complaining, boy. That orange cloud puts a roof over your head and food on your table!" I obeyed my Uncle Frank as we stood on the bluff overlooking the Monongahela River and the steel mills below. I stopped griping openly about the pollution, not only because I honored this particular elder, but also because he made an irrefutable point. I was about twelve years old and his statement made me acutely conscious of an ecology-economics dilemma.

Biography shapes ideology. On this assumption, a brief ecological autobiography of my youth can help uncover the motives, values, and biases embedded in this book. In my case, however, the autobiographical vignettes must be both ecological *and* socioeconomic, for the two are inseparable in my story (and probably in most other stories).

The steel mills in the lower Monongahela Valley of western Pennsylvania in the 1940s and 1950s were an environmental catastrophe. Thick, putrid clouds of pollutants bellowed almost continuously from the McKeesport Works across the river to our row houses on the bluffs in West Mifflin and Duquesne. "Dirt" and "soot" from the mills were ubiquitous; snow sometimes seemed to fall gray and always turned dirty early. Chemical particles from the clouds sometimes penetrated the paint on cars and rare wooden houses; we wondered about their effects on our lungs and burning eyes. The persistent noises, day and night, from the blast furnaces and the freight trains were often deafening. But the flames from the furnaces provided a safety feature: a bright, orange glow to nearly every night. The trees in the woods along the steep hillside to the river were stunted, but we did not know enough to ask why. The Monongahela River, a sewer for the mills, was biologically dead for maybe twenty miles, at least from Clairton to the point in Pittsburgh, and beyond that down the Ohio. Once, in fact, the discovery of a dead, undoubtedly alien catfish in a mill intake made the McKeesport *Daily News*. Even the sun was unusually hazy and the humidity abnormally high in summer: the industrial shroud apparently had created a microcosm of the greenhouse effect. The abundant slag—waste from the steelmaking process—was used to fill in several deep hollows and their natural habitats.

Yet, we were dependent on the "damned mills" (a typical term). They provided jobs for my grandfathers, my father, the fathers of nearly all my friends, all my uncles, most of my older cousins, and even me for a couple of summers. The operation of the mills meant the satisfaction of all our basic needs (and little more at that time). As a latent function, the mills enabled a community of extended family and intimate friends of broad ethnic diversity. We were all migrants dumped together by economic necessity, but we lived together in surprising harmony by social necessity and often a gradual appreciation for one another's ethnic customs.

Leaving the Valley was almost out of the question for our elders. The alleged mobility of labor meant the dislocation of community and employment insecurity, and these were sufficient disincentives for resettlement and environmental griping. So we took the "bitter with the better" because we didn't know any better, and we kept quiet about the environmental degradation. Indeed, many would have been violent, like a few of the present-day ecologically displaced, with anyone who suggested closing or cleaning up the sources of pollution, if that meant the possible loss of jobs or income.

Yet the mills for some of us also represented "the enemy," the "mill owners"—whoever they were. "They" were the oppressors (though people used vulgarisms not ideological descriptions) who got rich, we were told, by squeezing the blood and sweat from our fathers and forefathers and returned only a pittance of our due.

There was certainly an element of truth in that simple analysis. It was no accident of fate, I remain convinced, that the Duquesne Carnegie Library was the first major building in town to be condemned and demolished. Though that event occurred long after I left town, and despite the social benefits of the building, I could not resist a grin of vindication. The "library" had a swimming pool, pool hall, and basketball court, as well as a small collection of books; it never sounded odd to us to say that we were "going to the library" to swim, play basketball, and shoot pool. But the library was also a memorial to our forebears' nemesis, the iron and steel monarch, Andrew Carnegie. And our community's collective consciousness, I suspect, could not bear to let that dishonor to our forebears' memory remain unvandalized or, finally, left to stand. In my family, we were never allowed to forget that my maternal grandfather, a young newcomer to America, was an embattled veteran of a significant proletarian insurrection, the great Homestead Steel Strike of 1892. We remembered. One aunt later served as the curator of the only family heirloom, a button torn in combat from the uniform of a Pinkerton detective.

Our families wanted economic justice (though I never once heard a steelworker use that term)—higher wages, better pensions, safer working conditions, fair grievance procedures, things like that. Nothing noble here, simply self-interest. But our economic situation did generate some empathy and support for other "working-class" people elsewhere, particularly the nearby coal miners whose jobs were tough and whose union leaders we perceived as tougher. Racial justice, however, was another matter. Segregation in western Pennsylvania at that time was partial, often covert, and always brutal. It pervaded the churches, the "integrated" schools, the library, the mills, and the union. Blacks almost always had the least desirable and lowest paying jobs. Friendships, however, sometimes broke the color barrier, and some of us had a chance to share a taste of the agony and anger of our friends. We were eager for a new day of equality.

Yet, even in this caste system, blacks and whites had one major thing in common: we all wanted economic justice. Despite hints of corruption and the fact of discrimination in the union, most of us felt that our prime hope was in the counter force of organized labor.

Strikes seemed frequent in the Steel Valley as I was growing up. And they were times of both trauma and tranquility. No one I knew had sufficient savings to endure the economic hardships of a strike. Financial and related anxieties, therefore, ran high. However, I do not recall hearing many workers call for an end to a strike until the union said they had the best possible offer. Strikes also meant, however, that whole families could be together at "normal" times and groups of parents and kids could play together. Plus, the skies were blue, the river gradually turned a similar hue, and the mill noises ceased. We had a hint of the meaning of that strange hymn referring to "peace in the valley." Whatever the ambiguities of the strike, including financial losses incurred during the strike, we knew that it was a necessary strategy. The strike provided a larger measure of economic justice.

My nuclear family, however, was somewhat unusual in one respect in that setting: my father and I hunted and fished, reflecting his family's rural roots. I delighted in roaming the woods, fields, and streams, sometimes in search of "game" but mostly for the inherent pleasure. I regularly used a couple of guns, ironically, years before the state considered me fit to drive a car. I shot a shameful share of mammals, snakes, and "game" birds. We even had an English Setter, a genuine anomaly considering the social prestige of that hunting breed. My father and I also built a simple cottage in the wooded valley of Stahlstown in the Allegheny Mountains, at the confluence of three streams (cheap land, since below the floodplain, as we discovered), so that we could spend more time in our preferred pursuits. Hunting was not an economic necessity for my family, but we were sufficiently proficient that it was an economic asset.

More important, hunting was a rite of male passage, an exercise in primordial machismo. Success in the hunt brought acclaim from significant adults, male and female. It was a sign that I was fast becoming "a good provider," an indicator of male worth in that subculture. By that definition, when I became a deer slayer, I was a "man," fit to take my place in the mill—a role that I was obsessed to avoid.

My problem was that I gradually did not need hunting or fishing success as a sign of male maturity. Other signals were sufficient. Moreover, I was slowly acquiring a troubled conscience. I preferred to be a delighted observer rather than a destroyer of nature. Killing eventually seemed to detract, almost depressingly, from the pleasures of the wild, and killing or harming anything for pleasure seemed incompatible with even my primitive understanding of Christian love. Reading Albert Schweitzer in my late teens confirmed these emerging convictions. Thus I abandoned the gun in my early twenties. But it took more years to be persuaded to give up the rod (and I remain, I confess, psychologically unpersuaded and, therefore, sorely tempted to backslide).

Birds especially intrigued me. They were the most attractive creatures I saw prior to puberty. I dreamed of having a camera to get close-ups of birds and other wildlife, but I quickly discovered that my new Brownie Hawkeye was not up to my wild expectations. I found it miraculous that the beauty of the indigo bunting and the grace of the sparrow hawk could withstand the carnage of careless industrialization. I was impressed that even on the moonscape-like slag dumps, the adaptable killdeer nested (but fed elsewhere). To me, the birds were symbols of resistance against industrial imperialism—and I began to see it as a worthy role to support that resistance.

Contrary to stereotypes, none of my friends saw my interests in nature as beyond the pale of normalcy, perhaps because we shared otherwise the same passions and corruptions, but perhaps also because even the roughest and crudest of them had an instinctive aesthetic sense yearning to be nurtured. Thus they sometimes shared my awe. Once, the members of our baseball team, the Clovers (we were slightly more formidable than our name), followed me on a fall hike of twelve miles in search of slate-colored juncos, which I had advertised—incorrectly but innocently—as elusive and exotic migrants from the Alaskan tundra. Yet, neither my misinformation nor the drabness of the birds hindered biodegrading celebrations when we made the predicted discovery.

Our cottage in the Stahlstown valley enhanced the opportunities to follow my interests. However, even in this personal paradise, all was far from well. Signs of ecological degradation were evident, sometimes even ancient, and clearly expanding. There were no chestnut trees on Chestnut Ridge; the human-introduced blight created that misnomer. Logging had long ago eliminated most of the old trees, and the remains of old logging mills reminded me that the cycle would be repeated whenever the forest regenerated. A few abandoned farmhouses suggested tragic stories of agricultural exhaustion and human migration in earlier decades.

Recreational development was increasing, as our cottage itself signified. New summer homes and even a couple of estates meant the replacement of forests and fields with large lawns and ornamental plantings, along with "no trespassing" signs. Paved roads and steel bridges were replacing dirt roads, stream fords, and even woodland trails. Wildlife seemed to be declining with dehabitation and over-hunting. Nothing was really safe from gunners: even the rodenticidal broad-winged hawk was a prize, and the crows had just cause for their extreme wariness. Trapping seemed to me to be especially cruel and indiscriminate; I sprung every steel trap I found after discovering several with the chewed- or broken-off legs of raccoons, possums, skunks, and foxes. I sprung them almost vindictively after the ordeal of releasing my howling and biting dog from those springed clamps.

Four Mile Run was slowly becoming a twisting channel rather than a diverse ecosystem. Most recreational residents cut and mowed the banks and removed the unsightly but vitalizing "debris" from the stream bed. The trout were quickly caught after the state stocked the stream, but most "sportsmen" also killed their catches of native "trash fish" to leave a "better" habitat for the canned-in and easily conned creatures of the hatchery.

Soon even the pesticide revolution invaded the valley. Once, my father and I encountered two utility-line workers washing out two "empty" cans of herbicide in the stream. My father had objected when they sprayed the trees under the electrical lines; now he erupted. No harm, they said, the herbicide kills only plants and is benign for humans and other animals. Poisons hurt every living thing, my father countered. They left, job incomplete. A few hours later, several hundred fish floated belly-up along a mile or so of the slow-flowing stream.

Much has changed in the Steel Valley since my formative preteen and teen years. The results are painfully ambiguous. The steel mills are mostly silent, victims of complex economic dynamics and machinations. The orange shroud no longer hovers over the region. Pittsburgh even has a reputation for cleanliness. Maybe even the life of the river will someday be restored. Yet, the industrial residues of a century still permeate the land. Above all, my original community went down with the mills; it is a sluggish fragment of a once-bustling town. Unemployment, as I recall, exceeded 30 percent for a time. Many of a younger generation—mine—escaped almost compulsively in the sixties, and now many more of the remaining employables and their families have departed in economic desperation. A calloused brand of capitalism devastated my hometown economically and socially in the 1980s, just as it had done ecologically in earlier decades. Peace in an industrial valley has a heavy downside.

The current condition of the Stahlstown valley is far less dramatic or severe. Yet, the ecological trajectory from my youth slowly continues. The valley is now a simplified ecosystem.

Nevertheless, one thing at least has not changed. For those of us who are the scattered heirs of the ambiguous yet rich communities in the Steel Valley, ecological degradation and social injustice are not abstractions. They are traumatic experiences that permanently shaped our emotions and morals. Some of us never could stop complaining or seeking solutions to the economics-ecology and other ecological dilemmas that we lived. This book continues that complaint and search.

All of us, of course, have ecological autobiographies that have molded our motives, values, and biases. But it is not enough simply to discover the sources of our moral perspectives. That would imply a form of moral determinism. Instead, moral formation should be followed by ethical justification and transformation. The challenge of ethics is to examine our inherited values rationally, to revise or eliminate these values coherently in accord with empirical data and ultimate commitments, and to make choices that are consistent with our transformed values. This book represents a struggle to follow this normative process from a Christian perspective. But this ecological autobiography also warns readers that the pre-ethical prejudices from my early story undoubtedly continue to shape my theological, ethical, and political views.

CHARACTER OF THE CRISIS

"Ecology," says one TV commercial, is "definitely in!" When even the pop culture makes such a pronouncement, when even that once-abstruse word *ecology* is now so familiar that it can be used in a commercial, the signs seem favorable for environmentalists.

The prevailing perception of the public mood in North America and elsewhere is that the public now generally recognizes the existence of an ecological crisis and is ready to respond earnestly. Public opinion polls, for instance, now show high regard for ecological concerns. The supply of books, essays, and news reports on ecological issues is increasing significantly in response to an apparently strong public demand. In a revival of 1970s-style "ecopornography," some industrial giants are advertising themselves as sentimental caretakers of barn owl nestlings and wetland nurseries. Pollution-friendly politicians are hustling to remold their images as lifelong environmentalists. Major environmental organizations are now experiencing a boom in public acclaim.

Yet it could all be a fad. The environmental movement suffered the fate of faddism in the early seventies, while the ecological crisis intensified from neglect in the interim. That could easily happen again—including in the churches. Ecological concerns can be a priority for a time, perhaps a biennium or even a quadrennium, and then be neglected when a new and more glamorous issue seduces the attention of a mercurial church public and leadership.

Whether or not ecological angst is a fad, whether or not ecological concerns will be "definitely in" a few years or decades hence, the fact remains that the ecological crisis is definitely dangerous. The scale and scope of the problems are severe, and if present trends continue without sufficient human changes and constraints, the crisis and the difficulties of ameliorating it will again intensify, just as they did following the early seventies.

Moreover, whether or not the nineties will be the "turning point" in new attitudes and policies, as so many environmentalists hope, it definitely should be. In fact, the turning point should have been a lot earlier, since some elements of the problem have a long lineage. Now, however, with vast human populations wielding awesome technological tools, the crisis is developing rapidly, often radically, and sometimes irreversibly. The planet and its diverse populations of species are in peril, poisoned and impoverished on a score of fronts simultaneously. Ecological problems are serious and persistent, and the appropriate responses from Christians and other citizens should be correspondingly serious and persistent. Thus the ecological crisis warrants a prime place on the Christian moral and political agenda, ranking with the quest for economic justice and international peace.

The ecological crisis, however, is unlike many other events for which some reserve that word. It is not usually a clearly visible and sudden upheaval with fairly plain causal connections. It is rather, to use the title of Stewart Udall's book in the early sixties, a "quiet crisis"—a gradual and subtle debilitation, often without clearly visible causal connections to human actions. However, the harmful consequences for life can be as decisive as a cataclysm.

The ecological crisis is, in simplest terms, the decline and loss of ecological integrity as a result of human actions. What is meant by ecological integrity? In essence, ecological integrity refers to the "holistic health" of the ecosphere and biosphere, in which biophysical support systems maximally sustain the lives of species and individuals, and, reciprocally, in which the interactions of interdependent life forms with one another in their ecosystems preserve the life-sustaining qualities of the support systems. The concept is relative and dynamic, since not only do all human actions have ecosystemic effects but "natural" change is also a normal part of the process. The concept also implies moral constraints on human behavior to maintain the dignity of all life to the fullest possible extent. This whole book can be considered an exposition on the meaning of ecological integrity and the crisis that is disrupting and could destroy it.

For the Christian churches, however, the ecological crisis is more than a biophysical challenge. It is also a theological-ethical challenge. The crisis is partly rooted in philosophical, theological, and ethical convictions about the rights and powers of humankind in relation to the rest of the biophysical world. According to one popular conception—actually, a misconception and stereotype—of "dominion," humankind is a distinctive creation designed for domination. We are a species segregated from nature and possessed with an ultimately sanctioned and unrestricted right to exploit the bountiful supply of nature's "raw materials" provided for human benefit. Nature is simply matter, resources waiting to be re-formed for human utility. This viewpoint embodies the fundamental failures at the roots of the ecological crisis: the failure to adapt to the limiting conditions (the carrying and recuperative capacities) of our earthly habitat, the failure to recognize the intricate and interdependent relationships involving humankind and the rest of the ecosphere, and the failure to respond benevolently and justly to the theological and biological fact of human kinship with all creation. Without doubt, Christian traditions bear some responsibility for propagating these failed perspectives. Consequently, the ecological crisis is a challenge to Christians to eradicate the last vestiges of these ecologically ruinous myths.

Yet, the ecological crisis is equally a philosophical-ethical challenge for every religion and culture, since distorted dogmas of dominion also come in other religious and secular versions unrelated to Christianity. In fact, a modern technocratic version seems far more manipulative of nature than any ever devised in Christian history.

A crisis, however, is not only a tense and threatening time. It is also a kairotic moment, a decisive situation which challenges us to choose and to change. A crisis assumes that we are not fully fated, that we have partial but real moral and technical powers to remedy our plight and decide our historical destiny, and that *now* is the right time for turning toward a new direction. That seems to me to be clearly the character of the ecological crisis. As a response to this crisis, this book attempts to chart some Christian ethical and political directions for a new course.

PURPOSES AND PROGRESSION

This book is an *interdisciplinary* study in *Christian ecological ethics*. My main purposes are to develop at least the rudiments of an ecological ethic grounded in Christian theology, and to show some of the major

19

implications of this ethic for the formation of patterns of behavior and public policies in our time.

In doing an interdisciplinary study, I have stepped on a lot of academic turfs: history, theology, biblical studies, philosophical ethics, ecology, social sciences, and the like. This process is treacherous, because one inevitably exceeds the limits of one's competency by a wide margin. Yet, the process is unavoidable since Christian ethics seems to be inherently and overtly interdisciplinary. Moral problems do not fit into discrete, disciplinary categories, any more than life itself does. Moreover, Christian ethics is hard to imagine—if it is even conceivable—apart from dialogue with other relevant disciplines and responsiveness to empirical problems. Perhaps, however, there is a reciprocal justice in this interdisciplinary approach: ethics itself is one of the most common turfs stepped on by other disciplines, and usually under the cover of some claim to objectivity. Even "scientific" recommendations on public policy, for example, regularly make ethical assumptions and assessments and too often do so in the guise of value neutrality. In any case, Christian ethics must be interdisciplinary, and should be so openly, gratefully, and cautiously, without the pretense of mastery in other disciplines.

As a study in Christian *ecological* ethics, this endeavor cannot be described as simply a different application of Christian *social* ethics. Though ecological ethics incorporates and depends on social ethics, it is not simply a branch or subdivision of the latter. It includes the social sphere, but it also deals with a broader context where the standard values and norms of social ethics are often at least truncated and sometimes inapplicable. Thus Christian ecological ethics is not simply the values and norms of social ethics applied to an ecological context that is conceived as an area of intrahuman responsibilities. It is also a relevant revision and extension of these values and norms, applied to an ecological context that is conceived as moral problems of human relations with all other beings and elements in the ecosphere. If so, Christian ecological ethics warrants a place not under but rather alongside of and interrelated with social ethics.

Moreover, if ecological ethics is given its due, significant redefinitions of moral responsibilities and relationships will be necessary in all branches of Christian ethics. Everything from the definitions of "neighbor" and "sin" to the nature of rights and duties will need to be extended and revised. The implications for the reconception of the ethical task may not be radical or revolutionary, but they are major.

Christian ecological ethics is now only an emerging discipline. In fact, I doubt that even the name is widely recognized, since even the few practitioners of this discipline have not yet assigned a common ascription to what they are doing. Written works are still in relatively scarce supply, but I hope they will soon be a common commodity in response to a strong demand. This book is intended to be a contribution to that emerging specialty.

I prefer, incidentally, to use the word *ecological* rather than *environmental* to describe this ethic. The latter often seems to have anthropocentric connotations, suggesting moral concern only for the *human* environment, rather than for the context of all life.

The succeeding chapters are designed as a reasonable progression in the argument—an argument often in critical response to the major claims and questions now arising in Christian and other environmental circles. The progression moves

from an identification and analysis of the key moral problems in the empirical dimensions of the ecological crisis;

to a critical examination of how and why Christian traditions have responded or failed to respond historically to ecological concerns;

to a clarification and revision of the relevant theological affirmations;

to a formation of the ethical values and norms that are compatible with the theological affirmations and relevant to ecological realities;

and, finally, to the implications of these theological-ethical foundations for the directions of Christian advocacy in the dilemmas of public policy-making.

This progression corresponds roughly, I think, to the types and order of questions that much of Christian social ethics in the twentieth century has been raising concerning social problems. The structure of this particular progression, however, is designed to meet the special problems that the ecological crisis poses for Christian ethics.

Chapters 1 and 2 outline the major ethical issues in eight dimensions of the crisis, from pollution to extinctions. Chapter 2 concludes with a summary of nine "ecological virtues," which the empirical data suggest are imperative if we intend to resolve the crisis.

Chapter 3 responds critically to the widespread complaint in the circles of environmentalists that Christian anthropocentrism is the primary or at least a significant culprit in the crisis.

Chapters 4 and 5 explore the ecological implications of nine doctrinal affirmations, in order to show that the Christian faith has the potential to offer a solid, ultimate grounding for a strong ecological ethic.

21

Chapter 6 argues that love is the integrating center of Christian faith and ethics and explores the dilemmas and possibilities of applying a multidimensional understanding of Christian love in an ecological context. Loving nature is the key issue, it seems to me, in Christian ecological ethics and politics. *Nature* is defined throughout as simply the biophysical world, of which humans are parts and products.

Chapter 7 claims that justice is a vital dimension of Christian love, an essential means in both social and ecological contexts of defining responsibilities and ordering relationships. It argues for human environmental rights and prima facie biotic rights for all species and members of species.

Chapter 8 focuses on the implications of theologically grounded conceptions of love and justice for Christian advocacy in public policy. The intention is to offer guidelines to Christians and others in formulating and assessing specific policies. Six key areas are discussed: the economics-ecology dilemma, sufficient public regulations, global cooperation, responsibilities to future generations, the guardianship of biodiversity, and the linkages among justice, peace, and ecological integrity.

My own ethical perspective in the following pages cannot be described fairly as simply biocentric, ecocentric, or anthropocentric, to use the current code-words. None of these perspectives in isolation fits reality. All three have critical contributions to make to an adequate Christian ecological ethic. I, therefore, have tried to incorporate elements from all three into an integrated ethic.

CHAPTER ONE

DIMENSIONS AND DILEMMAS OF THE ECOLOGICAL CRISIS:

THE POLLUTION COMPLEX

The "environmental problem," many call it. But that description is a monumental understatement, comparable to calling a nuclear conflagration a fire. The ecological crisis is not a single, discrete problem, but rather a massive mosaic of intertwined problems that adversely affect humans and "every creeping thing." Each of the multiple problem-specialties includes an array of sub-specialties, so that our minds are overwhelmed by the volume, complexity, and connections of what we humans know about the ecological crisis, and we are awed by how little we know. The crisis is local, expressed in a variety of forms in each place, and global, as the forms in each place are carried by the winds and water to far-off places. Even the Eskimos in the Arctic, for example, bear in their bodily tissues the chemical contaminants used in the southern hemisphere. The ecological crisis is truly a hydra-headed monster.

Ecological problems, moreover, are not simply scientific, technical, political, or strategic questions. They are fundamentally moral issues, because they are human-created and soluble problems that adversely affect the good of humans and otherkind in our relationships. Ecological perspectives assume moral values, and they entail dispositions and actions that can be evaluated as morally right or wrong. Ecological problems, then, are moral challenges, which no person or group can responsibly ignore or neglect.

This chapter is an examination of three dimensions of the ecological

23

crisis which together constitute the "pollution complex": toxic pollution, global warming, and ozone depletion. The next chapter examines five other dimensions of the crisis: over-population, resource exhaustion, maldistribution, reductions and extinctions of species, and genetic engineering. This classification is, of course, not sacrosanct or even consensual. Ecological problems are so numerous and interconnected that the standard problem of every classification being an abstraction and oversimplification is exacerbated. I justify this one simply as a convenience for moral discussion.

The focus here, however, is not on the ecological "facts" and interpretations in themselves. The empirical reports—in books, periodicals, newspapers, educational programs, and the like—are now abundant and ubiquitous. In the light of this data glut, my focus is on the *major moral implications* of the facts. What do the ecological data suggest about moral problems and responsibilities? That is the key question. Even so, I can hope to respond to this question only in a general, introductory, and illustrative way, for the moral issues are numerous and often very particularized.

The following chapter, an extension of this one, concludes with an outline of nine ecological virtues. I propose them hypothetically until I later can establish their theological and ethical bases. If humans are to secure ecological integrity, these virtues are the characteristics or traits that are conducive to that goal and that, therefore, individuals and societies—indeed, the whole human community—ought to cultivate.

POLLUTION: POISONING OUR NEIGHBORS

It's not nice to poison your neighbors! That is a major part of the moral case against pollution, as John Passmore indicated.[1] Waste generation is another part. Pollution represents the failure to satisfy the moral obligation to prevent or minimize harm to our neighbors, both human and otherkind.

Pollution can be defined as the harmful or fatal effects of human actions, direct or indirect, that place natural and/or synthetic elements in ecosystems where they should not be at all or in amounts that surpass an ecosystem's capacities for normal assimilation. On this definition, trees don't pollute, contrary to a former president; they perform essential ecosystemic functions like recycling. However, humans do pollute in a variety of ways that exceed popular understandings.

Pollution, therefore, is a generic term to cover a multitude of overlapping "sins," including:

* *Oil spills,* from crude to used forms, not only in infamous cases like the *Exxon Valdez* in Prince William Sound and acts of war in the Persian Gulf, but in perhaps greater amounts cumulatively, and often intentionally, in every harbor and sea, at most extraction sites, and down countless sewers.

* *Ground-level ozone* smog in urban centers, resulting from the chemical reactions of sunlight with hydrocarbon and other emissions from motor vehicles, power plants, and other industrial sources. Serious respiratory ailments and damage to vegetation are among the major effects.

* *Toxic and other hazardous discharges* from petrochemical plants, refineries, paper mills, and other industrial sources. The Environmental Protection Agency documented 10.4 *billion* pounds of toxic substances dumped *legally* into the air, waters, and soils by major manufacturers in 1987 in the United States alone—and several thousand producers covered by the laws had not yet reported, while many smaller polluters were not covered.[2] Some of these discharges are known carcinogens. Their effects range from skin and eye irritations to birth defects, mental and neurological impairments, and many thousands of premature deaths. The impacts on nonhuman life are no less disastrous. Though generally complex and subtle, the biological consequences of pollution are sometimes obvious. Lake Erie, for example, was rendered biologically defunct in the 1970s by industrial sewage and sludge, and even now that great lake is a significantly transmuted ecosystem.

* *Acid rain* originating from sulfur dioxides and nitrous oxides emitted by motor vehicles, smelters, and especially electrical utility plants using high sulfur coal. When combined with water vapor and oxygen in the atmosphere, these emissions become mild sulfuric or nitric acids, which fall to the earth as acidic rain, snow, fog, or particles. Acid rain kills aquatic life in lakes, streams, and bays; it destroys forests and other vegetation and thereby deprives wild animals of their habitats; it damages crops (causing economic losses); and it corrodes buildings and historical monuments.[3] The effects are widespread, but the most notorious examples are the high smokestacks of coal-burning utilities in the Ohio River Valley and Great Britain, which help to

prevent local pollution but which spew acid rain, respectively, in northeastern North America and Scandinavia.

* *Radiation exposure* from the numerous waste dumps of nuclear power plants and weapons production facilities.

* *Nerve and mustard gas residues and wastes* from the Rocky Mountain Arsenal.

* *Pesticides* used abundantly in agriculture to maximize crop yields. Since the Green Revolution, the bulk of commercial agriculture worldwide has become chemically dependent, particularly to fertilize crops and to destroy insects and vegetation harmful to the crops. Pesticides, however, often destroy indiscriminately, killing not only some of the targeted species, but also "beneficial" species, like earthworms, bees, and particularly the natural predators of agricultural pests. Meanwhile, most of the world's major crop pests have rapidly evolved resistance to pesticides, prompting a spiraling escalation of chemical warfare against agriculturally noxious weeds and insects.[4] Humans are adversely affected directly and indirectly. Directly, "between 400,000 and 2 million pesticide poisonings occur worldwide each year, most of them among farmers in developing countries," resulting in 10,000 to 40,000 deaths annually.[5] Indirectly, through contamination of the soil, waters (including aquifers in many places), and food chains with environmentally persistent poisons, human tissues have accumulated carcinogens and other toxins with chronic effects.

* *Synthetic chemical residues*, including carcinogens, in food products like fruits and vegetables, often applied for cosmetic effects—and often arriving from Third World countries using pesticides banned in but exported by the United States and other industrial nations.[6]

* *Accidental emissions* from chemical and radioactive facilities. The disasters at the Union Carbide Plant in Bhopal, India, in 1984 (at least 2,500 direct deaths and perhaps 45,000 serious injuries) and the Chernobyl nuclear power plant in the Soviet Union in 1986 are notorious examples, but thousands of smaller, environmentally harmful industrial accidents occur annually.[7]

* *Metallic and other wastes*—copper, lead, mercury, iron, zinc, and the like—from mining and smelting that are often dumped indiscriminately and destructively in waterways.

* *Non-point pollution* (diffused, non-specific sources) from human habitations and life-styles. It often destroys or destabilizes marine

ecosystems through rain water run-off or indiscriminate dumping, and contaminates groundwater by leaching through the soil. These millions of singularly minor but cumulatively massive leaks include: excessive silt from erosion and construction sites, synthetic chemicals and fertilizers (nitrogen and phosphorus, which cause marine algae to grow profusely and harm other forms of aquatic life) from farms and residential gardens, de-icing salt and oils from roadways, and hundreds of billions of pounds annually of human excrements where treatment facilities are not available.

* *Legally and illegally dumped toxic chemicals* in landfills, like Love Canal and literally tens of thousands of lesser known places worldwide.

* *"Solid" or "municipal" waste,* otherwise known as garbage or trash. This form is largely the pollution of profligacy. It has generated a trash crisis in the United States and other affluent countries, with frantic searches by municipalities for additional landfills and more effective incinerators, along with new initiatives for prevention and recycling. Various estimates claim that the United States produces 150 to 230 million tons of solid waste annually. New York City alone is credited with 24,000 tons daily. Solid waste includes paper in all forms (the largest percentage by weight), glass bottles, aluminum cans, other valuable metals, plastic products, ozone-depleting chlorofluorocarbons, food wastes, old furniture, antiquated appliances, grass clippings, and, the current symbol, disposable diapers. In theory, solid wastes are distinguishable from hazardous wastes, but the two are often hopelessly intermixed; toxins are a small but treacherous part of solid waste under current systems of indiscriminate disposal. The trash crisis not only utilizes valuable land, requires major expenditures of scarce public dollars, and wastes vast quantities of reusable resources like paper and metals (which then leads to further lumbering and mining), but also has a variety of other health and ecological effects. Ecosystems are often damaged by the placement of open dumps and "sanitary landfills" (an almost cynical euphemism). Open dumps nourish infestations of disease-bearing rats and fleas, and all forms of waste dumps frequently contaminate the soil and groundwater. Most facilities for incineration not only degrade air quality, but also produce tons of toxic ash and, thus, additional disposal problems. Because biodegradable garbage decomposes very slowly in oxygen-

starved dumps, and because much contemporary waste, like some plastic products, is not even biodegradable in any time span less than scores of years or even centuries, future generations will bear the agonies of our generation's profligacy. The moral question, then, is not only how to dispose of our wastes responsibly, but how to prevent them, by radically reducing the volume and by treating disposables not as wastes but as recyclable and compostable materials.

The multiple and serious effects of pollution—probably millions of directly and indirectly caused deaths and a host of physical and mental impairments among humans, present and future, as well as comparable consequences for other species and their habitats—confirm that pollution is a major *moral* problem. It demands moral solutions. If the solutions are to be commensurate with the problem, they almost certainly will require fundamental changes in how societies assess and control the economic exchanges and consumption patterns of their citizens and institutions. Poisoning our neighbors and wasting common commodities are not matters of privacy or free marketeering or national sovereignty; they are serious moral offenses against others that demand public regulations and prohibitions.

One major change demanded is in the scope of cost-benefit analysis, including risk assessment. Some form of cost-benefit analysis is an inherent, although frequently implicit, element in any ethical approach that is concerned about the consequences of actions. Yet, this form of analysis as commonly employed in most allegedly value-free circles generally has major deficiencies. For instance, the arbitrary assignment of quantifiable, usually economic, values to non-quantifiable entities, like living beings, only veils value assumptions. Moreover, cost-benefit analysis is usually insufficiently inclusive and, therefore, unjust. It frequently fails to give adequate, if any, moral consideration to all of the benefits and costs or all of the beneficiaries and losers in a social decision to tolerate toxins and other pollutants in kind or degree.

Some pollution and, therefore, some risks are unavoidable in a modern society, but that statement only starts the questions. What, for instance, is a "safe" dosage or "negligible" or "acceptable risk" for carcinogens, radiation, and other toxins? How is that safety level calculated and with what degree of confidence? What does that safety level mean when translated into mortality rates or human misery? What is safe or negligible when toxic effects are measured cumulatively (the long-term consequences of regular low dosages) or synergistically (the combined effects on life forms of thousands of toxic and non-toxic chemicals interacting in the environment)? Answers to these questions are not only value-dependent, but are largely unknown. In the light of human ignorance and the potentially severe consequences of inevitable human error, a morally adequate cost-benefit analysis should proceed with high, health-conscious caution. The burden of proof, for instance, should probably rest not on public agencies to prove that new and existing synthetic chemicals are harmful, but on the producers to give reasonable and reliable evidence that these compounds are tolerably safe and nonpersistent in the environment. "Chemicals, unlike persons, are not innocent until proven guilty, but suspect until proven innocent."[8]

Similarly, an adequate cost-benefit analysis presents a serious challenge to nuclear energy. The risks of nuclear catastrophes may be as small as optimistic nuclear advocates contend—one in so many hundreds of thousands of operating hours or years—but the risk estimates are only educated guesses and hopes. Yet, on those rare occasions when the risks become costs, which the risk assessments themselves predict will occur, the potential magnitude of the damage is so severe, as Chernobyl illustrates, that the risk seems morally unjustifiable.[9] The rejection of the risk is really the rejection of a possible or probable cost. Additionally, the risk problem is aggravated when the interests of future generations are given their due. Plutonium wastes are lethal during the lives of tens of thousands of generations, but they are stored in facilities or containers that will endure for a few decades or at best a few centuries! In the light of the waste problem, nuclear energy is "safe" or "acceptable" only so long as the interests of future generations are discounted, only so long as the risks and costs are unjustly postponed to the future.[10]

Moreover, whose costs and benefits are morally relevant in determining the level of toleration for pollutants? Do only national or regional interests count? Do the economic interests of chemical complexes and agribusinesses take precedence over other contenders? Is the prevention of job losses in particular places more important than health and ecological effects? What about the interests of poor and power-deprived groups near whose residences polluting industries and dumps are disproportionately situated?[11] What about the interests of Third World peoples whose lands are often used as cheap dumps for First World hazardous wastes and who are often the importers of toxic chemicals, like DDT, which have been declared illegal in developed countries?[12] What about the rights of nations that are the involuntary recipients of air- and water-borne pollutants, like acid rain, from other nations? What are the moral claims of future generations? What are our moral responsibilities to other species and their habitats? A morally adequate cost-benefit analysis is comprehensive, considering all these questions. To be just, it must give due consideration to all the costs and benefits for all relevant parties. Its evaluations should be local and global, economic and environmental, immediate and long-term.

Another major issue revolves around a question of economic justice: who should pay for pollution? One common and generally sound answer is the "polluter pays principle,"[13] which proposes taxes, tariffs, user fees, penalties, and other charges to reduce or deter the use of polluting products and processes and to provide public resources for law enforcement, environmental rehabilitation, and fair compensation for those who are losers in the unavoidable battles of NIMBY ("Not In My Backyard").[14] This principle has numerous applications. It covers hefty penalties for using or dumping illegal toxins, and similar taxes on the production and use of legal products. It also suggests progressively graduated taxes on production and consumption, that is, the more used, the higher the rate—for instance, graduated rates for garbage disposal beyond a certain maximum, or on the consumption of electricity and water, or on the fuel consumption of automobiles. Where practical and prudent (and they aren't always), these and many other applications of the principle could significantly reduce waste and pollution.

The polluter pays principle is essentially an effort to calculate the full and fair costs of a product. The costs of production and distribution should be measured not only in terms of the internal operations of a corporate entity, like a petrochemical plant or agribusiness, but also in terms of what economists call the "externalities," the social and ecological effects of a business operation, which entail public expenditures in, for example, health care and clean-up costs. The waters, soil, and atmosphere are not free dumping grounds. If the public in general ends up paying these "hidden" costs of doing business, then, as Daniel Rush Finn and Prentiss Pemberton argued, pollution is "piracy of the common good" and the cleanup is "a subsidy of the corporation," even "legalized theft."[15]

Almost inevitably, however, the incorporation of pollution costs into the price of products would be passed on to consumers, raising their costs significantly (though more accurately). Generally, that process is fair, since consumers receive the benefits, participate with the producers in the guilt, and ought to share in the burdens of pollution. Yet, this valid answer also raises another question of justice: what about the adverse economic effects on the poor in the First and Third World nations who cannot avoid purchasing the products of pollution in a pollution-pervasive world? This question cannot be neglected. Resolving the problem of poverty is an inherent part of any responsible solution to the problem of pollution and other ecological ailments. Otherwise, environmentalism can be described credibly as a luxury of economic elites who are morally insensitive to the plight of the poor.

The moral challenge of pollution, however, is not exhausted by structures of penalties and deterrents, or determinations of who should pay and how much. It also calls for strategies of prevention—avoiding costly medical care and environmental clean ups by eliminating or drastically reducing the sources of the problems. Prevention means banning or abandoning some poisons and wastes (like DDT, CFCs, and some plastic products) as too dangerous and/or persistent, and regulating and reducing the production of others to stay within the bounds of sustainability.[16] Thus, in agriculture, integrated pest management uses a variety of techniques, including biological controls, not to eradicate crop-damaging insects and weeds, but rather to prevent serious economic losses. Pesticides are used only as a last resort, not routinely.[17]

Similarly, the goals of industrial and municipal waste management should be to reduce the production of waste to the maximum extent possible, and then to segregate, recycle, reuse, and compost the remainder to the maximum extent possible. Recycling not only reduces the demand for primary resources and landfills, but is also economical. It is far cheaper, for example, to reprocess aluminum—requiring only about 5 percent of the energy—than to transform bauxite into aluminum. Disposal in landfills and incineration should be last resorts for the unsalvageable and non-hazardous, rather than standard operating procedures.[18]

Strategies of prevention, of course, would require significant transformations in the patterns of production and consumption in affluent (and effluent) societies. Life, admittedly, would be less consumptive, more frugal, more restricted, and less convenient, but also safer, more efficient, and potentially ecologically richer. In any case, affluent societies have little choice but to move rapidly toward this goal if we are to live within the bounds of ecological sustainability for humans and other species. The tragic ambiguity of contemporary agriculture and industry is that our benefactor has also become our destroyer. These enterprises have produced a rich variety of goods, services, jobs, investments, and technological innovations, many of

31

which deserve commendation and gratitude. In the process, however, they have also stimulated wasteful production and consumption, exploited renewable and nonrenewable goods, and served as the primary contributor to the toxication of the environment.

Nonetheless, big business and agribusiness are not the only culprits in pollution. No citizen of the affluent nations is guiltless; all who have consumed the benefits from the productivity of these enterprises—through purchases, jobs, or investments—are implicated in the problem. Hazardous substances, for example, are made and used because most consumers want the products and tolerate the by-products thereof—from unblemished apples and plastic containers to air-polluting automobiles. These facts, however, imply not only moral guilt but also moral power: consumers, employers, and investors are to some degree regulatory forces to control and prevent hazardous and wasteful products and by-products. The moral challenge to all of us is to sustain for the future as many benefits of our economic institutions as possible, while eliminating their socially and ecologically destructive capacities.

GLOBAL WARMING: CLIMATE CHANGE
AND EXCESSIVE CONSUMPTION

Maybe it won't happen. Maybe the greenhouse effect is "just hot air"[19] from the propaganda mills of environmentalists. Maybe the global temperature in the next fifty years will be lower than expected and the effects less than feared, because the climatologists failed to properly incorporate into their models variables like cloud cover and oceanic dynamics. Maybe acid rain(!) from sulfur dioxide will delay or reduce the warming.[20] Maybe moving deliberately and avoiding precipitous actions are wise, since the changes necessary to minimize global warming could be disruptive of industrial economies. After all, the evidence is inconclusive, based on supercomputer simulations, and everyone acknowledges that more data and analysis are necessary. Yet a remarkable consensus has emerged among climatologists and other atmospheric scientists that global warming and some dire, attendant effects are high probabilities. A go-slow policy, waiting for conclusive evidence that may not appear until it is too late to act, is therefore a high-risk strategy. That is a key ethical issue surrounding global warming.

Global warming—or, more accurately to indicate agency, human-induced climate changes—is a form of pollution, but one that has major atmospheric and global effects. The problem is of gigantic *really that much?* proportions. Since the peak of the last Ice Age, perhaps 18,000 years ago, the earth's average temperature has warmed only about 5 degrees centigrade.[21] Thus, an average increase of 1.5-4.5 degrees centigrade (even if, as some current estimates claim, the increase will likely be at the lower end of the scale) in less than a century is a drastic shift. "If the temperature rises 4° C, the earth will be warmer than at any time since the Ecocene period, 40 million years ago."[22] The problem, however, is not climate changes in themselves; these, like the Ice Age itself, are natural, inevitable, and generally gradual, except for catastrophes—and global warming qualifies in that catastrophic category. The problem is the suddenness and radicalness of the change. Climate changes, if they occur, are likely to be too swift and massive for gradual cultural adaptations by humans and biological adaptations by many other species of plants and animals.

Global warming is caused primarily by human-induced imbalances of carbon dioxide and other trace gases in the lower atmosphere. The earth's atmosphere functions like a greenhouse, with trace gases (in low concentrations of less than 1 percent) playing a crucial role in making the planet habitable. The sun's rays penetrate the atmosphere and warm the surface of the earth. But when heat radiation is reflected from the earth, the trace gases absorb or trap some of it and maintain life-fostering temperatures. The main trace or greenhouse gases are carbon dioxide, water vapor, nitrous oxide, methane, and synthetic chlorofluorocarbons (CFCs, also the main problem in ozone depletion). Carbon dioxide, the seemingly innocuous and certainly abundant by-product of fossil-fuel consumption, contributes about 50 percent of the greenhouse effect. It never rose above atmospheric concentrations of 280 parts per million (ppm) for 160,000 years prior to the Industrial Revolution; it now exists at about 350 ppm.[23] The combined effect of the others, however, is now close to CO_2. Methane, for example, generated primarily from the decomposition of organic matter in landfills, swamps, rice paddies, cattle pens, and the like, is at least 20 times more effective than CO_2 in absorbing heat radiation. All are increasing in the atmosphere.

Except for CFCs, the operation of the greenhouse gases and their effects are "natural," "normal." The problem is excess—the human generation of more carbon dioxide than the plants and oceans can absorb, thus increasing the amounts of this gas in the atmosphere and gradually increasing the temperature of the earth's surface. Through the complex dynamics of photosynthesis, plants absorb and convert into energy for growth about 100 billion tons of carbon annually, but an approximately equal amount is returned to the atmosphere by the processes of plant respiration and decay. Roughly equal amounts are absorbed by the oceans and soil—but more than they exude. Yet, there is a net annual gain of approximately 3 billion tons of carbon dioxide in the atmosphere or an increase of 1.5 ppm annually. The net increase is caused primarily by the excessive burning of fossil fuels (oil, coal, natural gas) and the excessive cutting and burning of tropical forests, which is also reducing the total absorptive capacities of photosynthesis.[24]

The social and ecological effects are extraordinarily hard to predict. Climatology is still an inexact science, and its tentative conclusions are debatable. The effects of numerous variables in a complex web of interactions are far beyond present human capacities for prediction. Moreover, some environmentalists have clearly exaggerated the case, envisioning apocalyptic scenarios as certainties, in order to encourage terrified conversions to the environmental cause. However, the reasoned predictions and reasonable fears of a responsible and restrained corps of analysts cannot be dismissed; their conclusions deserve to be taken seriously and treated as if they are probabilities. If so, global warming as a human-created and avoidable problem threatens a moral crisis of historically unprecedented and cataclysmic proportions.

The potential consequences are diverse and interrelated. If sea levels rise as a result of the warming expansion of ocean volume and possibly some polar ice cap melting (now regarded as less likely)—even if only a foot or two by 2050, rather than the six to twelve feet or more suggested by some, the changes would be significant. It would mean—especially during storm surges—the inundation of some ecologically or agriculturally rich coastal plains, deltas, and estuaries, the deeper erosion of shorelines, and the salination of some coastal freshwater lakes and aquifers.[25]

Shifts in weather patterns are likely and would be experienced differentially, with the greatest changes in temperature and precipitation likely in the middle and upper latitudes. On the basis of an average global temperature increase, some places would be hotter and some colder. Some would experience droughts and others floods. In different places (we hope), tropical storms and snowstorms might increase in frequency and severity. Temperature-affected ocean currents, like the Gulf Stream, might shift, drastically affecting the climes of North Atlantic regions.

Weather changes, moreover, would cause biological changes. For instance, agricultural belts would probably shift; the grain-growing regions of the midwestern United States and China would probably change or disappear. Temperate forests would likely decline, disappear, or shift settings. Thus, the title of a *Washington Post* article asked the right question, euphonically: "Will Palm Trees Replace Pines Along the Potomac?"[26] The rapid dehabitation for many other plants and animals, both marine and land species, is probable, since they often have narrow temperature tolerations and other dependencies on specialized conditions. Many species might not be able to adapt by migration, and very few would be able to adapt so quickly by evolution.

Human communities would also need to adapt rapidly. Health and economic hardships are likely, with increased scarcities of land, food, and fresh water. Environmental refugees from uninhabitable places and greater population densities on available land are probable consequences. All this—plus much more, including some probable surprises—in less than a century! Who dares imagine the truly long-range effects if excessive carbon emissions persist? The prospects, apart from apocalyptic fears, are intimidating.

The tragedy of our situation is that the time may have passed to prevent global warming entirely. Fortunately, it is not too late to mitigate its extent and effects. A moral response to this emerging tragedy seems to demand no less.

The World Commission on Environment and Development argued that "choosing an energy strategy inevitably means choosing an environmental strategy."[27] That is true; the reverse is also true, for the two are reciprocally connected. To reduce global warming and secure other ecological benefits, an energy and efficiency revolution is necessary. Carbon dioxide emissions from the burning of fossil fuels in automobiles, other vehicles, industries, and residences must be cut by at least 50 percent (some say 80 percent or more[28]), deforestation must be reversed, and CFCs eliminated. Such major changes will be economically dislocative and complex, requiring imaginative and morally sensitive strategies to minimize harm.

The essential components of an effective response are well-known.[29] Conservation—the radical reduction of fossil fuel consumption through frugal life-styles, mass transportation, and other methods—is the cheapest and safest way. Energy efficiency in automobiles, appliances, lighting systems, and the like offers a cost-effective and environmentally effective means to save energy, sometimes with dramatic potential. Energy-efficient automobiles, for example, can now get more than 60 mpg, and the possibilities are significantly greater with new technologies.

Alternative sources of safe, reliable, renewable, and ecologically benign (relatively) energy are also necessary. Some, like large-scale hydropower and geothermal energy, may destroy critical ecosystems. Others, however, are promising, particularly wind and solar power, including photovoltaics. Indeed, if the full externalities of fossil fuels and nuclear energy are taken into account, these emerging alternatives may be cost effective now. Perhaps ethanol from fermented feedstock is one answer in the short run to powering motor vehicles,[30] but that resource may reduce scarce croplands and forests. New fuels, like hydrogen, seem preferable to many environmentalists. Clearly, increased research and development in new technologies are imperative, and, where necessary, should be stimulated by governmental subsidies. Equally, deforestation must be reversed and reforestation of native species must be accelerated. And, fortunately, the prohibition of CFCs, since the Montreal Protocol of 1987, seems to be a strong possibility in the international community, as public pressures increase and new substitutes are found. These steps are the primary parts of an effective, moral response to global warming.

Since global warming is a peculiar form of pollution, nearly everything I said earlier in the moral discussion of pollution applies here as well. The polluter pays principle, for example, is compatible with a "carbon tax," which proposes graduated rates for different fuels based on the level of their carbon emissions.[31] Similarly, the problem of economic justice is critical in strategies for reducing the consumption of fossil fuels. What will be the effect on poor countries that may need fossil fuels in order to develop a higher standard of living? In this case, it might be fair to accept their need to burn a disproportionate share of fossil fuels for a fixed time, while developed nations reduce their consumption even further to make up the difference. This suggestion is probably politically unrealistic, but it points to the urgent need for fair distribution of benefits and burdens.

Global warming raises the question of moral risk-taking more insistently than does any other problem of pollution. How much environmental risk should be taken in the midst of uncertainty? A department of the U.S. Chamber of Commerce claimed that caution—meaning the maintenance of the status quo—is the best policy. Arguing that global warming predictions are grounded not in fact but in hypothesis and speculation, it described the proposed solutions as "draconian." The Chamber's department did not deny the danger but appealed for more data. Until then, the forecasts should be taken seriously, but the nation should take no "inappropriate action"—that is, steps that require us to pay "unneeded social, environmental, and economic costs."[32]

In the light of the potential magnitude of the problem, such a response may be dangerously unresponsive. The best moral response seems to be to take the steps necessary to reduce global warming and to do so quickly. If the fears are exaggerations, the nations will still reap major social and ecological benefits, because every initiative to combat global warming, like energy conservation and reforestation, can be justified as essential on other grounds. If global warming is no exaggeration, the nations will have reduced its most debilitating consequences by acting decisively. The National Academy of Sciences calls this strategy "a planetary insurance policy" at "cheap" rates.[33] The greater risk by far is to do business as usual.

Global warming is truly a global problem. Like some other ecological dilemmas, its causes are international and its effects planetary—and its cures must also be international and planetary. A major moral challenge for the coming decades, therefore, is whether the human community can develop the political will and institutions to express what it already is in fact and value: the human community.[34]

OZONE DEPLETION: WHAT PRICE CONVENIENCE AND LUXURY?

Ozone depletion can be described as a peculiar form of pollution, one with global effects and a particular target: atmospheric ozone. Speaking simply, one can make a distinction between "bad" ozone and "good" ozone. At ground level, especially in urban centers, ozone is the main constituent of dangerous smog. But in the stratosphere, the unheralded ozone layer makes life on earth possible. Though existing only in minuscule atmospheric proportions, a few parts per million or billion in different places, the ozone layer is nature's sunscreen: this three-atomed molecule of oxygen is the only gas that absorbs much of the hazardous ultraviolet radiation (especially UV-B) from the sun, which otherwise would destroy all life.

Yet, the ozone layer is being dangerously depleted, as even most governments and corporations now readily acknowledge. Though

37

fluctuating annually and seasonally, a continent-size hole was discovered in 1985 over Antarctica, and a smaller one exists over the Arctic. Overall, the average ozone depletion during the last decade may be around 4 to 6 percent, and increasing. Natural chemical reactions continuously destroy and replenish atmospheric ozone. But the balance is now being upset by the emissions of certain synthetic chemical compounds. The primary ozone-eaters are chlorofluorocarbons (CFCs), which cause more than 80 percent of the damage by releasing chlorine. Fire-extinguishing halons, however, contain bromine, an even more effective ozone-depleter than chlorine. Two solvents are also notable contributors: methyl chloroform and carbon tetrachloride.[35] The effects are broad-ranging and durable: CFC molecules can destroy tens of thousands of ozone molecules during their atmospheric lifetimes, and the prime lifetimes of the most widely used ones are from 75 to more than 125 years.

The several forms of CFCs represent a major industry, creating hundreds of millions of pounds in products and tens of billions of dollars in income. The products are almost ubiquitous, because they are nontoxic, inexpensive, and versatile. CFCs are used in air conditioning (especially auto), aerosol propellants (now banned in the United States and some other nations, but still the largest use worldwide), refrigerator units, food packaging and containers (like Styrofoam cups and burger containers, whose use is declining because of public pressures), cleaning solvents (to remove manufacturing residues in computer chips, metals, etc.), and foams (as found in housing insulation and comfortable cushions and seats). The products are often useful, some very valuable, but not generally essential for human needs. They are luxuries and conveniences that could be abandoned and replaced by tolerable alternatives to save the ozone layer and other life-support systems.

By allowing dangerous increases in the atmospheric penetration of UV-B, ozone depletion probably means some harm to all lifeforms. For humans, the results might be increased cancers (especially skin cancers and possibly multiple millions of cases), respiratory ailments, cataracts and other eye diseases, possible birth defects, and damage to immune systems (thereby resulting in greater susceptibility to some diseases). Other animals might experience similar or unique effects. In plants, many of which are sensitive to UV-B, ozone depletion might interfere with the growth process, thus reducing agricultural yields in crops and forests and affecting ecological relationships. The aquatic food chain may also be adversely affected. In some species of phytoplankton, the minute free-floating

38

plants that are the foundation of marine life, radiation increases could cause mutations, reduced reproduction, or death.[36] These results would disrupt ecological relationships and shift the distributions of species. The causes for concern and action are numerous.

Like global warming, ozone depletion is a peculiar form of pollution. Consequently, virtually all of the ethical issues relevant to pollution are relevant to ozone depletion. The polluter pays principle, for example, suggests a tax on ozone-depleting products, to discourage use and encourage alternatives. Similarly, equity for poor nations raises the question of a morally legitimate extension of time for them in international anti-depletion agreements to gain whatever economic benefits from CFCs that the wealthy nations have been reaping for decades. This idea is already embodied in international agreements like the 1987 Montreal Protocol. Yet, some other form of compensation—particularly technical assistance for producing substitutes—seems far preferable.

Moreover, as with global warming and some other forms of pollution, a basic ethical issue is responsibility to future generations. The effects will be felt far more by future generations than by present ones. Though CFCs are soon likely to be banned in most nations as cost-effective substitutes become available and governments and their citizens respond to alarms, the reality is that CFC-induced ozone depletion will persist. Presently and prospectively manufactured CFCs will continue to float into the stratosphere and persist in their dysfunctions for over a century. This fact provides no argument for procrastination. Indeed, it is a reminder that time is of the essence. The longer we wait to prohibit CFCs, the more disastrous and long-lasting the effects of ozone depletion will be. If our generation has responsibilities to future generations, both human and otherkind, then eliminating the ozone eaters as soon as possible is a matter of urgency.

Ozone depletion confronts us forcefully with a set of morally relevant questions about life-styles, which are also applicable to most other forms of pollution: What products and functions of CFCs are really necessary or valuable for the "good life"? Are the luxuries and conveniences really significant contributors to human enrichment? What should we be willing to sacrifice now for the sake of social and ecological integrity in the future? If the functions of CFCs are really necessary or valuable, what substitutes can be found that will perform the same functions adequately, not necessarily equally or as cost-effectively? How can we reduce or redesign our wants?[37] One imperative for an ecologically declining age is: Ask what you can do *without* for your country—and the peoples and other populations of your planet.

CHAPTER TWO

DIMENSIONS AND DILEMMAS OF THE ECOLOGICAL CRISIS:

EXCEEDING THE LIMITS

Pollution is a prominent and multipronged part of the problem, but it is certainly not the only ecological problem, contrary to popular conceptions. Other dimensions of the crisis are no less significant. This chapter examines five other forms of humanity's ecological excesses and abuses: resource exhaustion, overpopulation, maldistribution, reductions and extinctions of species, and genetic engineering. Whatever else these five interrelated dimensions of the crisis have in common, they are all expressions of humankind's tendency to exceed the limits of our rights and nature's capacities.

This chapter ends with an outline of nine ecological virtues applicable to all dimensions of the ecological crisis.

RESOURCE EXHAUSTION: LIVING BEYOND PLANETARY MEANS

An elementary lesson of ecology is that we live on a finite, essentially self-contained planet. There are no infinite bounties or inexhaustible resources. Though the limits are usually and sometimes significantly extendible by means of human technology, like recycling, still everything is limited—be it mineral resources, waste-absorption capacities, or space for species. Virtually everything of material value can become scarce—if it is not already so by nature—by overuse or abuse. Even so-called renewable resources, like naturally regenerative plants, animals, and soils, can become functionally nonrenewable when pushed beyond their levels of tolerance. Ecological prudence, then, is adaptation to the forces and restraints of nature that cannot be changed, no matter how sophisticated our technology becomes. This lesson is applicable to every dimension of the ecological crisis, but it is especially evident in resource exhaustion.

The ecological crisis represents, in large part, humanity's failure to learn this lesson. Speaking anthropocentrically, we are living beyond our means, beyond the limitations of our annual "solar energy income,"[1] the regular regeneration of renewable goods. We are living off our "solar savings"[2] (fossil fuels) and restricted capital (like nonrenewable minerals), and doing "environmental deficit financing"[3] with renewable goods. If sustainability implies living within the bounds of the regenerative capacities of the earth, with a sense of responsibility for future generations, then present practice is characterized predominantly by *un*sustainability in the use of both nonrenewable and renewable resources.

Nonrenewable resources include fossil fuels (oil, coal, gas) and industrially significant minerals (iron, manganese, copper, nickel, silver, tin, bauxite, and the like). By definition, they will run out; the only question is when, the short or the long term?

In *The Limits of Growth,* a book which influenced many of us in the early 1970s, the Club of Rome warned against exponential growth in the use of nonrenewable resources, argued that this growth would lead to shortages and high costs in the relative short term, and claimed that the limits to growth would be reached within the next century.[4] Since then, discoveries of new mineral reserves have pushed ahead the danger point of scarcity, from the perspective of many analysts. For instance, deposits of substantial sea bed reserves of major minerals— like manganese modules containing iron, copper, nickel, and the like—may be recovered cost-effectively with emerging technologies. Yet, serious problems remain. The high quality reserves of some minerals are disappearing. The extraction of low-grade ores is more energy intensive, thus increasing costs and prices, with particularly adverse effects on the poor. Moreover, with increasing scarcity, economic pressures are likely to arise to explore and withdraw minerals from environmentally sensitive areas, thus entailing signifi- cant ecological damage (since mining is anything but a delicate operation). If growth in the consumption of these minerals continues (for example, by the Third World increasing its level of consumption to its fair share from a present perspective), shortages and associated effects are likely to develop sooner rather than later.

[handwritten margin note: scarce = high cost of extraction]

41

Similarly, since *The Limits of Growth,* new discoveries of oil deposits have continued, but these resources are declining rapidly. Alaskan North Slope oil, for example, is probably half depleted, and that fact is prompting pressures to drill in other "promising" places in Alaska—notably the pristine and sensitive ecosystem of the Arctic National Wildlife Refuge, for a total production of oil of probably less than two years of annual U.S. consumption.[5] With the end of the Oil Age only a matter of decades away, with politically and economically manipulated shortages and price increases periodically giving us previews of critical events to come, the search for alternative energy sources intensifies. These include old and new sources: nuclear, low-grade coal, natural gas, oil shale, wind, geothermal, solar collectors and photovoltaics, wood and other biomass, hydroelectric, and the like. Some are promising, particularly solar. Others have actually or potentially severe ecological effects, particularly nuclear, alternative fossil fuels, and some major hydroelectric dams. All have limited potential.

In the light of these and other developments, it seems clear that *The Limits to Growth* was wrong in its estimations and calculations. That is to be expected in predictions based on numerous variables. Yet, it also appears to have been right in principle and on its main point: in view of the declining availability of nonrenewable resources, the industrial growth that we have known in the past century may not be sustainable for much beyond another century, and probably not that long. Indeed, if this prediction is an underestimation of resources, the fact remains that nonrenewables *will* eventually run out or become too cost-ineffective to extract.

Of course, human ingenuity is impressive. Recycling is widespread and has far greater potential. Substitution of one mineral for another is technologically possible in many cases. But eventually, what nonrenewable will substitute for the substitutes? Substitutes are not guaranteed; "progress" is not inevitable. "The faith in the infinite substitutability of nonrenewable resources" is probably, as Herman Daly and John Cobb suggest, a myth.[6] Indeed, without reasonable expectations, it is "recklessly optimistic."[7] Nonrenewables are exhaustible by definition. And that fact raises serious ethical questions about their use in relation to future generations. How, for instance, shall we apportion nonrenewables among generations, and how far ahead should moral consideration be extended?

Renewable resources, on the other hand, are by definition annually or periodically regenerative through natural cycles. Functionally, however, they can become nonrenewables for decades or centuries, or

42

even permanently, through unsustainable use. Humanity's present plight includes the exhaustion of many of the world's renewable resources.

Agricultural lands in many places are gradually becoming degraded, mainly as a consequence of poor agricultural practices, including salination from long-term irrigation and insufficient crop rotation and fallow periods. Wind and water erosion reduce the fertility, stability, and, therefore, the productivity of soils: "Each year, the world's farmers lose an estimated 24 billion tons of topsoil from their cropland in excess of new soil formation. During the eighties, this translated into a loss of 240 billion tons, an amount more than half that on U.S. cropland."[8] These figures are significant because it sometimes takes centuries to rebuild an inch of lost topsoil, and because these losses represent millions of tons of foodstuffs not being available to feed starving peoples.

In arid and semi-arid areas, moreover, human-induced desertification or severe drylands degradation is proceeding dangerously—threatening perhaps 35 percent of the world's land mass, particularly in the Third World.[9] Under the spurs of desperate poverty and overpopulation, the direct causes include overgrazing of rangelands, erosion from farming on marginal lands, and devegetation for fuelwood (the main energy source in many poor countries). One major consequence is starvation, when migration is not feasible, as in the west African Sahel.

Even in the First World, however, population and production pressures accelerate not only agricultural land degradation but also its disappearance. Rich crop and pasturelands, as well as natural areas, are eliminated for urban and suburban development. Some affluent communities in the United States are now seeking to control these encroachments by zoning requirements. That process, however, can be parochial and parasitic. It sometimes means that the local protectorate provides a shelter for the affluent from the hefty burdens of urbanization, while the sheltered continue to benefit from urban services in employment, commerce, and culture. The "relevant whole," to use James Gustafson's term, for resolving these inequities is not the local community; it is probably the region or state.

Usable water—the essential and seemingly ever renewable resource—is becoming locally scarce in many places. Safe water is simply not available in many parts of the Third World. And elsewhere, what isn't contaminated by pesticides and other pollutants is often being used unsustainably.[10] The great underground and nonrenewable reservoir in the central United States, the Ogallala Aquifer, is half-depleted from irrigation of croplands. Overpumping for agricultural, industrial, and municipal purposes has severely diminished the flow and ecosystems of great rivers like the Colorado, the Rio Grande, and the Platte. Competition for water has become a way of life in the arid regions of California and Arizona; emerging shortages, however, may dramatically change that way of life.

Fisheries, a prime source of protein for many people, also show serious signs of unsustainable use.[11] Overfishing by technologically sophisticated fleets has substantially reduced the numbers of some species, like haddock and halibut in the North Atlantic. The destruction of coastal wetlands, like salt marshes, a principal nursery of sea life, is also a major contributing factor.

Deforestation is occurring far faster than regeneration in some key forested regions of the world—at a time when reforestation is demanded by the threat of global warming. That is true in the temperate, old growth forests in the United States' Pacific Northwest and especially in the rain forests of the tropics, notably the Amazon. Indeed, regeneration of the massive Amazonian rain forest may not be possible beyond a certain threshold of destruction, because the loss of the forest may change the hydrological cycle and, thus, the climate. Current estimates suggest that perhaps up to 50 million acres of tropical forests are cleared annually.[12]

This litany of woes only nicks the surface of resource exhaustion. Countless horror stories and statistics—and some successes, including the recent reduction of soil erosion in the United States—from around the globe could be recited, but numerous other sources provide that service. The central point behind all of these declines, however, is that the present generation is living beyond planetary means. The maximization of current benefits for a minority of the present generation is being achieved by the reduction of potential benefits for future generations. If humans have responsibilities for future generations, economic systems that stress the virtues of sustainability and frugality are essential.

POPULATION PROGRESS: BEYOND EARTH'S CARRYING CAPACITY

The biblical injunction to "increase and multiply" may be the only one that humankind has obeyed faithfully! But the effects are no jesting matter. The world's human population is at this writing roughly 5.3 billion and growing. Current projections indicate that the figure probably will rise to 10 to 11 billion by 2025, and may reach 14 billion by 2100, when some—not all—predict it will stabilize.[13] Most are familiar with the standard rhetoric: It took humankind so many millions of years to reach one-half billion in numbers by 1650, but less than 200 years to become 1 billion in the early nineteenth century. One hundred years or so later (1930), the human population became approximately 2 billion, and thirty years after that (1960), 3 billion. Human numbers are expected now to double in 35 to 40 years. To put the matter sharply, it took humankind thousands of centuries to produce one billion people living simultaneously on the planet, but that number can now be reproduced in little more than a decade. This growth is not descriptively an explosion but it is certainly a dramatic—and seemingly a dangerous—progression.

Ironically at first sight, the numerical increases are occurring at the same time that birth rates are stabilizing or declining in most parts of the world. The annual death rates, however, also have been declining, because of improvements in most places in health care (for instance, immunizations), sanitation, and food production. Moreover, because persons of reproductive age make up a large and growing percentage of the population in many developing countries, the absolute numbers will grow even if the average woman produces fewer children.[14] Most of the major increases are expected in Africa, the Middle East, Latin America, and the Indian subcontinent—generally regions where economic resources are already stretched dangerously thin. The absolute numbers will also grow gradually in most affluent nations, even with their lower birthrates. And that fact may have an even greater impact on the world's economic and ecological systems.

The determination of an optimal human population is an exceedingly difficult task. The answer depends on our ends, as John Passmore notes.[15] Fortunately, however, it is not necessary to answer this question to recognize that population expansion is a serious problem. It is enough to say that if we want to realize and sustain social justice and ecological integrity, the size of the human population can jeopardize these goals and appears already to be doing so to different degrees in different places.[16] We seem to be pressing the limits of life-supporting resources, if we have not already surpassed them. A few optimistic analysts argue, contrary to the bulk of the evidence, that the earth can sustain many times the present population, because of its alleged practically unlimited resources and the greater potential for

45

technological creativity in a large and expansive population.[17] Most current demographic interpreters, however, are at least anxious and many are alarmed. The size and rate of population growth can have—and is having—serious social and ecological consequences.

One current consequence is that many poor nations are losing the race between socioeconomic well-being and population expansion. They are like runners on a conveyer belt moving in the opposite direction: they must run desperately just to remain in the same place or make slight progress. Their dilemma of development can be stated simply in a real—not hypothetical—scenario: if a country's productivity increases by 2 percent and its population rises by 3 percent, then its per capita income declines by 1 percent.[18] And this formula does not include the problem of maldistribution. Hence, some poor nations are achieving net decreases or insufficient increases in their standards of living, partly because their industrial and agricultural productivity is erased by expanding numbers.

Population growth exacerbates the problems of improving education, cultural creativity, employment, health care, sanitation, housing, and available food.[19] These problems are especially acute in the emerging megacities of the Third World, which are experiencing what used to be called the population *implosion*. Moreover, growth increases the vulnerability of these nations to natural dynamics like floods and droughts, and increases the potential for social conflict, within and among nations, as growing numbers compete for static or shrinking resources.[20] The Malthusian theory that population, growing geometrically, will outstrip the means of subsistence is actually or potentially a gruesome reality in some regions of the planet.

Another major consequence is that excessive population growth accentuates every environmental problem. The ecological reality is that the earth has limited resources to sustain and improve the quality of life. While these limits can be extended through human creativity, such as technological improvements in agricultural productivity, the potential for extension itself is limited. The earth has a carrying capacity, and population growth can exceed that capacity, as it has done often in densely populated places. Increased demands for sufficient nutrition and other basic needs can lead to excessive exploitation of nature's resources: the overuse of croplands and the overgrazing of grasslands (thus contributing to erosion and desertification); the reduction of fresh water supplies; the expanded consumption of energy resources; increased pollution; the accelerated destruction of forests and other ecosystems and their inhabitants.

46

Fuelwood, for example, is a basic energy source in many parts of the Third World, especially urban areas. But a "population-driven overharvesting" of fuelwood threatens shortages by 2000 in areas occupied now by 2.4 billion people.[21] That overharvesting also means the degradation of ecosystems and the reduction or extinction of their species.

Historically, migration was a response to overpopulation and other environmental problems. That strategy, however, is decreasingly feasible. Increasing numbers of environmental refugees are aggravating social and environmental problems elsewhere, and adequate places to migrate are becoming increasingly rare.[22] Overpopulation is not the only or often the main cause of environmental degradation, but it can be and often is a major contributing factor.

Overpopulation, moreover, is not the main cause of poverty or poverty-related environmental destruction. Maldistribution, accompanied by the grandiose consumption of the affluent, probably has that distinction. The actual and potential resources of the earth are probably sufficient to provide sustainable and adequate goods for all humanity and other species, present and future, though only so long as human population in absolute numbers remains within the earth's carrying capacity. Poverty is not only about numbers, but also about the inequitable distribution of resources within and among nations.

In this context, current population problems must be understood in relation to patterns of consumption and available resources. Not only additional numbers matter, but so does the per capita consumption of each additional number. If so, population progression is not only a problem for the Third World; it is also, and perhaps more so, a problem for the First World. The reason is that the average additional person in affluent nations, particularly the United States, consumes far more and places far greater stress on the world's natural resources—some say 20 to 30 times more, on the average—than their counterparts in some poor nations. In terms of per capita resource consumption, the United States is probably the most overpopulated nation in the world.

Thus population growth reduction is an urgent moral demand on *all* nations, and it is accompanied by a moral demand on affluent nations for reduced consumption and equitable distribution. One moral criterion for determining a national population and family size is not how many children we can afford (which in my case, as I discovered ex post facto, was 0.6) or "our" children's "superior" social value. The first criterion is a manifestation of economic classism and the second of the eugenic fallacy. Rather, a major criterion is what *the world* can afford—and there is increasing evidence that the rest of the world cannot afford North American consumption, let alone additions to it.

From a Christian perspective, the nations are in fact and value an international and interdependent community of moral equals. The relevant whole for moral responsibility is not the family or the nation, but the global community. That perspective has many implications. One seems to be that the prosperous should not recommend any population policy for the poor that they are not willing to follow themselves. If excessive population is related to global resource consumption, then the United States and other rich nations have some major rethinking to do about morally balancing their reproduction and consumption policies. The stamp of moral authenticity is granted only when we practice what we propose.

What strategies are likely to be effective and morally reasonable to defuse the so-called Population Bomb? To answer this question, it must be clear that if the human population exceeds the carrying capacity of the earth, then the only alternative to decreasing the birth rate is increasing the death rate—through famine, pestilence, war, and the like. That is the terrible but only choice!

A host of solutions has been proposed by alarmed exponents of population control, frequently on the assumption that we are now in a "lifeboat" situation and must take drastic actions immediately or soon. The desperation tactics include the withdrawal of family allowances for welfare recipients or foreign aid for nations that are not adequately controlling their numbers; the elimination of tax deductions, educational benefits, or using other penalties for large families; the prohibition of early marriages; compulsory abortion or sterilization after a certain number of children; incentives or bribes, like the infamous transistor radios in India, to encourage vasectomies or tubectomies; triage in the distribution of food aid (that is, writing off parts of the Third World as a lost cause, in a highly nationalistic scheme);[23] "a transferable birth quota plan," which can be sold to the benefit of the affluent;[24] the temporary sterilization of a national population through antifertility chemicals in the water supply; and even suggestions of infanticide. Some of these alleged solutions are insults and injuries to the poor, even assaults on physical integrity, and all of them are affronts to human dignity and freedom. Where they are not punitive or discriminatory to poor nations and individuals, they are reminiscent of a police state.[25]

Yet, the critical question remains: Could the world or parts of it reach such desperate straits that policies such as these are the best possible alternatives? In emergencies or extremities, what is normally, even repulsively, wrong can be justified as right, as a last resort if the end is essential.[26] Ethicist Roger Shinn offers some wise words on this moral dilemma:

[handwritten note: Who is to say?]

> Conflicts of values . . . are part of almost all serious moral decisions. So it is with population policy. A desperate world may use coercion to limit population. . . . But the dilemma is a bitter one. . . . Human dignity demands limitation of population. But some methods of limitation destroy dignity.
>
> In any crisis society qualifies personal rights, but *part of ethical wisdom is to avoid crises that permit only destructive choices, and another part of wisdom is to maintain a maximum of human integrity even in crisis.*[27]

That answer seems reasonable. The moral solution is *prevention,* with the least possible amount of coercion and offense to human dignity. If, as I assume, the world is not yet in a lifeboat situation, then the nations must make hard choices *now*, while the options are still somewhat open, to avoid harsh choices by future generations.

What, then, are some morally and practically reasonable means of alleviation and prevention now?

Contraception certainly must be the centerpiece of a population control policy. The modern world knows what to do—and has the technical and organizational skills to impart that knowledge. The moral opposition to artificial birth control seems to me to be morally indefensible. Technological interventions in natural processes are legitimate in a multitude of ways, including medical procedures; it is hard to see any morally relevant difference in this one. Contraception seems to me to be not only morally acceptable but morally essential, not only for the good of couples and families, but for the common good of nations and nature. A right *not* to procreate is reasonable, but a right *to* procreate without limits under current and emerging circumstances seems indefensible, despite the U.N. Declaration of Human Rights. Concern for human well-being suggests that the means of contraception ought to be chosen pragmatically, based on safety, simplicity, and efficacy. Indeed, the need for our time is stronger government assistance for contraceptive education and research and development.

[handwritten note: Yes!]

Yet, contraception is not sufficient. Population control needs to be part of a strategy for socioeconomic justice, which, according to demographic transition theory, appears to be an essential precondition for population stabilization and reduction. Socioeconomic conditions seem to be prime factors affecting birth rates, with improvements in the quality of life associated with reduced births. Thus equality for women—for instance, in education, employment, and social status—should have the latent function of reducing birth rates. Equally, improved economic security for the citizens of poor nations should have similar effects. Poverty, according to this theory, breeds population progression in some cultures, since large families provide a means of economic assistance in family economic production and security in old age. Improved housing, hygiene, nutrition, education, employment opportunities, and social security systems, then, should decrease the economic need for more children.[28] Of course, there is no decisive evidence, let alone guarantee, that the demographic transition theory will work in Third World nations as it apparently did in the First. Nonetheless, socioeconomic justice is valuable in itself, and should be pursued apart from its demographic effects.[29] Substantial economic assistance from First to Third World countries should be a major component of any population strategy.

To paraphrase a famous manifesto, a specter is haunting the globe—the specter of population progression, which will require a holy alliance of nations to exorcise. That specter is a threat to rich and poor families and nations, as well as to future generations of humans and other species. Only if present and near-present generations of humans propagate less will future generations of humans and other species likely have the chance to propagate at all.

MALDISTRIBUTION: THE LINKAGE BETWEEN ECONOMIC INJUSTICE AND ECOLOGICAL DEGRADATION

The World Commission on Environment and Development made a rather startling statement about the impact of economic disparities on environmental conditions: "This inequality is the planet's main 'environmental' problem."[30] This statement might be a rhetorical exaggeration, but it is not sufficiently so to be worthy of argument.

In making this linkage a major theme of *Our Common Future*, the Commission sanctions an important corrective to those advocates of environmental integrity or economic justice who view their respective concerns in isolation and fail to see maldistribution as a prominent dimension of the ecological crisis. The fact is that economic inequalities are major contributors to environmental problems, and vice versa. Maldistribution is not simply a problem that exists parallel to environmental degradation; rather, it is both a cause and an effect of that degradation in an interacting and vicious circle. Realistically, therefore, a preferential option for the poor entails a preferential option for ecological integrity—*and* vice versa.[31]

Radical disparities in income and resources, among nations and within nations, are fundamental features of the modern world. The symbols of the First and Third Worlds and now the hemispheric North and South are intended to convey that reality. While a minority of less than 25 percent of the world's population lives in comfort and luxury, many in gluttony and frivolity, consuming and wasting more than 75 percent of the world's goods, still another minority lives in chronic and desperate poverty. Their numbers have been estimated at 1.2 billion or more than 20 percent of the world's population.[32] Similarly, an overlapping 20 percent, especially in southeast Asia and sub-Saharan Africa, suffer from malnutrition or are seriously ill from ailments like malaria and diarrhea, according to the World Health Organization. While the First World can now provide even artificial hearts for a few, the Third World often lacks basic vaccines and drugs for elementary immunizations and cures.[33]

For these desperate people, poverty means deprivation and dispossession—homelessness or primitive housing, illiteracy, malnutrition, debilitating illnesses, lack of property, vulnerability to natural calamities, and, in many millions of cases annually, death from hunger and hunger-related diseases. Yet, poverty also means powerlessness, subordination, humiliation, and manipulability. In sum, massive numbers of humankind lack sufficient resources to satisfy their basic needs and to enable social participation.

Even worse, desperate poverty is growing in many places. Spurred by population growth and debt crisis, per capita income declined by 8 percent in Latin America during the 1980s,[34] and similar trends have been evident in other poor countries.[35] Even in the paragon of prosperity, the United States, the lot of the poor gets no better, and may be getting worse.[36]

Moreover, even in poor countries where adequate resources are potentially available for basic needs, internal corruption, mismanagement, and injustice often contribute to the concentration of available wealth—land, food, cattle, even water—in the grasp of the affluent few, and the deprivation of the many. Sandra Postel of the Worldwatch Institute outlines one way that economic and ecological declines frequently grow in poor nations:

> Next to population pressures, perhaps no other factors foster more degradation than the inequitable distribution of land and the absence of

51

secure land tenure. In an agrarian society, keeping a disproportionate share of land in the hands of a few forces the poorer majority to compete for the limited area left, severely compromising their ability to manage sustainably what land they do have.[37]

Thus the plight of the poor is not solely a North-South or First World-Third World phenomenon; it has its own internal dynamics in the elitist corruptions of every nation. Avarice is a universal phenomenon.

The situation is exacerbated by the fact that in the international economic system, more wealth is percolating up from the Third World than is trickling down.[38] This neocolonialistic effect, though often not the intent, is especially evident in the international debt crisis—now generally estimated at the surrealistic figure of more than $1.3 trillion that the nations of the Third World owe the commercial and governmental institutions of the First. As nations struggle, often unsuccessfully, to service their debts and to confront other problems like falling export prices, the results include declining incomes, increased deprivations and malnutrition, and absurdly high inflation (more than 3,000 percent annually in some Latin American countries).

These economic disparities also have severe ecological effects. Poor people are forced to use their natural resources beyond the point of sustainability simply to survive in the present. For instance, the intensive use of croplands and the extension of agriculture to marginal lands wear out the soil and contribute to erosion and desertification. Similar consequences arise from overgrazing on grasslands. The forests, waters, fish, and other resources also are jeopardized for the future. Moreover, the debt crisis imposes a public austerity that deprives Third World governments of the financial resources necessary to control ecological problems, like deforestation, and to enforce regulations.[39] Finally, the poor suffer disproportionately from ecological maladies. Poor nations and low-income regions of the United States, particularly African-American and Hispanic communities, are often the preferred dumping grounds for toxic wastes: "The rich get rich and the poor get poisoned."[40] Thus poverty is a driving force behind ecological deterioration. Then, in a vicious cycle, this deterioration reduces the availability of resources and further propels the extension of poverty. And the process begins anew.[41]

Clearly, global environmental problems cannot be resolved adequately unless economic maldistribution is remedied. Otherwise, the world's poor are forced to overexploit their natural goods in order to stay alive.

In *Keeping and Healing the Creation,* the Presbyterian Eco-Justice Task Force makes a useful distinction between "pollution from poverty and pollution from prosperity."[42] The distinction also holds true for other dimensions of the ecological crisis. While most of the world's ecological degradation is a by-product of affluence, poverty increasingly contributes an unhealthy share. The two categories cannot be separated causally, as the Task Force knew. Environmental destruction from prosperity, for example, contributes to environmental destruction from poverty, since the excessive use of the world's finite resources by the overdeveloped world is a significant force in depriving the poor of sufficient resources for their essential needs, and thereby practically compelling them to choose between death and ecological degradation. Ethicist Joseph C. Hough describes the situation accurately: "In the long run, it is not those who have too little who will destroy the land. It is those few who have too much."[43]

If profligate prosperity is a causative factor in abject poverty, then this connection implies that economic disparities of such magnitude are also moral inequities. In an interdependent and resource-limited planet, a global and finite society in fact and value, the deprivation of necessities for any is an issue of justice. Scarcity is no excuse in this context. Scarcity is a useful market concept that too often has been transmuted into a pseudo-moral principle to rationalize inequities. In reality, the world's actual and potential goods appear to be sufficient to supply the provisions for the basic and creative needs of all humanity and other species, present and future, *if* justice prevails and sustainability is practiced.[44] Yet, there can be little doubt that the realization of these "ifs" will require monumental changes in the life-styles and political economies of the prosperous.

Biologist Charles Birch's often-quoted maxim describes sharply the moral responsibilities of the prosperous: "The rich must live more simply so that the poor may simply live."[45] In general, that means substantially reduced production, consumption, and accumulation in the First World in order to enable sufficient production, consumption, and accumulation in the Third World. On a planet with natural limits on economic growth, so that reducing poverty by creating a "bigger pie" is no longer a convincing alternative, it means restricting economic growth in affluent nations in order to provide the materials for essential economic development in poor countries.[46] It means fair trade, land reform, and enhanced efficiency. It means a political economy that exists *for* all people, giving priority to necessities over superfluities. It does not mean sharing in poverty, but it does mean

53

sharing in solidarity to eliminate poverty. It is an emphasis on being more rather than having more.[47] In short, for the nations which celebrate the cornucopia, this responsibility means frugality—the currently subversive virtue, for frugality is considered economically depressive in a market ethos that is obsessed with the conviction that humans live by GNP alone.

Economic justice demands economic systems that supply the material conditions for human dignity and social participation for all, within the limits of the earth's carrying capacity and the integrity of its ecosystems. Substantial debt forgiveness and "debt for nature" swaps (debt exemptions in exchange for the preservation of tropical forests) are important as interim solutions, but they are insufficient as long-term resolutions. Only authentic economic equity among nations is sufficient to halt the spiraling degradation of nature. Global economic justice is an essential good in itself, but it is also an essential condition of ecological integrity. Yet, satisfying the demands of justice and sustainability will be extremely difficult and traumatic, even "unrealistic" at this juncture. Our moral dilemma, the "predicament of the prosperous," is that "neither the human family nor the rest of nature can afford the modern world; and yet we cannot extract ourselves from it and achieve a different order without a period of wrenching, costly change"—costly for the rich and poor alike.[48] A major moral challenge for our time is to find tolerable solutions to that dilemma.

RADICAL REDUCTIONS AND EXTINCTIONS OF SPECIES: THE LOSS OF BIODIVERSITY

The term *renewable resources* is an anthropocentric euphemism. These natural provisions for human needs and wants are also an astonishing diversity of living beings struggling for sustenance and space in complex and interdependent relationships. This dual status of other species confronts humanity with a host of rarely recognized, daily dilemmas. This is the moral context in which the radical reductions and extinctions of species must be interpreted.

Plausible estimates among biologists are that somewhere between 5 and 30 million species of plants and animals, from insects to elephants, phytoplankton to redwoods, exist on the planet. The actual figure is not known even to the nearest order of magnitude.[49] Taxonomists have classified far less than 2 million species, and little is known about many of them. Yet, major losses in this rich biodiversity are feared in the next several decades. Some competent analysts suggest extinction rates of 20 to 50 percent, with the bulk in the rapidly declining and degraded rain forests where perhaps half of the probable species reside. Other species probably will be reduced substantially in numbers and populations, thus also reducing the internal, genetic diversity—and survival power—of each species.[50] This process is not simply a hypothesis; it is a current reality. Most analysts believe that the number of extinctions is now in the thousands annually. Similarly, the numbers of many bird species that migrate between North America and the South American tropics, including the vast majority of warblers, flycatchers, and vireos, are declining steadily (as most birdwatchers can verify anecdotally). Ironically, many unique and irreplaceable species are being diminished and extinguished even before they are humanly discovered and classified!

Extinctions and reductions of species are not new phenomena. Human-induced extinctions and near-extinctions have been tragic parts of human history. In the United States, the stories of certain charismatic species are well-known: the bison (once perhaps 60 million _not extinct_ strong), trumpeter swan, peregrine falcon, Carolina parakeet, Labrador duck, black-footed ferret, American chestnut, passenger pigeon, California condor, ivory-billed woodpecker, great auk, jaguar, red wolf and gray wolf, and heath hen (once an abundant food source for the eastern colonists).[51] Thousands of prominent and many more obscure species worldwide have suffered similar fates. What is new is the trend and prospect of megaextinctions of species and populations. The massive scale of anthropogenic extinctions in a matter of decades exceeds by far any previous acts in human history, let alone the millennial slowness of evolutionary extinctions. Extinctions are not reversible. They are final and forever. They mean not only the loss of regenerative potential, but also the loss of new evolutionary emergences.

The causes of these decimations are many. Every dimension of the ecological crisis—pollution, overpopulation, maldistribution, resource exhaustion—takes a heavy toll, and global warming and ozone depletion probably will do the same.[52] Overhunting endangers some species, as it did the American bison. The African elephant, for example, is jeopardized in most places by ruthless poaching to provide the affluent with ivory piano keys, billiard balls, and carved curios. Similarly, poachers overkill black bears in Tennessee for the alleged aphrodisiac effects of their gallbladders, golden eagles for the religious value of their tail feathers, and rare cats like ocelots and leopards to cloak the conspicuously rich. Trophy hunters, in the quest to display their conquering powers, try to kill the fittest of "big game" mammals, thus further weakening the genetic reservoirs of the often declining herds. "Accidents"—often really indiscriminate or careless destruction—also cause heavy losses. Oil pits and ponds that look like freshwater to flying ducks kill hundreds of thousands of migrating waterfowl annually in the western United States. Indiscriminate fishing drift nets—thirty to forty miles long—capture not only the targeted marine life but also seals, sea birds, threatened fish, and turtles. Off-road vehicles, like beach buggies, destroy the nesting sites of terns and plovers. Additional examples are abundant.

The major, direct cause of the decline and extinctions of species, however, is habitat destruction, degradation, and fragmentation. Relatively few species, unlike humans, are habitat generalists. The vast majority are specialists, dependent on particular habitats, sometimes with very precise survival requirements in temperature, altitude, food, shelter, nesting materials, and so on. Each of hundreds of species of fig trees, for example, is dependent on a different species of wasp for pollination. Seventy-five or more species of birds in North America are dependent on dead trees and branches for food and nesting sites. Thus, the destruction of habitat—which may be a single type or size of tree or grass—will mean the extinction or numerical decline of a species. And if the species is a "keystone," on which many other species are dependent in the intricate bridgework of nature, whole ecosystems may decline or disintegrate.

This habitat destruction is growing in intensity and extent throughout the world. No habitat is secure—not grasslands, tropical forests, temperate forests, deserts, arctic or alpine tundra, oceans, rivers, estuaries, or any other habitat. Consequently, no species is truly safe—not even humans who depend on other creatures for all our needs, from nutrition to oxygen.

Under the pressures of overpopulation, maldistribution, and economic expansion, natural habitats are being converted for "development." Development takes many forms, including farms, industries, oil facilities, logging mills, suburban residences, shopping centers, and the like. The problem is particularly acute in tropical rain forests. They are now being burned, bulldozed, and logged for cattle ranches (often exporting their beef for fast-food chains), mines, smelters, hydroelectric projects, "farms" for coca (cocaine), exotic woods (especially from Southeast Asia), and short-term subsistence farms on nutrient-poor soils for poor settlers. In the process, indigenous peoples are also displaced from their homelands. Though much tropical deforestation is a consequence of greedy exploitation by economic elites, much is also a consequence of agricultural clearance by poor people trying to feed themselves and indebted nations trying to produce exportable goods for foreign exchange.

In the United States, the old growth forest in the East is long gone, and it is severely depleted and fragmented in the Pacific Northwest. The northern spotted owl, threatened with dehabitation by the logging of the last vestiges of ancient forest, is the scapegoat for a timber industry that has been undercutting its job base for decades by overcutting its raw materials and is now undercutting potential local jobs by exporting unprocessed logs to Japan. Brazil is only starting to do what the United States did and is doing, but the ecological consequences will be far worse.

In most developed areas, habitat destruction often leaves behind habitat fragmentation—remnants or islands of the original ecosystems that are generally too small or too isolated to support long-enduring populations of many species. The genetic pool depends on input from migrants to avoid harmful inbreeding. Without wildlife corridors connecting these patches, highways and other human developments function as fences for some species and make them vulnerable to local disasters. Adequate habitat is the key to survival for all species.

But why protect biodiversity? This is a key moral question. One answer is strictly anthropocentric and instrumentalistic. Biodiversity has immense, largely untapped potential for human benefits. Species and their genetic adaptations can make major contributions to agriculture, medicine, and industry, potentially worth billions commercially. Tropical forests have been described as pharmaceutical laboratories, with various plants and insects embodying chemical structures that offer the potential of new medical drugs, maybe even cancer cures. New foodstuffs and new disease-resistant and higher yielding crops are possibilities. Even "green gasoline" can be derived from plants that, like fossil fuels, contain hydrocarbons rather than carbohydrates and grow well in strip-mined areas.[53] Wild species are "a storehouse for human welfare."[54] Biodiversity is an essential condition of sustainable development, according to the World Commission on Environment and Development.[55] Consequently, humanity cannot afford to destroy these rich resources; they are sources of long-term economic wealth and human well-being, which far surpass any short-term gains from destroying them.

57

This rationale for biodiversity cannot be dismissed. It is a valid argument as far as it goes. It is even a moral argument insofar as it focuses on human welfare. It also can be strategically effective, counteracting the standardized economic arguments—jobs, profits, tax revenues—given for the destruction of habitats. But this rationale's strength is also its weakness: it is strictly anthropocentric and says nothing about human responsibilities to other creatures. Many species may have no significant value for humanity. What happens then? And even if they do have value for humans, what responsibilities, if any, do we have to them?

Thus another answer is that whatever instrumental values otherkind have for humans, they are valuable in themselves as unique works of God and/or evolutionary processes. How are they to be treated as biological relatives? Do they have moral claims on us? Are concepts of justice and rights applicable to nonhuman species and/or individuals? Are they entitled to living space, sustenance, healthy habitats? What conditions, if any, are necessary for overriding these rights? I will raise some additional and related questions when discussing a related issue, genetic engineering. Answers to these questions can have significant effects on ecological attitudes and behavior. They, therefore, will occupy us at some length in later chapters.

Another critical moral issue revolves around the question of national or regional sovereignty. Who "owns" the "renewable resources" of particular locales, or who has the rights and responsibilities of oversight? Are initiatives to preserve tropical rain forests, for example, the proper response of all humankind, or outside interference in the internal affairs of other nations? Are the creatures of the earth part of the "commons," like the high seas, belonging to none but a resource for and a responsibility of all? From any perspective that affirms the earth as a global community in fact and value, in which all parts are related to and affected by all other parts, the answers are at least that all people have legitimate interests in protecting the species of any place on the earth, and all nations have responsibilities as global stewards to preserve and use sustainably the species in their territory for the good of the whole, human and otherkind. These rights and responsibilities apply universally, not only to the Amazonian tropical forests but to the Olympic Peninsula's temperate forests, not only to the elephants of Africa but also to the much rarer desert bighorns, gray wolves, and grizzly bears in North America, not only to charismatic species but also to obscure invertebrates and flowers.

58

GENETIC ENGINEERING: RESTRAINING HUMAN POWERS

[handwritten: What does the Bible say regarding this?]

No one can say that genetic engineering (or recombinant DNA technology) is a part of the ecological crisis—yet. But this revolutionary power has the potential to become a serious ecological problem in coming decades. Genetic engineering is the extraordinary scientific capacity to manipulate and modify the genetic constitution of cells and organisms, even to the point of cloning multiple copies of revised organisms and crossing the reproductive barriers among species. Some suggest that genetic engineering is not new in principle; its forerunners include selective breeding in domestic animals and plant hybridization. Yet, its methods and its results—especially cloned genes and transspecies hybrids—seem to be not merely extensions of its forerunners but also qualitative differences. If so, the moral issues may also be distinctive.

In Christian ethics, genetic engineering has generally been discussed anthropocentrically as a problem of biomedical ethics and, to a lesser degree, agricultural benefits for humans, but it is also a problem of ecological ethics for humans vis-à-vis all other creatures. Like most sophisticated technologies, this one promises both potential blessings and curses, both power for good and power for evil. And the key word here is power, for genetic engineering is in large measure a question of the ethics of using and abusing power.

On the one hand, the potential products of genetic engineering could improve the human prospect. They include health benefits: new medications, vaccines, and therapies, perhaps at lower costs. In the case of a few hereditary disorders traceable to a single gene, genetic therapy might be able to replace the defective gene.[56] In agriculture, genetic technology could provide higher yields and faster growth from crops and stock; drought-resistant, herbicide-resistant, and pest-resistant crops; biopesticides and petroleum substitutes from plants. The list could go on at length. Euphorically and uncritically, Norman Myers describes the positive side of a bioengineered future:

Among the marvels of genetic engineering that we can confidently anticipate within the present decade [1980s!] should be, for instance, a crop plant that supplies us with edible leaves, high-protein beanlike seeds, large nutritious tubers, and useful fiber from the stalk. Genetic engineering will help us to grow a super-tree that matures in just a few years instead of several decades, incorporating a whole bunch of *desirable timber traits* in its wood. Genetic engineering will enable us to *devise bugs*

59

that degrade environmental pollutants, and even help us to extract more minerals from the ground. Genetic engineering will *create new life forms* (there is no better phrase for the process) that will with their *tailormade attributes serve our needs* in scores of ways.

In short, biotechnology offers us the possibility of building a sustainable future based on renewable resources. Its potential could well bring us closer to material well-being for all citizens on Earth than has been achieved through human ingenuity during the whole of human history.[57]

On the other hand, genetic engineering has a negative side that can harm the prospects of humanity and other creatures. Indeed, Norman Myers' vision may be not only an exaggeration (as were his expectations for the 1980s) but also a dangerously anthropocentric hope. Genetic engineering can be hazardous to the health and wealth of the earth.

It portends some major environmental risks, such as monocultures—the reduction or elimination of multiple genetic strains of plants and animals. Agricultural hybridization has stressed genetic similarity, in order to maximize productivity and other humanly desirable traits. Now, cloning makes possible the genetic identity of agricultural plants and animals. In contrast, genetic diversity in nature is a survival strategy for species, increasing the chances that some members will adapt to different habitats and to environmental changes, such as climatic conditions or newly evolved predators. In fact, "defective" genes from a human perspective may be survival mechanisms under changed conditions. In this context, genetic uniformity means high vulnerability. As natural biodiversity disappears or declines, genetically engineered strains, as in maize, may not be able to adapt to adversities and may also disappear or decline. Humans know too little about ecological dynamics to take such risks.[58]

Another danger is the introduction of new life forms into the biosphere—either accidentally or deliberately by experimental curiosity or biological warfare. This was the stuff of science fiction and horror films, but it is now not totally far-fetched. Some engineered organisms, without coevolved natural predators, could be pathogenic or otherwise harmful to humans, other species, or ecosystemic relationships. That is not unprecedented, as illustrated by the damaging effects to ecosystems from the introduction of alien species into vulnerable environments—rabbits in Australia, the Nile Perch in Africa's Lake Victoria, rats in Hawaii, and gypsy moths in the northeastern United States.

Yet, the science fiction accounts probably are heavily inflated. One distinguished ecologist, Paul Ehrlich, claims that the danger of a superorganism with ecologically catastrophic potential is "almost certainly exaggerated;" "A universally lethal pathogen seems virtually impossible." If such an organism is to cause widespread havoc, it would need to be a superior competitor and relatively resistant to predation. Ehrlich doubts that such an organism could maintain a viable population worldwide. Nevertheless, he is not sanguine: engineered organisms, like other exotica, could cause local or temporary ecological disasters.[59] Other scientists see even greater risks—including unexpected mutations and the accumulation of local disasters—and urge extreme caution and stricter regulations.

Even without these risks, however, genetic engineering raises serious questions about the legitimacy of human powers vis-à-vis other species of plants and animals. Much of the hype celebrating the new technology implies that nonhuman species are simply "machines" to be reconstructed or information bits to be reprogrammed and upgraded, without controls or bounds. It is the finale in the ideology of the mastery and management (requiring ever more management because of mismanagement) of nature for human advantages. While moratoria and bans are justifiably proposed on modifications of human germ or reproductive cells (which would affect all succeeding generations, unlike therapy on somatic cells, which affects only individuals), the same alterations are frequently assumed as morally valid for nonhuman species. Are otherkind simply "matter" or DNA to be reorganized, or are they in some sense subjects, intrinsic values whose physical integrity ought to be respected? Should natural species' barriers be honored, so that nonhuman species can propagate their own kind in perpetuity and not some genetically altered kind? Is uncontrolled genetic engineering on nonhuman species a license for the ecological equivalent of genocide? Human civilization depends on interventions in and humanly beneficial improvements upon nature, but is the whole of nature to be defined by human purposes and subject to human improvements? What are the limits? What alternatives are available and satisfactory? Since members of other species cannot be informed or give informed consent, what justifications are necessary for genetic alterations, and who should function as advocates for their interests?

These are among the key questions that ecological ethics should direct to the new biological technology. Answers, of course, depend on value assumptions. My own view is that the transmutation of species warrants nothing resembling blanket sanctions. It is not the norm but the rare exception on which the burden of proof rests. The genetic reconstruction of some species may be justified for compelling human needs in medicine, agriculture, or ecological repairs (for example, oil-eating microbes), *so long as* it can be reasonably tested and verified that tolerable alternatives are not available, genetic diversity is not compromised, and ecosystemic integrity is not endangered. More refined criteria for interventions in nature will be noted in a later chapter, but the above-mentioned ones are sufficient here to suggest some necessary limits on recombinant DNA.

The point is that the biosphere cannot be reduced to an instrument for human welfare; it has its own integrity which, in the final analysis, is also the integrity of the human species as part of nature. Convenience, comfort, commodities, and commercialism are not adequate excuses for distorting a species' genetic heritage and ecological connections. In a rather far-fetched example, a mosquito that doesn't suck blood would be a source of comfort on a warm evening near a marsh or swamp. But the biodiversity of the marsh or swamp would be severely simplified, because the "mosquito" would no longer be a mosquito and it would, therefore, no longer serve such vital ecosystemic functions as providing the blood-derived nutrients on which so many species, including humans, are directly or indirectly dependent. Respect for evolutionary legacies and ecological relations (about which even the biological sciences know remarkably little) are strong reasons for strong constraints on the new technology.

Yet, so long as human economic "needs" are defined as insatiable or expansively acquisitive, particularly in material possessions and commodities, it will be nearly impossible to define the bounds of genetic or other interventions in nature.[60] Some new "want" in the garb of an urgent "need" will always emerge to justify a new transgenetic creature and another step toward the total artificialization and simplification of nature. This dynamic suggests that the preservation of biodiversity depends on a narrower redefinition of human needs and the "quality of life" in affluent societies. Alterations in the genes of species may not appear valuable or imperative with alterations in the definition of human needs and patterns of consumption.[61]

Genetic engineering is a vast, awesome, and potentially dangerous power, socially and ecologically. It must be controlled to prevent abuses. Indeed, that need is not in dispute: national and regional regulations have long been operative. But *who* should control? Certainly not the bioengineers themselves! They have professional interests and temptations, and some will succumb to corruption and folly. Abuses of this power are inevitable, as the Christian doctrine of sin warns us. "Pure" science has never meant moral purity. And certainly the controllers should not be the private enterprises that dominate present research and development. Their primary interests are maximizing profits and, therefore, preventing access to "trade secrets" and the duplication of their products (thus the desire for patents on their genetic re-creations, which will probably accentuate the dependency of poor nations and small farmers). The only reasonable answer seems to be various forms of public control, with legislative oversight, regulatory agencies, and a knowledgeable and vigilant citizenry. In fact, international guidelines and structures of enforcement are probably necessary,[62] since all nations have vital stakes in bioengineering outcomes.

No matter who has control, a healthy dose of humility is indispensable in an area where hubris now dominates.[63] Humility is the antidote to arrogance in our interactions with the biosphere. Despite the extraordinary intellectual and technical achievements in bioengineering and other biological disciplines, human knowledge is fragmented, our ingenuity is limited, and our moral character is ambiguous. We know very little about biological connections and the consequences of human interventions. Practically, we do not have the powers to master all natural dynamics, and, ethically, we ought not to exercise all of the limited powers that we do have. Otherkind also have interests, which, as I will argue later, ought to be respected. Humility prevents the exaggeration of human value at the expense of the undervaluation of other creatures. It punctures the pretensions in zealous theological ideas like cocreatorship. Humility reminds us that the miracles of genetic engineering are trivial in comparison with the surrounding magnitude of evolutionary and ecological miracles, which deserve preservation.

THE ECOLOGICAL VIRTUES

Values cannot logically be derived from facts, but facts can suggest the values that are imperative if we intend to be appropriately responsive to the facts. Thus, in the light of the moral problems associated with the various dimensions of the ecological crisis, what attitudes and habits will enable individuals and communities to respond remedially to these problems? Or, what are the characteristics and traits that are conducive to the goal of ecological integrity and that, therefore, we ought to cultivate?

The answers are what I call the "ecological virtues." They are the patterns of personal and social perspective and behavior that, if followed, can make ecological integrity a reality. These virtues overlap to some degree, but they are sufficiently distinctive to warrant separate consideration. All are necessary and interactive. An outline of them is an appropriate summary of this and the preceding chapter.

The nine ecological virtues are as follows:

1. *Sustainability* is living within the bounds of the regenerative, absorptive, and carrying capacities of the earth, continuously and indefinitely. Its prime concern is long-range intergenerational equity: "A sustainable society is one that satisfies its needs without jeopardizing the prospects of future generations."[64] Sustainability is the most celebrated ecological virtue today in the circles of environmentalists, and justifiably so, because a primary characteristic of ecological problems is *un*sustainability. The peoples of the earth are living beyond natural means, and future generations will be major victims of our generation's excessive consumption, toxication, destruction, and reproduction.

But sustainability is not the all-sufficient ecological virtue, that some proponents suggest. It includes distributive justice for the present generation in some definitions,[65] though certainly not all, but it does not imply justice logically. Justice, in any case, is a virtue that deserves to stand on its own alongside sustainability, not as a sub-division of it. Similarly, sustainability implies the preservation of biodiversity, but primarily on anthropocentric grounds, for the sake of the well-being of future human generations.[66] Sustainability then is an indispensable virtue, but not the only or all-encompassing one.

2. *Adaptability* is closely related to sustainability. Recognizing ecological limits, adaptability is the accommodation to those forces and constraints of nature that cannot be changed. As the clichés say, it does not "defy gravity"; it does not "tempt fate"; it does not "live on the edge." It does, however, expect the uncontrollable and unpredictable but inevitable, like droughts and floods, fires and earthquakes. And it allows for these and other eventualities in its calculations, so that communities can respond flexibly. Adaptability is part of the ethics of the fitting: it is living within the bounds of natural limitations and cycles, avoiding unnecessary risks, and allowing room to recover from novel problems.

Adaptability is an ecological virtue because so many ecological problems evidence the lack of it—for instance, reducing an ecosystem or a species' population to a remnant that can be annihilated by a single natural disaster, reducing the genetic composition of an agricultural grain to a monoculture, or risking the ecological dangers of nuclear energy or global warming. Not everything requires adaptability; many things can be changed, but some things ought not to be changed. Moral wisdom is knowing the difference.

3. *Relationality* is the acute sensitivity to the fact that everything is connected with and has consequences for everything else. We can never do merely one thing, says one aphorism. This virtue is derived from the elementary lesson of ecology: the intricate interdependence and systemic cycles of all life forms in their environments. Relationality is a corrective response to assumptions of isolation and fragmentation that have caused ecological disasters by neglecting relationships—for instance, the connections between ozone depletion and CFCs, global warming and the burning of fossil fuels, population growth and resource depletion, or habitat destruction and species' extinction. Relationality is a counsel of caution to be responsive to the environmental impacts of our activities. It also means being aware of the multiple dimensions of the ecological crisis and their linkages, and acting in ways that the solution to one social or environmental problem does not cause or aggravate another social or environmental problem. Relationality requires us to think holistically.

4. *Frugality* connotes thrift, moderation, efficiency, simplicity of life-style, and stringent conservation. As the antithesis of consumerism and prodigality, it thrives on the control of consumption, the reduction of waste, and comprehensive recycling. It is the key to sustainability, equity, and biodiversity. Voluntary frugality also, therefore, is the economically subversive virtue from the perspective of the affluent and effluent societies. It means, as the current slogan says, "living lightly on the earth." Frugality is a virtue that applies only and progressively to the prosperous.

5. *Equity* here is simply a synonym for justice in the distribution of the world's goods and services, so that all human beings have the essential material conditions for human dignity and social participation. Since economic deprivation is a major cause and effect of ecological degradation, justice is a necessary condition of ecological sustainability. This virtue applies also to the fair distribution of costs and benefits for pollution and other forms of ecological degradation (for example, the "polluter pays principle"). Equity is an anthropocentric value, but one that is intimately associated with ecological integrity.

6. *Solidarity* is, as Pope John Paul II effectively argued, the moral response to the reality of human interdependence.[67] Solidarity today

must be global and environmental. The classical moral principle of subsidiarity rightly assigned the performance of a social task to the lowest social unit capable of performing it effectively. On particular environmental concerns, that unit might be the nation, the state, the city or town, a voluntary association, or even the family. But considering the macrocosmic dimensions of the current crisis, the lowest social unit capable of responding effectively is the international community. The problems cannot be understood or fully resolved on a lesser scale—as global warming, ozone depletion, and the fall-out from Chernobyl illustrate. The world is now the relevant whole for much moral decision-making. The nations' actions and destinies are bound together. Global solidarity, then, is the virtue that seeks to institutionalize—economically and politically—global responses to the ecological crisis.

7. *Biodiversity* is both a fact and a value. It is the extension of solidarity to the whole biosphere. It is perhaps also implied by some of the other virtues, such as relationality and equity, but it is too important and has been too neglected to be reduced to a sub-category. Respect for biodiversity is a commitment to sustaining viable populations of all other species in healthy habitats until the end of their evolutionary time. It is, therefore, characterized by antagonism to the radical reductions and extinctions of species. This virtue, unlike sustainability, seeks to save other creatures for their sake, not solely for the sake of humanity.

8. *Sufficiency* represents the overtly political wing of the ecological virtues. It means that solutions must be proportionate to the intricacies and magnitude of the problems. Thus sufficiency is the opposite of the standard syndrome of too little and/or too late—such as minor penalties for major pollution, or regulatory agencies like the EPA with inadequate resources and powers, or an emphasis on voluntary actions when only public coercion will work, or legislation that reduces the severity of a problem but does not prevent it at the source, or an obsession with economic growth when only a new economic order can resolve the crisis. The virtue of sufficiency simply impels us to find solutions that are a match for the problems.

9. *Humility* is the self-realistic virtue—and the self-deflating one for the arrogant—that recognizes the limitations on human knowledge, technological ingenuity, moral character, and biological status. It avoids overconfidence in human powers to control nature, exaggerations of human authority and rights over nature, and undervaluations

of other creatures and their rights. Humility is a guiding norm for all the other virtues. I will discuss humility further in chapter 6.

* *
** **

A critical question is: Can Christian theology and ethics support and nurture these ecological virtues? That is one of the implicit questions in the next several chapters. As the next chapter indicates, however, the question is not mere rhetoric. There have been considerable doubts and debates about Christianity's ecological credentials and potential.

CHAPTER THREE

THE ECOLOGICAL COMPLAINT
AGAINST CHRISTIANITY

T he ecological complaint is the charge that the Christian faith is the culprit in the crisis. Christianity is the primary or at least a significant cause of ecological degradation. It is so human-centered that it is inherently, or at least has been historically, indifferent or hostile toward nature and, therefore, antiecological. "Man" is the center of all created values for Christianity—it is alleged. The ecological complaint accuses Christianity of advocating the human domination and/or damnation of the biophysical world for the sake of material exploitation or spiritual elevation (a curious contradiction suggestive of Christian diversity, which most of the complainants never notice in their singularly indiscriminate assaults). Consequently, claim the complainants, Christianity should be superseded or abandoned, in favor of a new or another religion, perhaps from the East or traditional native American cultures, or at least Christianity must be radically altered.

These charges are widespread and persistent, though some think they are declining in breadth and intensity. Most Christians who are environmentally involved have heard or read the complaint with dulling regularity, and many accept its basic case as valid. Those, however, who believe that the complaint is a half-truth or distortion of the truth would like to move beyond self-defense to a collaborative offense with the accusers against environmental deterioration. But that goal is not easily reached. The residue of the complaint seems as environmentally persistent as an oil spill, and new globs keep popping to the surface.

In recent years, the complaint appeared again in a prominent place, the *Time* magazine issue on the Endangered Earth as Planet of the Year. Though in subdued garb, *Time*'s version of the complaint mistakes hypotheses for firmly established facts and displays some of the faded fashions from the late 1960s:

> The Judeo-Christian tradition introduced a radically different concept [from other religio-cultural traditions]. The earth was a creation of a monotheistic God, who after shaping it, ordered its inhabitants, in the words of Genesis: "Be fruitful and multiply, and replenish the Earth and subdue it: and have dominion over the fish of the sea and over the fowl of the air and over every living thing that moveth upon the earth." The idea of dominion could be interpreted as an invitation to use nature as a convenience. Thus, the spread of Christianity, which is generally considered to have paved the way for the development of technology, may at the same time have carried the seeds of the wanton exploitation of nature that often accompanied technological progress.[1]

But the ecological complaint has far deeper roots than popular news magazines. It has scholarly sources and has been a worthy subject of scholarly debate. Oftentimes, the complaint has been called "the Lynn White thesis," but not because this cultural historian was the first or only one to state it. Many others had expressed similar sentiments, sometimes much earlier. Alan W. Watts, for example, contended that while Christianity is not inherently antinature, it is an "urban" religion that fits poorly with nature and has encouraged technological transformations of nature.[2] Arnold Toynbee blamed it all on Judeo-Christian monotheism, which allegedly desacralized nature and which should be supplanted by a once-universal, nature-reverencing pantheism (actually animism).[3] Nonetheless, Lynn White, Jr. was the first to popularize the idea—and popularize it with a vengeance he (or more accurately, his fans) did! The famous Lynn White essay, called "The Historical Roots of Our Ecologic Crisis,"[4] is considered by many to be a classic of environmental literature, almost as well-known perhaps as Aldo Leopold's *Sand County Almanac*. "Historical Roots" has been reprinted in numerous books and periodicals—including the handbook for the first Earth Day in 1970.[5] I can see at this moment on my bookshelves six sources in which the essay is reprinted. The thesis has been popular and widely accepted as "gospel."

What is Lynn White's version of the ecological complaint? White (incidentally, "a churchman") argued that the distinctive Western tradition of modern technology and science is "deeply conditioned," historically and presently, by Christian beliefs. Despite the claim that contemporary North Americans are living in a post-Christian age, the traditional substance of Christian values remains the same in our culture. We continue to live in a context of "Christian axioms," like "perpetual progress"—which, contrary to White, is widely regarded by Christian theologians as a heresy. Primarily but not exclusively in its Western forms (specifically, Roman Catholic and Puritan Protestantism), Christianity is "the most anthropocentric religion the world has seen," since it operates on the assumption that "God planned all of this explicitly for man's benefit and rule: no item in the physical creation had any purpose save to serve man's purposes." Modern science and technology, which operate on assumptions about the mastery and exploitation of nature, emerge out of Christian attitudes that are almost universally held by Christians. Christianity bears "a huge burden of guilt" for our crisis, and "we shall continue to have a worsening ecologic crisis until we reject the Christian axiom that nature has no reason for existence save to serve man." White concludes by calling for the value of ecological egalitarianism, "the democracy of all God's creatures," allegedly following St. Francis who should be the patron saint of ecologists. Since the root of the crisis is religious, the remedy must be essentially religious, particularly a reformed Christianity (a point that many of White's fans fail to emphasize).[6]

White's original thesis has been repeated often and by many, sometimes far more harshly and unambiguously than White himself expressed it. Consequently, the effects of the allegations have been multiplied. One example is Donald Worster's claims about "Christian pastoralism" in his justly celebrated history of the science of ecology, *Nature's Economy.*

Worster berates "Christian pastoralism," which he says is quite unlike the classical arcadian pastoralism with its emphasis on the simple moral life in peace with the earth and its creatures. In contrast, Christian pastoralism allegedly idealizes the role of the Good Shepherd in relation to his flock of faithful believers, defending them against the hostile forces of nature—wolves, lions, bears—and leading them to greener pastures.[7] He argues, using White as an authority:

> This second variety of pastoralism illustrates nicely what observers have long noticed about Christianity (and its Judaic background): of all the major religions in the world, it has been the most insistently anti-natural. In the mind of the average Christian, argues historian Lynn White, Jr.,

nature's chief function is to serve man's needs. In extreme cases, nature is seen as the source of demonic threats, fleshly appetites, and animal instincts that must be rigorously repressed. No religion, this authority on the medieval period believes, has been more anthropocentric. None has been more rigid in excluding all but man from the realm of divine grace and in denying any moral obligation to the lower species. . . . This general animus against nature in Christianity seems to have been most pronounced in Roman Catholicism and, ironically, in its arch opponent on so many other matters, the Puritan wing of Protestantism. Christian apologists in recent years have sometimes pointed to one outstanding exception: [St. Francis]. . . . But such rare exceptions have not disproved the essential truth in the observation that Christianity has maintained a calculated indifference, if not antagonism, toward nature. The good shepherd, the heroic benefactor of man, has almost never been concerned with leading his flock to a broad reverence for life. His pastoral duties have been limited to ensuring the welfare of his human charges, often in the face of a nature that has been seen as corrupt and predatory.[8]

A virtual tradition of responding to Lynn White has emerged among Christian professionals writing on environmental concerns. White has been a prime provocateur, goading some theologians and ethicists to become "defenders of the faith" or, more frequently, critics and reformers of the church, who often are the true defenders of the faith. He awakened many of us from our doldrums. It is probably true that "White's paper, perhaps more than any other single factor, was responsible for making the Creation and the need for its stewardly care an issue in the Christian press."[9] If so, that fact alone means that the churches owe Lynn White a profound debt of gratitude.

I have no desire here to follow in this tradition of responding to Lynn White. In some respects, that would be anachronistic, perpetuating and duplicating the now-hackneyed harangues of yesteryear. Nevertheless, the ecological complaint against Christianity persists, and it demands ongoing responses to new versions if Christians and their churches are to interpret their faith soundly and to have credibility and pride of place in the circles of environmentalists. The issues are part of an ethos, not a single essay, and the necessary responses are far more numerous and complicated than can be expressed in this chapter. They will require the contributions from many of the broadly-defined theological disciplines, including systematics, social ethics, sociology of religion, biblical studies, and church history. Nevertheless, perhaps I can add here some different touches and angles that will prompt deeper research.

71

A CONFESSION OF SIN

A satisfactory response to the ecological complaint against Christianity must begin with a forthright confession that at least much of the complaint is essentially true. Christianity does bear part of the burden of guilt for our ecological crisis. Ongoing repentance is warranted. It will not do to draw a neat distinction between Christianity and Christendom, between the faith itself and perversions of it by its practitioners.[10] That distinction may be formally or logically true, as I agree, but it is facile and unconvincing when applied to history. We cannot so easily distinguish between the faith and the faithful. The fact is that Christianity—*as interpreted and affirmed* by billions of its adherents over the centuries and in official doctrines and theological exegeses—has been ecologically tainted. A normative Tradition exists formally (as we all assume in our efforts to articulate it), but the practical reality is that the historical traditions have disagreed on what that normative Tradition is. Moreover, even the sourcebook of that Tradition, the Bible, has treated ecological relationships peripherally and pluralistically. The bottom line is that Christianity itself cannot escape an indictment for ecological negligence and abuse. Functionally, a few alleged "Christian axioms" have been part of the problem, while other, more central ones have been neglected.

Ecological concerns have rarely been a prominent, let alone a dominant, feature in Christian theory and practice. That is true in both the so-called Eastern and Western churches, though less so in the former. In the mainstream traditions in the West, Protestant and Catholic, the ecosphere has generally been perceived as theologically and ethically trivial, if even relevant. The biophysical world has been treated either as the scenery or stage for the divine-human drama, which usually alone has redemptive significance, or as a composite of "things," which have no significant meaning or value beyond their utility for human interests—aesthetic, scientific, recreational, but mostly economic interests, particularly human production and consumption.

For most theologians—Augustine to Luther, Aquinas to Barth, and the bulk of others in between and before and after—the theological focus has been on sin and salvation, the fall and redemption, the divine-human relationship over against the biophysical world as a whole. The focus has been overwhelmingly on human history to the neglect of natural history, even to the point of forgetting the profound influences that natural history exercises on human history. This focus has often been associated with significant dichotomies in Christian attitudes toward the "world": body and soul, material and spiritual, nature and supernature, nature and humanity, secular and sacred, creation and redemption, even female and male—the latter usually being the superior, and the interdependencies poorly understood.

The radically ascetic *contemptus mundi* tradition, with its obsession for the salvation of the soul and its disdain for biophysical realities, carried this dualism to extremes. Though most Christian thought in the Middle Ages accepted the concept of the Great Chain of Being, with its emphases on the plenitude, continuity, and hierarchy of creation, that tradition contained conflicting tendencies, one on ascent to the Creator and the other on immersion in the creation. Most Christian spiritual writers stressed the former. Thus, while formally valuing the hierarchy of being, they were functionally dualistic—focusing on contemplation of the divine and advocating withdrawal from the biophysical world.[11] *Contemptus mundi* can hardly be blamed for direct environmental abuse or overuse, but its indirect effects were serious: it dismissed the theological and ethical relevance of the biophysical world from which it was alienated, and thereby gave tacit (rarely explicit) permission for environmental destruction to proceed as an ultimately and morally immaterial matter.

The sin of omission is evident in the *contemptus mundi* tradition, but this sin cannot be restricted to that strain of Christianity. *Contemptus mundi* represents an extreme form of a dualism that is present in different degrees in most historical strains of Christian thought and practice—a dualism that has neglected or negated nature, a dualism that has been an ecological sin of omission, and a dualism that has contributed to and/or often sanctioned various ecological sins of commission.

These ecological sins of omission and commission continue into the present. For instance, only during the last thirty or so years has an ecological concern arisen with some visibility among modern Christian theologians and ethicists, and then only among a small minority, some of whom still argue from a strictly anthropocentric base. Today, for the bulk of Christian theologians and ethicists, ecological consciousness and concern remain relatively minor. Fortunately, the situation is now improving, but Paul Santmire's description of the theological times seems to me to be still close to accurate: "According to a large number of contemporary Christian writers . . . Christian theology never has had, nor should it have, a substantial ecological dimension. These writers are convinced that Christian theology must focus primarily—even exclusively—on human history, not on the history of nature."[12]

Historically and presently, the theological mainstreams, though by no means every tributary or every element in the mainstreams, have displayed, as Donald Worster charges, "a calculated indifference, if not antagonism, toward nature." Anthropocentrism has been and remains a norm in the dominant strains of Christian theology and piety, and it has served as both a stimulus and a rationalization for environmental destruction in Christian-influenced cultures. Again, Paul Santmire seems to be on target: "In the nineteenth and early twentieth centuries, Protestant theology by and large washed its hands of nature . . . and thereby gave the spirit of modern industrialism its de facto permission—sometimes its de jure encouragement—to work its will on nature."[13] I would add only that the same description seems applicable also to Roman Catholic and Orthodox theology and ethics.

The central thrust of the ecological complaint against Christianity, therefore, should not be discounted. Christianity has done too little to discourage and too much to encourage the exploitation of nature. Though it is no comfort, it is still worthy of note that humans were often not treated much better than other animals in most periods and manifestations of Christianity's morally ambiguous history. Yet, the complaint is an overgeneralization. It tends to reduce the explanation of the complex ecological crisis to a single cause, to exaggerate the authority of Christianity in cultures, to minimize the fact that non-Christian cultures also have been environmental despoilers, to overlook the number of dissenting opinions in Christian history, and to underestimate the potential for ecological reform in Christianity. Some of these weaknesses, in fact, could be harmful, if they hinder our search for causes, effects, and solutions to the crisis. With this view in mind, I turn now to five corrective responses to the ecological complaint.

NO SINGLE CAUSE

The single cause theory for the emergence of our ecological crisis is pathetically simplistic. Lynn White generally recognized that fact, but he too succumbed finally to oversimplification. And most other complainants have been undeterred by fears of reductionism. They often have structured their complaint on a single, flimsy biblical passage (Gen. 1:28) dealing with "dominion," and have ignored the

74

fact that the Christian faith and its cultural influences have been far more complicated and ambiguous than that. Theirs is proof-texting of the worst sort. They have accused Christianity of being the parent of ecologically debilitating forms of industrialization, commercialism, and technology. However, in historical reality, many complex and interwoven causes were involved—and Christian thought was probably not the most prominent one. In fact, Christians and their churches frequently resisted these developments (though not always for morally defensible reasons).

Eco-historian Carolyn Merchant in her excellent book, *The Death of Nature,* argues against the oversimplification of causation in anti-ecological attitudes and behavior. Focusing on the emergence of modern science and technology in Europe between 1500 and 1700, she explicitly refutes much of the ecological complaint:

> In the 1960s, the Native American became the symbol in the ecological movement's search for alternatives to Western exploitative attitudes. The Indian animistic belief system and reverence for the earth as a mother were contrasted with the Judeo-Christian heritage of dominion over nature and with capitalist practices resulting in the "tragedy of the commons." . . . But . . . European culture was more complex and varied than this judgment allows. It ignores the Renaissance philosophy of the nurturing earth as well as those philosophies and social movements resistant to mainstream economic change.[14]

Merchant contends that Christian-rooted images of the earth as a living organism (vitalistic, organistic, and arcadian philosophies) served as important ethical and cultural restraints against the denudation of nature[15]—particularly against the "rape" of Earth and the pollutive effects of mining, the drainage of the fens and the destruction of their biological diversity, the deforestation resulting from the growth of shipbuilding and other industries, and urban pollution from coal-burning.[16] The major factors in the emergence of antiecological attitudes and actions were not Christian axioms, but rather population pressures, the development of expansionistic capitalism in the forms of commercialism and industrialization (particularly ship-building, glassworks, iron and copper smelting),[17] the triumph of Cartesian mechanism in science (which meant the "death" of nature, since it represented the defeat of organic assumptions, and the victory of the view that nature is "dead," inert particles moved by external forces),[18] and the triumph of Francis Bacon's notions of dominion as mastery over nature.[19] Resistance to these developments was strong, and generally operated on Christian value assumptions other than exploitative dominion. Many saw it as wrong to meddle with God's design, and some interpreted dominion as the role of caretaker of God's creation.[20] The prevailing values prior to the scientific-technological revolution in this period were typically medieval Christian assumptions other than exploitative dominion: "The Chaucerian and typically Elizabethan view of nature was that of a kindly and caring mother provider, a manifestation of the God who imprinted a designed, planned order on the world."[21]

Merchant's thesis generally corresponds with that of Clarence Glacken in his classic ecological history, *Traces on the Rhodian Shore.* The contemporary distortion of dominion as a sanction for control over and radical modification of nature began to crystallize in this period. The scientific-technological-industrial revolution had many causes, and religion was not a dominant one.[22]

Merchant's thesis is also reminiscent of R. H. Tawney's classic, *Religion and the Rise of Capitalism.* The post-Reformation economic order was not embraced with enthusiasm; it was resisted by many of the leaders from the several churches—Catholic, Lutheran, Calvinist, Anglican, and Anabaptist.[23] Calvinistic Puritanism, and later the other churches following suit, did eventually give sanctions to some of the new commercial and industrial developments. They did not create these conditions, but they responded favorably to *some* of them (reflecting the socioeconomic makeup of their membership). Tawney states his theory clearly: "The 'capitalist spirit' is as old as history, and was not, as has sometimes been said, the offspring of Puritanism. But it found in certain aspects of *later* Puritanism a tonic which braced its energies and fortified its already vigorous temper."[24]

This assertion does not mean, however, that classical Puritanism would have blessed the ecological devastations caused by contemporary industrialization and technocratic development. Quite the contrary! The Puritans advocated the virtues of thrift, moderation, frugality, sobriety, and diligence[25]—noble values, indeed. These values, of course, led to an accumulation of capital among many of the adherents of Puritanism (to the point of distorting the social perspectives of some segments of this movement). Yet, these very values represent the antithesis of the modern norms of effluent and opulent capitalism, and these very values also represent the essence of the modern environmental movement's norms of sustainable lifestyles. Ironically, the chief ecological virtues of the modern environmental movement correspond with the virtues of classical Puritanism (and, of course, with much earlier forms of Christian austerity), which many in the movement regard as the source of the current crisis!

Thus the ecological complaint against Christianity appears to be a serious historical oversimplification. In fact, dangerous modifications of the environment are not necessarily dependent on any philosophical or theological concept like dominion. Technological developments and industrialization, which often create ecological problems, have their own momentum. They occur often without a philosophical base,[26] or they may grasp and distort an existing concept, like dominion. I shall have a little more to say about that process of rationalization in the next section.

CHRIST AND CULTURE

The ecological complaint against Christianity is an exaggeration of religious influences on culture. It credits Christian faith and institutions with more cultural authority than they usually, if ever, exercised. This response is probably an extension of the previous one, but it still merits separate consideration.

Religion is not generally the prime mover or shaper of culture, not the decisive and independent variable that controls culture. Yet that is the myth which many of the ecological complainants assume. Religious influences vary from situation to situation; the conditions and dynamics of causation and power are extraordinarily difficult to analyze. The typical situation involves some level of reciprocity between religious and other cultural institutions, as Tawney showed with Puritanism: "Puritanism helped to mould the social order, but it was also increasingly moulded by it."[27]

Cultural influences on religion are frequently, probably even generally, greater than vice versa. Even the great ecumenical councils of the church during the Patristic age were presided over by the emperors; decisions were ratified and coerced by imperial authorities intent on using the unity of the church to preserve their sovereignty and the harmony of the empire.[28] And more than a few popes, patriarchs, and pastors have been bounced around by princes, politicians, and parishioners. The process of acculturation, however, is generally more gentle, or at least subtle. Cultural accommodation is inevitable and, to some degree, desirable; the faith is and, within limits, ought to be acculturated, in order to relate to the diverse conditions of people. That is what indigenization of Christianity in contemporary cultures is all about. All forms of Christianity are shaped by their cultures in everything from language and rituals to values and architecture. We are partially captives of our contexts. Our theological constructions are always more or less social constructions. Our creeds always reflect the relativities of the cultures from which they emerge. The danger, of course, is that cultural aberrations may creep in (in fact, always do) and distort our expressions of the faith itself. This has been a perennial problem in Christian history, and various forms of "civil religion"—conservative and liberal—have been regular outcomes. The questions of how Christ and culture are related sociologically and ought to be related theologically are complex; various typologies have been proposed (the church-sect debate), but none more impressive than H. Richard Niebuhr's five types.[29] The Christian faith and institutions have undoubtedly influenced the mores of Western cultures, but these cultures have also—and maybe more so—influenced the expressions of the faith.

thought he was saying

On ecological concerns, the Christian traditions probably affected the various cultural forces at work historically, but they were hardly the historical root of our ecological crisis. As I noted earlier, the variables are far too many to make such a simple assessment. Moreover, cultural forces often adopt and distort religious concepts, and use these honorific ideas as rationalizations or "justifictions" for their projects. Francis Bacon clearly used the notion of dominion in this way.[30] Examples of this phenomenon are abundant in the sociology and history of religion.

From the Puritans on, the idea of dominion was widely used as a rationale for antiwilderness attitudes on the American frontier. But the idea was dramatically embellished from its ambiguous meanings in scripture and tradition, and exaggerated far beyond its classical importance. The idea served the interests of social forces intent on economic gain and manifest destiny. Consequently, conquering the American wilderness became a religious crusade, according to Roderick Nash, in the name of national pride, ethnic identity, and progress on behalf of God. Many—not all—of the pioneers perceived themselves not only as "agents of civilization," but also as "Christ's soldiers," converting the moral wastelands of wilderness into gardens of paradise, transforming the demonic barrens into civilized beneficence.[31] Christian concepts and words were employed, but their meanings changed. Wilderness became a sinister symbol of cursed chaos; the concept lost its diverse and ambiguous meanings in classical Christian expressions.[32] Dominion experienced a similar fate: it

78

became isolated from the moderating and controlling influences of the whole corpus of Christian thought, and served as a license for elimination with extreme prejudice. The practices under the rubric of dominion were alien to the biblical and most traditional understandings of the concept. Instead of trusteeship or benevolence, as it had been interpreted in some earlier Christian contexts, dominion became a rationale for exploitation. Whatever else this dynamic might illustrate, it shows clearly the influence of culture on religion, particularly the distortion of religious values for social goals.

The ecological complaint raises other questions about the relationship between Christ and culture that the complainants ought to consider. If the Christian faith and institutions are the source of our ecological crisis, why did Eastern Christianity not have the same transformative effects on its cultures as Western forms allegedly had?[33] If Christian doctrines like dominion are the root cause of the rampant technological-industrial destruction of nature, why did the effects not show up much earlier in history? Why were prominent Christians often in a resistance movement against these forces? If Christian doctrines are the basic cause, how is it possible for the same doctrines to produce both the technological destruction of nature and the ascetic tradition of *contemptus mundi?*

These rhetorical questions are intended simply to suggest the complexity of the problem. Christianity is no monolith: it has had multiple strains with radically different emphases. Moreover, multiple cultural forces are at work in the process of social change, and some of them manipulate religious ideas and values for their interests. The ecological complainants should remember that there are Christian-influenced cultures and culture-influenced Christian churches, but there is no such thing as a Christian culture. The norms of the faith and the practices of the culture are always at least in tension. Remembering this reality will help to prevent simplistic causal theories about Christian values being decisive influences on cultures.

ECOLOGICAL SENSITIVITY IN CHRISTIAN HISTORY

The ecological complaint against Christianity overlooks the complex, ambiguous, and diversified character of Christian history. The complainants tend to assume a monolith and, therefore, perceive only the majority or dominant opinions. They miss the varied voices—albeit minorities—for ecological sensitivity in Christian history. These voices are not always prominent, though sometimes they are. And they are frequently ambivalent—even contradictory—mixing anthropocentric and biocentric values inconsistently. But the important point is that these voices are present and persistent. The evidence is sufficient to justify the claim that the Christian faith has coexisted comfortably and coherently with ecological values.

I will cite here a few vignettes of ecological sensitivity in historical Christian thought and practice. Not even pretending to be an historian, I can do little more than provide a spattering of data, but they are sufficient, I think, to confirm my point. I hope, moreover, that church historians will follow the example of Professor George H. Williams, historian emeritus of Harvard Divinity School (and a "nature lover"!), and give more attention to this field. There probably is no "hidden tradition" of ecological sensitivity in Christian history,[34] but there is much in the known traditions that has been bypassed and could be highlighted as a boon to a generation yearning for ecologically sensitive precedents.

Paul Santmire in *The Travail of Nature* argues that one strain of Christian thought is characterized by an "ecological motif," which emphasizes human rootedness in nature and celebrates God's presence in the biophysical world.[35] This strain, he claims, includes Irenaeus, Augustine, Martin Luther, and John Calvin. In Luther and Calvin, for instance, one must look to the circumference rather than to the center of their thought for vital signs of the "ecological motif." Even there, it is sometimes ambiguous, but the important consideration is that the motif is present[36]—and present to a sufficient degree to contend that the Reformers never sanctioned interpretations of dominion as license for abuse. Santmire shows that Christian theology, while neither ecologically bankrupt nor affluent, offers the promise of a strong base for ecological responsibility. Santmire's selection, however, is necessarily limited. Other theologians with ecological sensitivities might have been included: John Scotus Erigena (*Perisphyseon*), John Wesley, H. Richard Niebuhr, Paul Tillich, and many of the early Greek theologians.[37]

In fact, Eastern Orthodoxy provides significant evidence against the ecological complaint. In their theology and piety, the Orthodox churches have prominently and proudly retained the expectation of the redemption of all creation and the sanctification of all matter through the incarnation.[38] These and other relevant doctrines have by no means been embodied consistently or regularly in the practices of the Eastern churches; they too are not immune to the ecological complaint; they too are guilty of sins of omission and commission. Nonetheless, through the ideals of living in humility in recognition of humanity's place *in* nature, and seeking to minimize the alienation between humanity and the rest of nature in anticipation of the final transfiguration, Eastern Orthodoxy has a great deal to teach the Western churches about the ecological implications of the Christian faith. I shall have occasion to cite several examples of these contributions in subsequent pages.

Christian piety also has retained important signs of ecological sensitivity. Joseph Sittler claims that the church "has intuited and sung and prayed beyond her doctrines." An affirmation of creation has "squeaked into her life via liturgy, paratheological documents, and hymnody"[39]—as well as psalms (like Ps. 104), poetry, legends, and art.[40] The ecologically conscious hymns include some commonly used classics: the Benedicite (the apocryphal Song of the Three Children, used historically in the Office of Lauds in the ancient liturgical churches of East and West, read daily by Francis of Assisi from his breviary, and strongly reminiscent of his Canticle of Brother Sun), *Cordus Natus Ex Parentis* ("Let Creation Praise Its Lord, Evermore and Evermore"), "All Things Bright and Beautiful," "For the Beauty of the Earth," "This Is My Father's World," "All Creatures of Our God and King" (translation of Francis's Canticle of Brother Sun), and "I Sing the Almighty Power of God" (Isaac Watts).

But it was in some of the legendary exploits of the saints that historical Christian ecological sensitivity becomes most intriguing. The stories of saints' relationships with nonhuman creatures are an important indicator of ecological consciousness. The stories are significant not only in themselves, but also because they are remembered and celebrated as illustrative models of behavior for Christians to emulate.

1. Desert Fathers

The influential stories of the Desert Fathers contain a number of scattered accounts of human encounters with the "denizens of the desert." These monks of the third and fourth centuries withdrew into the deserts of Egypt and Syria to escape social decadence and to duplicate the harmonious conditions of a prelapsarian Paradise, to avoid distractions and to ascend the ladder of perfection, to face demons in spiritual combat, and to find God in soul-saving contemplation and severe asceticism. These hard-working, hard-

81

praying, and hard-fasting hermits—called "athletes of God"—were noted for their humility, charity, and simplicity.

Their life-styles are theologically and morally dubious to many of us. And their legends are not always the stuff that will delight naturalists. Occasionally, some animals are seen as demonically possessed and, therefore, destroyed. Often the stories are about divine protection from animals or saintly control over animals—thus suggestive of the powers of benevolent dominion in Eden. Some stories will legitimately offend herpetologists. Though a couple of mighty serpents patrolled the premises of one holy man as his guardians,[41] that type of relationship is rare. Some of the other fathers frequently killed poisonous snakes and other reptiles, sometimes in self-defense but not always. Abba (a title connoting a distinguished elder in piety) Appellen, for instance, crossed a river on the back of a crocodile, which came at his call. When he was across, Appellen killed the crocodile, asserting: "Death is better for thee than punishment for the souls which thou hast already slain, and wouldst slay."[42] In judging the Desert Fathers, however, it is important to allow for extenuating circumstances: they lived in a genuinely dangerous environment, without the benefit of hiking boots, secure tents, nearby hospitals, well-managed trails, and four-lane highways. It is not easy to love wilderness that is truly wild.

Yet, a few of the stories reveal authentic friendship between humans and other animals. Mar Paul, the so-called Prince of the Monks, was regularly visited in his cave by a hyena. For sixty years, a raven daily brought him a half-loaf of bread, but when Paul was visited by St. Anthony, the raven brought a full loaf. When Paul died during the visit from Anthony, two lions came running, wagging their tails in friendship at Anthony, and mourning the death of their friend. They dug a grave for Paul, kissed Anthony's hands and feet, and purred for a blessing.[43] Macarius the Alexandrian, and a vegetarian (as most were), was "a lover beyond all other men of the desert, and had explored its ultimate and inaccessible wastes."[44] Once desperate with thirst, he suckled milk from a congenial buffalo who followed him. On another occasion, Macarius healed the blind whelp of a hyena, who later brought him a sheepskin cloak in gratitude.[45] He even sentenced himself to six months of sitting naked in a mosquito-infested area for vindictively crushing a biting mosquito.[46]

My favorite Desert Father, however, was Abba Theon, healer of poor folks, onetime scholar, vegetarian, and indisputable "soul friend" of field naturalists:

His food consisted of garden herbs, and they said that he used to go forth from his cell by night and mingle with the wild animals of the desert, and he gave them to drink of the water which he found. The footmarks which appeared by the side of his abode were those of buffaloes, and goats, and gazelle, in the sight of which he took great pleasure.[47]

Despite a theology of world renunciation, not all of these anchorites could resist the temptation of consorting with the local inhabitants and loving it. And their deeds were remembered and celebrated and sometimes emulated.

2. Celtic Saints

The nature-loving tendencies of some of the Desert Fathers were influential throughout the monastic communities of Christendom. Some of the monks of sixth- and seventh-century France, for example, were famous for courageously protecting wild animals like boar, deer, and hares from royal hunters and providing sanctuaries on their lands.[48] But nowhere is the desert influence more strongly evident than among the early medieval Celtic saints. Even some of the stories of their exploits are probably borrowed from the hermits (though none about snakes; St. Patrick presumably solved that problem for his successors!). The legends of these Irish monks are filled with embellished accounts—even fantastic tales—of mutual affection and service between saints and animals. Some of these tales are manifestations of classical dominion, designed by hagiographers to show the saints' capacities to restore some of the innocence of Eden. However, compassion and care are the dominant features of these stories, as the following sampling illustrates.

Wild deer voluntarily substituted for oxen to pull a wagon of timber for Finian of Clonard, and another deer regularly carried the books of a monk in his antlers.[49] When St. Molaisse of Devenish wanted to write a book, a bird dropped a feather to make a pen. A wild boar used his tusks to build a cell for St. Ciaren of Saigir.[50] A fox carried the Psalter back and forth across the fields to two monks who could not leave their posts.[51] After a frigid night at sea, two otters warmed the feet of St. Cuthbert with their breath and dried him with their fur.[52] Every third day for thirty years, another otter brought to one monk a fish for dinner and twigs for a fire.[53] Birds and squirrels came to the call of St. Columban and sat quietly under his hand.[54] A mouse nibbled at the ear of St. Colman of Kilmacdaugh to wake him for his prayers, and a mosquito once voluntarily served as a bookmark when the saint was called away from his reading.[55] (Questions about how or to what effect are best suspended in the context of hagiography.)

The first monks of St. Ciaren the Elder of Osriage were a group of animals, including a fox, badger, wolf, and deer—all living together peacefully and all called "Brother." Apparently, however, there were occasional lapses of discipline, since the fox once stole and ate the Abbot's sandals. The sorrowful Brother Fox, however, did penance for his sin.[56] Through prayer, Kentigan restored a robin to life after it had been torn apart by some malicious boys,[57] and St. Moling did the same for a wren killed by a cat—and then commanded the wren to follow the saint's merciful example by disgorging a fly it had swallowed earlier.[58]

The Irish saints were often wandering penitents—the traveling yarns reaching their peak in the sixth century *Voyage of St. Brendan the Navigator.* Consequently, their influence spread with their travels throughout Europe. In the monastic communities of Europe, their legends were remembered, celebrated, and imitated—including the tales of their affectionate relationship with nonhuman creatures. Their sacramental sense of the natural world as the place of divine presence and revelation ran deep; their appreciation of that world as the creation of God was intense. When they established monastic communities, their site selections were generally places of "great natural beauty," symbols of Paradise.[59]

3. St. Francis

Francis of Assisi is frequently treated in the ecological complaint as a nearly isolated example of ecological responsibility in a sea of Christian exploitation of nature. That claim is indefensible. Though St. Francis probably should be regarded as the epitome of Christian love in an ecological context, since his life was a radical demonstration that humanity should concern itself with the welfare of all creatures,[60] he neither emerged nor departed in a vacuum. Though sometimes innovative, his expressions and actions were "some of the grandest and most explicit manifestations and elaborations of common presuppositions" of his time.[61] He was the foremost of a cloud of witnesses, often obscure and forgotten, who preceded and followed him. Judging from some similarities in the legends, the hagiographers of Francis probably borrowed from the hagiographies of the Celtic saints,[62] who, in turn, borrowed from the hagiographies of the Desert Fathers. A little hagiographic competition was going on here: my saint's better than your saint! Whatever the process, Francis may have been the best, but he was not the first Christian with an implicit or explicit biocentric ethic. And he would not be the last.

The stories about St. Francis and the nonhuman creation abound and are well known. Even those who rarely read have at least seen the bird baths. The stories were obviously enhanced to mythical proportions by his early admirers. A major intent of some of the hagiographers, as was the case with the Desert Fathers and the Celtic saints, was to demonstrate the saintly compassion and miraculous power of their hero to elicit affection and secure subservience from lesser creatures, as a sign of his holy innocence and, therefore, of his abilities to restore some of the original harmony of Eden.[63] The "obedient animal motif "[64] is really an expression of anthropocentric dominion. Yet, in Francis, as in some of the earlier saints, this motif shows clear signs of the mutual affection and service that Christian love ultimately is. The prominence, character, and general consistency of the animal stories leave little, if any, room for doubt that underneath the hagiographic puffery is a core of authentic biocentrism. Francis is "an embodiment of Christianity's ecological promise";[65] "the purest figure (gestalt) of Western history, of the dreams, the utopias, and of the meaning of living panfraternally that we are all searching for today."[66]

He genuinely loved the Creator, the creation, and its creatures, and he expressed that love with extravagant friendship, compassion, tenderness, kindness, and even sacrifice. He treated all things courteously in the tradition of chivalry. He befriended and blessed pheasants, cicadas, lambs, mice, rabbits, waterfowl, fish, turtle doves (for whom he once made a nest[67]), bees, worms that he gently lifted from his path, and certainly "sister larks" (the killing of which he wanted the Emperor to outlaw).[68] Addressing the notorious, human-devouring Wolf of Gubbio as "Brother," Francis reprimanded and converted him into a dispositional sheep in canine clothing, who gave Francis his paw in repentance and vowed never thereafter to hurt human or beast.[69] Francis even preached to his "little sisters" the birds, who listened reverently, and told them, "Your Creator loveth you so much, since he hath dealt so bounteously with you."[70] With his sacramental sense, his nature mysticism,[71] Francis "not only loved but reverenced God in all his creatures";[72] he saw in a chirping cicada the handiwork of the Creator.[73] But it is clear that Francis also passionately loved them all for themselves, calling them brothers and sisters in consciousness of kinship. And they often returned the affection. A falcon, for instance, regularly awakened him at night for prayer. Other creatures enjoyed cuddling with him and sometimes brought him gifts.

Francis's integrated affinities, however, did not stop with the animal realm; they were inclusive, cosmocentric. The sun, moon, water, fire, plants, and rocks were greeted as siblings, because he shared with them a common Source.[74] When he walked over stones, one hagiographer said, he did so reverently for the love of the one who is called the Rock. He told the wood-cutting friar not to cut down the whole tree but only to remove the branches, for the love of him who saved us on the cross. The gardening friar was instructed not to till the whole plot but to leave part for the wild flowers, in love of the one who is the lily of the valley and the flower of the field.[75] Despite these allegorical interpretations, the general tenor of his life-style, capped by The Canticle of Brother Sun, suggests that his ethic was loving respect for all his cosmic comrades in creation.

Francis comes to us in many respects as a stranger. He is an anachronism from the twelfth and thirteenth centuries. His behavior was often bizarre. His life-style was austere, even pathological by some contemporary standards. Most of these dimensions of his life are conveniently forgotten or passed over quickly—and often legitimately so. Yet, Francis is remembered and celebrated mainly for the breadth and depth of his love, particularly for the poor, the sick (for example, lepers), and other life forms (animal and plant). His love was integrated, whole. Concerning his love for nonhuman creatures, he has been remembered and celebrated not for poignant idiosyncracies that are optional supplements to the Christian faith or even hedgings on heresy, but rather for representing the model of what a fully blooming Christian love might be. His affinities for nature are understood not as an alien addition to the gospel, but rather as an appropriate and even essential extension of it. Only such a thesis can adequately explain the power that his story has exercised over every subsequent generation of Christians,[76] and the fact that he has been memorialized by Christians of all subspecies as the only ecumenical— and ecological—saint, as a beacon by which to be guided. What a people remember and celebrate is not trivial; it is a sign of their norms, their Christian axioms, and a goading judgment on their behavior.

4. Significant Others

Francis was by no means the last ecologically sensitive Christian. The breadth and depth of his affection for nature were certainly rare, maybe even unique, but that does not mean that his example was not followed in various degrees by countless of his ilk in succeeding generations. Most are ordinary, unsung, and now unknown women and men. Some are remembered in the histories. Only a few can be mentioned here. Thus, a haphazard litany follows.

The tradition of creation-centered spirituality, according to Matthew Fox, included such noteworthies as Hildegard of Bingen (1098–1179, actually a predecessor of Francis), Mechtild of Magdeburg (1210–1280), Meister Eckhart (1260–1329), and Julian of Norwich (1342–1415), who rejoiced in the blessings of the earth and its inhabitants.[77] The medieval bestiaries, produced by monastics, also deserve mention. The bestiary, while intended to be biologically serious (and was in its time), often contains fantastic descriptions of animals and comparable moralizations and allegories. Yet, there is truth in the judgment, particularly when due allowance is made for the times, that the bestiary is a "compassionate book" that displays "a reverence for the wonders of life, and praises the creator of them."[78] Members of the Evangelical movement in England in the latter part of the eighteenth century, especially Quakers and Methodists, were in the forefront of the struggle against cruelty to animals—just as their Puritan predecessors had been in the sixteenth and seventeenth centuries in combatting cock-fighting and bear-baiting.[79] One of their leaders was William Wilberforce, best known as a major voice in the antislavery cause.[80] Anglicans also joined in. In 1776, the Reverend Doctor Humphrey Primatt published *A Dissertation on the Duty of Mercy and the Sin of Cruelty to Brute Animals*, which argued from scripture that love is required in relations with other animals and cruelty is a heresy.[81] By the early part of the nineteenth century in England (and in the eastern cities of the United States), clerical denunciations of the maltreatment of animals had become commonplace.[82] That routinization, however, did not always come without cost: when one Anglican vicar in 1772 preached against the abuse of animals, his appalled parishioners concluded that he had either gone mad or turned Methodist![83]

We dare not forget, moreover, the most famous of a long line of country parson-naturalists, the Reverend Gilbert White of Selborne, England. His reverential nature studies in his parish were a major contribution to field studies in ecology, and his book, *The Natural History of Selborne* (1789), was by this century the fourth most published book in the English language, having appeared in well over a hundred editions![84] Two other rural pastors, Francis Orpen Morris and H. F. Barnes, were instrumental in protecting wild birds in England in the nineteenth century.[85] During this same period on the other side of the Atlantic, there was "Johnny Appleseed" or John Chapman, whom we do well to remember. This Swedenborgian missionary did more than operate apple nurseries: "In his religiously inspired mercies to wild creatures, he was one with Francis of Assisi and the desert Fathers."[86] Finally, we should not ignore the ecologically minded poets like Gerard Manley Hopkins ("God's Grandeur," "Inversnaid," "Binsey Poplars"), William Blake ("Auguries of Innocence"), and the obscure Thomas Traherne. The litany continues into the present,[87] with many practitioners of an allegedly antiecological faith being actively involved in ecological causes.

The list could be supplemented at length. That is why we need more historical studies of this substream of Christian ecological consciousness, which meanders through Christian-influenced cultures. The voices from the past are often ambivalent and sometimes contradictory, but they exist. They should be assessed in the context of their times, not anachronistically by late-twentieth century, avant garde ecological standards. They provide significant evidence against the charge that Christianity has been historically or is inherently an antiecological faith.

INTERRELIGIOUS MISCOMPARISONS

The alleged ecological superiority of other religions and cultures over Christianity may be partly a manifestation of Western parochialism and historical myopia. The claim of the ecological complaint that Christianity should be abandoned in favor of another religion or fully infiltrated by the ecological values of another religion demands a response, particularly since so many contemporary Christian environmentalists seem sympathetic to infiltration. The response, however, must be a cautious one, in order to avoid the danger of succumbing to comparative religious or cross-cultural polemics ("My faith is better than your faith"). No one benefits from those diatribes. Nonetheless, some delicate apologetics are in order as a witness for the defense.

Ecological crises are not peculiar to Christian-influenced cultures. Non-Christian cultures have also caused severe or irreparable harm to their ecosystems. Ethicist Thomas Derr describes the situation with bluntness:

Ecological mismanagement is not the property of areas of Christian influence, nor exclusively of modern technology. Over-grazing, deforestation [as well, I must add, as over-population, desertification, extinctions, erosion, etc.] and similar errors, of sufficient magnitude to destroy civilizations [and ecosystems], have been committed by Egyptians, Assyrians, Romans, North Africans, Persians, Indians, Aztecs, and Buddhists. Centuries before the Christian era Plato commented, in his *Critias*, on the deforestation of Attica. Since primitive times man has been altering his environment dramatically, in ways that upset ecological balances. Early hunters used fire to drive out their game. Agricultural people everywhere clear fields and dam streams and wipe out stock predators and kill plants that get in the way of their chosen crops. In the modern industrial era western technology is widely copied elsewhere in the world, including areas where Christianity has had little effect.[88]

Elsewhere Derr adds: "We are simply being gullible when we take at face value the advertisement for the ecological harmony of non-Western cultures."[89]

Derr's viewpoint is not unique. Others have made similar arguments and only slightly less bluntly.[90] I essentially agree. The situation forces the ecological complainants to ask themselves: If the ecological crisis is a consequence of Christian axioms, why have so many non-Christian-influenced cultures experienced—and are experiencing—the same crisis? If Christianity is so intimately linked with Western technological arrogance and industrialization, why have many non-Christian-influenced cultures been eager to adopt these same processes?[91] These rhetorical questions simply point us to a deeper source of our ecological crisis.

The near-universality of ecological problems suggests that the roots of the crisis are not in theological affirmations themselves, but rather in human character. Ecologist Peter Farb makes this point clearly:

It appears to be a characteristic of the human [evolutionary] line—perhaps the one that accounts for its domination of the earth—that from the very beginning *Homo* [*sapiens*] has exploited the environment up to his technological limits to do so. But until recently the harm this exploitation could cause was limited, for ancient man's populations were low and his technology primitive.[92]

Farb sees the problem as a genetic defect; classical Christianity might describe it as a volitional defect, a moral misuse of human freedom and creativity, or sin. The latter interpretation implies that humans are not doomed by determinism. Either way, however, the problem is far deeper than cultural conditioning or religious training, though these factors certainly have their effects.

89

If Farb and others are right, moreover, about the ecological effects of population growth and technological sophistication, it is a fallacy of misplaced comparison to compare indigenous communities with complex, pluralistic, anonymous, technologically "advanced" societies. It may be relatively easy for indigenous communities—often with small populations controlled in size by the medically unhampered dynamics of their ecosystems—to live in equilibrium with their environments. It is incomparably more difficult for crowded, technological societies to do so. Comparing one with the other is unfair. Though we have much to learn from the ecological knowledge and moral attitudes of indigenous communities, advocating their practices for technological societies seems largely irrelevant. If these communities grow in population and develop further technical skills, they too are likely to be tempted to follow the path to ecological disaster, for the problem appears to be dormant in the human condition.

Similarly, it is unfair to compare the ideals of one religion or culture with the realities of another. That seems obvious; comparing theology with sociology is absurd. Yet, such fallacious comparisons are commonplace. Other religions are nearly deified for their often romanticized ecological ideals, and Christianity is virtually demonized for its empirical defects. But when like is compared to like, both Christianity and some other religions can display some noble norms and models, and both have substantial grounds for repentance for practical deficiencies. Ambiguities, of course, will emerge in a process of fair comparisons. Traditional Christian anthropocentrism, for instance, has had some dire ecological effects, but it also gradually and painfully helped to produce, particularly in Puritan-influenced cultures, some very positive social consequences: the dignity of the individual, human rights, and democratic political structures (all linked with the idea of the "image of God" in Gen. 1:26-28!). That too should be noted in any fair comparisons.

Nothing said here implies that Christianity cannot benefit ecologically from dialogue with practitioners of other religions—Buddhists, Hindus, Native Americans, Jains, and others. The dismissal of dialogue is arrogant and self-diminishing. Dialogue can be enriching;[93] but it must be, at least potentially, *mutually* enriching. Interreligious dialogue should not be asymmetrical, between providers and recipients. Christians ought not to enter such conversations with bowed heads and hats in hand, waiting masochistically to be verbally whipped for their sins and begging for handouts of ecological wisdom from their benefactors. Instead, Christians should enter into dialogue as both givers and receivers and expect their partners to do the same. Dialogue is between equals, or else it is a monologue or tutorial. Both partners can benefit from such equality, and both need to benefit. All have sinned and fallen short of the nobility of morality, let alone the glory of God. Historically, for instance, there seems to be an "intractable ambiguity" about the ecological norms and practices of Native American cultures and religions,[94] but the same can be said about Christianity and other religions. In this context, anything less than symmetrical dialogue may bear the marks of condescension—treating other religious groups as inferior by the ironic deception of romanticizing their histories and norms, and pronouncing their superiority in some isolated respect.[95] Through symmetrical dialogue, however, both parties can be both benefactors and beneficiaries, making both our futures better than our pasts.

POTENTIAL FOR REFORMATION

Even if everything in the ecological complaint were true, even if Christianity stood totally indicted for its ecological crimes of the past, these hypothetical facts would not necessarily prevent Christianity from developing strong ecological ethics and actions for the future. Assuming enduring fidelity to the intentions of faith in the central affirmations found in the apostolic witnesses in scripture, Christianity is not otherwise bound to its past—to the various expressions of faith and other cultural accretions in its history. The past is provisional and parochial. The corruptions of the past need corrections for the future.

Historically, the Christian faith has shown a remarkable capacity for flexibility, for stretching—for extensions of the applications of its doctrines, for reinterpretations based on new insights into scripture and tradition, for incorporations of compatible (and often incompatible) elements from the cultures in which the churches have been embedded and also from other religious traditions. The Patristic theologians, for example, provide a prominent precedent. They appropriated the metaphysics and often the mythologies of their milieus as means of expressing their understandings of the faith. Their particular borrowings are not binding, but their process is certainly prudent. In fact, as critical approaches to the Bible demonstrate, the Bible itself is the most prominent precedent for the various forms of flexibility.

In short, the Christian church has a history of and a capacity for

91

self-reformation. "Always to Be Reformed" (*Semper Reformanda*) was a Protestant motto in the post-Reformation period. Similar, but less flamboyant and more restricted, understandings have been present in other Christian traditions. In the doctrine of the Holy Spirit, the church has found provisions for continuing revelation. New light, new truth is always breaking forth from the Spirit. These new revelations can come through both theological and ecological studies, intra-Christian or interreligious dialogue, and all other means of reasoning on human experience. The Spirit cannot be closeted. This capacity for change means that the church can readily incorporate new elements and reinterpret its main themes to develop a solid, ultimate grounding for an ecological ethic. That development, in fact, would be the very best refutation of the ecological complaint against Christianity.

In a sense, the church does need "new" theological and ethical bases for sustaining ecological integrity. This need, however, does not entail abandoning or replacing Christianity's main themes. Rather, it requires extensions and reinterpretations of these main themes in ways that preserve their historic identity and that are also consistent with ecological data. The next two chapters are an effort to show the significant ecological potential in some central Christian convictions.

CHAPTER FOUR

FIRM FOUNDATIONS:

DOCTRINES OF CREATION, COVENANT, DIVINE IMAGE, INCARNATION, AND SPIRITUAL PRESENCE

The Christian faith, despite the historical ambiguities in its ecological credentials, has the impressive potential to become an indestructibly firm foundation for ecological integrity. The faith contains all things necessary, all the values and virtues, for ecological integrity. Indeed, nothing short of that integrity is compatible, in my view, with authentic representations of the Christian faith. What, then, are the ecological implications of some central affirmations of Christianity? In what directions do these convictions point for ecological ethics and action? These are the questions discussed in the next two chapters.

Unlike philosophical ethics, which seeks to be an autonomous discipline—developing its values and principles on "reason alone," independent, practically and logically, of "religion "[1]—Christian theology and ethics do not have the luxury of debating about autonomy. These disciplines cannot function independently; they are interdependent, reciprocally critical and influential. Christian ethics, for instance, contributes to theology by making ethical evaluations of theological formulations. That is what classical liberalism did in envisioning "a morally credible deity"[2]—descriptions of God that corresponded with moral sensitivities about love and justice and the richest Christian experiences of God in scripture and tradition. Theology, in turn, critiques ethics on its consistency with theological affirmations. Above all, however, theology provides Christian ethics with its groundings, the interpretations of God in relation to the creation on which ethics structures its basic values and norms.

Thus the two are not only interactive; they should also be coherent, internally consistent, adequately comprehensive, and integrative of experiential data.

On these assumptions, the next two chapters are efforts to show the significant promise of ecologically and ethically "reformed" theological affirmations as a foundation for Christian ecological ethics and actions. Ecological responsibility does not require the abandonment or replacement of Christianity's main theological themes. "New" or "radical" or "imported" theologies are not necessary. What is required, however, are reinterpretations, extensions, and revisions, as well as cast-offs of cultural corruptions, in ways that preserve the historic identity of the relevant Christian doctrines and yet integrate ethical insights and ecological data. In fact, in most cases, the necessary "reforms" have long been part of some segments of the Christian tradition. The "reforms," then, are often rediscoveries of ancient wisdom embedded in parts of scripture and tradition. Other proposed reforms are simply reasonable extensions of Christian doctrines to their horizons—a process that compels corrections, additions, and excisions. The process is relatively conservative, though the product may appear radical to some (and perhaps reactionary to others). The revisions are more akin to pruning and trimming than to a "root and branch" transformation. The important point, however, is that Christian theology can remain loyal to the intentions of faith in the historic affirmations of the church while developing a genuinely ecological theology. I doubt, in fact, that the former is possible without the latter.

This chapter focuses on the ecological implications of five historic Christian affirmations concerning *creation, covenant, the divine image and dominion, incarnation,* and *spiritual presence.* The next chapter gives attention to *sin, divine judgment, cosmic redemption,* and *the church.* These are only fragments, even though major ones, of what I think needs to be incorporated into a truly systematic ecological theology. A "creation theology" is insufficient as an ecological grounding; other doctrinal foundations need to be included. I, of course, do not pretend that the list of topics or the discussion of each topic is exhaustive. Others might make a different selection and would certainly offer different stresses and interpretations. That is the nature of classical Christian diversity. My purpose is adequately served if I can show that a reasonably and modestly reformed Christian theology can provide in its central affirmations—and not simply in peripheral elements—an ultimate, sustaining foundation for ecological integrity.

CREATION: GOD'S COSMIC AND RELATIONAL VALUES

The first statement of the classical creeds—the Apostles' and Nicene symbols—is a confession of faith in God as the Maker of heaven and earth. It is the foundation of all that follows. It is an affirmation of divine sovereignty, universal providence, creaturely dependence, and—implicitly and recessively—ecological responsibility.

God is the Pantocrator, the sole governor and final benefactor, the sovereign source of all being and becoming, the ultimate provider and universal proprietor, the originator and systemic organizer. All elements and inhabitants of this planet and solar system, and every planet and solar system, from the sun and moon to lakes and mountains, from protozoa to humans, are finite creatures—creations of God and finally dependent on God's providential preservation and parental care. In wisdom, God creates all things, provides food and shelter for all life forms, gives the breath of life and takes it away (Ps. 104). God alone is the owner: "The earth is the LORD's and all that is in it, the world and all those who live in it" (Ps. 24:1)—a claim that ancient Israel interpreted as imposing ethical restrictions on the use of the land by its temporary occupants, the human "aliens and tenants" (Lev. 25:23).

The logic of the doctrine of creation does not permit a nature-grace dichotomy. That fact, however, has not deterred Christian churches from restricting in practice the scope of grace to matters of personal salvation, and the means of grace to ecclesiastical functions—Word and sacraments—performed through ecclesiastical functionaries.[3] These typical restrictions distort the doctrine of creation, as Joseph Sittler argued brilliantly. Grace is not only the forgiveness of sins but the "givenness" of life,[4] both redemption and creation—"a double gratuity."[5] The whole of nature—the biophysical universe—is not the antithesis of grace, but rather an expression of grace, that is, God's free and faithful loving kindness that characterizes God's nature and acts. God *is* love. The creative process, therefore, is an act of love, and its creatures are products of love and recipients of ongoing love (cf. Ps. 136:1-9). This fundamental affirmation has critical implications for a Christian ecological ethic, as I will argue in chapter 6. Here, however, it is sufficient to note that the church's explication of grace or love must be comprehensive, characterized by a "Trinitarian amplitude" that covers the whole and all the parts of creation as the "field of grace."[6] The elimination of a nature-grace dichotomy, and its replacement with an understanding of nature as a manifestation and beneficiary of grace, endows all of nature with an intrinsic moral significance.[7]

From this perspective of radical monotheism in the doctrine of creation, there are no lesser divinities—not the sun and moon (against the worship of which Genesis 1:14-18 was a reaction), not golden calves and other "graven images," not sacred groves or ancient trees, not mighty mountains or volcanoes, not fearsome beasts or demons, not caesars or pharaohs or heroes, and not even Gaia or Mother Earth. In this view, polytheism, animism, astrology, totemism, and other forms of nature worship are not only idolatry, but also, as the prophets regularly suggested, vanity and stupidity (cf. Isa. 40:12-28; 44:9-20; 46:1-11; Acts 14:15). The Creator alone is worthy of worship. In fact, in manifestations of the pathetic fallacy, the Old Testament occasionally calls all creatures, biotic and abiotic, to praise their Maker (Pss. 148, 96, 98). Nevertheless, though only the Creator is worthy of worship, all God's creatures are worthy of moral consideration, as a sign of the worthiness imparted by God and, in fact, as an expression of the worship of God. The monotheistic doctrine of creation does not desacralize nature: "Nature is still sacred by virtue of having been created by God, declared to be good, and placed under ultimate divine sovereignty."[8]

The classical doctrine of creation *ex nihilo* (out of nothing) should be understood in the context of this radical monotheism. It was derived especially from New Testament sources (Rom. 4:17; Heb. 11:3) and was intended to enhance the affirmation of God alone as the source of all being. Nothing in creation is independent of nor identifiable with God. The doctrine rejects, on the one hand, metaphysical dualism, which usually posits dialectical forces of Good and Evil (the latter often responsible for creation) or God the Orderer and the primordial chaos. On the other hand, it rejects pantheism, which identifies Creator and creation.[9] Though not implied by the first Genesis story of creation and probably irrelevant to the text,[10] creation *ex nihilo* probably corresponds with the intention of the priestly author of Genesis 1.[11] The doctrine appears vacuous from the perspective of philosophical speculation. It is hardly an explanation of origins, but that is precisely its point and value. The doctrine is not designed to be an explanation; rather, it is designed to prevent explanations that compromise the affirmation of divine sovereignty. Creation *ex nihilo* is a denial of ultimate dualism and pantheism, and an affirmation of divine sovereignty and mystery.[12] It represents humility in the face of ultimate mysteries that transcend human possibilities of understanding.

The same sense of mystery is present in the first and primary story of creation in the Old Testament (Gen. 1:1–2:4).[13] The story is not, nor was it intended to be, an account in natural history, natural science, or metaphysics. It is not compatible with scientific data, nor was it intended to be, nor should it be interpreted to be. In fact, the second story of creation in Genesis 2, with its significantly different ordering of the creative process, illustrates that the biblical compilers were not significantly interested in scientific accuracy or intratextual consistency. The priestly writer (P) of Genesis 1, like his counterpart (J) in Genesis 2, was transmitting and transforming a varied tradition, which included ancient myths of origins.[14] The text represents not an empirical inquiry but rather an existential one. It is not a speculative cosmogony but rather a confession of faith.[15] Genesis 1 is not interested in creation methodologies and processes: "The Bible discusses not *how* the world was made but rather *who* made it."[16] The text is a "mythopoetic" proclamation of God's sovereign Reign and relationships with the whole creation; it expresses a different order of truth than scientific inquiry.[17] It is a theological affirmation that "permits every scientific view that is genuinely scientific and not a theological claim in disguise."[18] Consequently, Genesis 1 opposes two contrary forms of fundamentalism: pseudo-scientific positivism or reductionism and biblical literalism.[19] The writer displays humility in the face of ultimate mystery about origins by concentrating on the proclamation of Israel's faith in the Originator.

Since God is the source of all in the Christian doctrine of creation, all creatures share in a common relationship. This kinship of all creatures is symbolized in the second Genesis story of creation by the formation of both humans and other animals from the same element, the earth (2:17, 19). It is symbolized in the first creation account by the fact that humans and other land animals are created on the same day, "a subtle literary indication of affinity."[20] This affirmation of relationality is, moreover, enhanced by the theory of evolution, which describes humans as related to every other form of life through our common beginnings in one or more living cells and through our subsequent adaptive interactions. We evolved relationally; we exist symbiotically. Human existence depends on coexistence with the rest of creation. Equally, the doctrine of creation implies that nature is not alien to humans; we are interrelated parts and products of a world that is continually being made and nurtured by God.

On the assumption that one ought to value God's relational design, this theocentric—and biological—kinship has often been interpreted in Christian history as having ethical implications. Thus, St. Chrysostom argued: "Surely, we ought to show them [nonhuman animals] great kindness and gentleness for many reasons, but above all, because they are of the same origin as ourselves."[21] Similarly, St. Francis called other creatures—from the sun to stones, from worms to wolves—brother and sister, "because he knew they had the same source as himself."[22] In this vein, one of the fundamental tasks of Christian ecological ethics is to determine the moral responsibilities entailed by the reality of theocentric and ecological kinship.

The creation is also "good"—indeed, as a whole, "very good." This has been an enduring affirmation of the Christian church in following the lead of Genesis 1—though oftentimes, as we have seen, it has been a mere formality as Christians have shown disdain or indifference for nature, matter, and "the world." Nevertheless, the assertion itself is strange and troubling to anyone who is sensitive to the agonies of natural evil. How can the creation be "very good" in the light of the suffering and death that are built into the system? Indeed, how can the Creator be "very good" in the light of the ambiguous character of creation? Despite the awe that the biosphere inspires and the good that it sustains, the other side of ambiguous reality is that evil is an inherent part of the system, not an alien force. Empirically speaking, suffering and death came into the world not through sin but rather through natural processes. Death occurred universally long before the evolution of the first human with the post-instinctual, moral capacities to exercise free judgment, the precondition of a sinful condition. Is this claim of goodness then a sign of moral insensitivity or romanticism? Partly both, I fear. Yet, the claim of the goodness of creation is not so easily abandoned. It expresses a truth that is not only essential for ontological meaning and theological integrity, but also for ecological ethics.

Though exegetes differ, the meaning of the goodness of creation in Genesis 1 appears to be both moral and aesthetic. A crafter has completed a project, according to Claus Westermann, and the results are successful. The achievement is beautiful and functional. It works according to the design, and it can fulfill God's purposes in creating the system.[23] The work of creation is a product of the divine wisdom—intelligible, coherent, and purposeful, though mysterious to all creatures. God is pleased, satisfied, even delighted with the results of the creative process (Ps. 104:31), because they correspond with divine intentions and expectations. Thus the ecosphere (indeed, the universe) is valued by the Source of value in all its moral ambiguity—including the predation and prodigality that are inherent parts of the dynamics of evolution and ecology, including the inseparable intertwinings of beauty and ugliness, including the combination of destruction and construction in floods and quakes, including the ordered chaos in the structure of ecosystems, and including the "purposive randomness" with elements of creative chance structured into generally predictable processes.[24] But God has a mysterious purpose, and God values the creation in its ambiguous state because it contributes to that purpose.

Divine valuations, however, in scripture and in the logic of the doctrine of creation are not solely or even primarily anthropocentric. The universe was not created mainly for "man," contrary to the humorously arrogant pronouncements in most periods of Christian history. The creation and its creatures are declared to be "good," according to Genesis 1, *before* the emergence of *Homo sapiens*. All animals are blessed with fertility, commanded to "increase and multiply" (Gen. 1:22; 8:17). And prior to the Flood, all are expected to be vegetarians (an intriguing moral idealization of nature, perhaps indicative of "troubled consciences" about killing even to eat and also of a consciousness of the flawed state of existence). Indeed, the story as a whole represents at least "a partial displacement of [the hu]man from the central place in the drama of becoming."[25] In Psalm 104, the components of creation are celebrated, and God is praised for comprehensive benevolence *apart from* any human values. Similarly, in Job 38–41, the author not only stresses human humility in the presence of divine mystery, but also assumes God's positive evaluations of the whole creation *apart from* any human utility. God's compassion covers the whole creation (Ps. 145:9). Thus, the creation and its creatures have divinely-imparted value independent of human interests, and this value exists even in a wild, virginal state, prior to and apart from the taming, technological transformations of human managers.

Divine valuations appear to be cosmocentric and biocentric, not simply or primarily anthropocentric. As a gift of divine love, the world was created as a habitat not only for humanity but also for all living beings. Old Testament scholar Claus Westermann states this perspective forcefully:

> The simple fact that the first page of the Bible speaks about heaven and earth, the sun, moon, and stars, about birds, fish, and animals, is a certain sign that the God whom we acknowledge in the Creed as the Father of Jesus Christ is concerned with all these creations, and not merely with humans. *A God who is understood only as the god of humankind is no longer the God of the Bible.*[26]

The logic of the doctrine of creation itself leads to a similar conclusion. Its stresses on divine sovereignty and universal providence imply that the Creator is concerned about the whole of creation and all

99

its parts, not only the human parts. Ethically, since fidelity to God implies respect for divine valuations, Christians are called to honor and nurture what God honors and nurtures, and that includes the whole good creation.

For the Christian faith, however, the affirmation of the goodness of creation is also an expression of ultimate confidence in the goodness of God. The world now has an interim goodness. It is not to be despised or rejected or transcended; it is to be appreciated and valued as an expression of the goodness of God. It overflows with marvels and sustains diverse forms of life, for a time. Yet, it is also a world of systemic alienation, in which all life is temporary and destructive of other life. Empirically speaking, the classical theological propositions that the Creator and the creation are "very good" are virtually indefensible, in my view, apart from an eschatological expectation. The creation needs liberation and reconciliation. Thus the Christian church has always linked creation and redemption, though in most of its historical forms, it has strangely excluded otherkind from the realm of redemption. Christ is the mediator of creation (John 1:1-3; I Cor. 8:6; Col. 1:15-17; Heb. 1:2-3). To say with the Nicene Creed that "all things were made" through Christ is to affirm that the creation as a whole has a redemptive purpose from the beginning. The creation is going on to perfection, ultimately. It is very good because it is being brought to fulfillment by a good God—an expectation that, as I shall argue in the next chapter, enhances Christian responsibility for ecological protection.

THE ECOLOGICAL COVENANT OF RELATIONALITY

The Noachic or Rainbow Covenant (Gen. 9:8-17) is often interpreted as a powerful biblical symbol for ecological responsibility. But the story of the Flood as a whole (Gen. 6-9) is morally ambiguous, like so many other stories in scripture. The primitive portrait of God is hardly flattering; this is no compassionate deity! An angry God, infuriated by human wickedness, creates a worldwide ecological crisis, saves a remnant of every animal species, and then vows, in apparent remorse, never to do it again, no matter how severe the provocation. Nevertheless, the story symbolizes a cosmic covenant that is built into the earthly ecosphere and the effects of which are empirically verifiable. There is a rational order of interdependence—which Christians also see as a moral, purposive order of relationality and ecological integrity—that appears to be universal and that demands respectful adaptability from moral agents. This myth conveys a truth that must be incorporated into any ecologically sensitive Christian theology and ethics.

In the Noachic covenant (the rainbow being its sign), God is portrayed as making an unconditional pledge in perpetuity to all humanity, to all other creatures, and to the earth itself, to preserve *all* species and their environments. God will be inclusively faithful. The commitment is self-binding, unending, and unrestricted. All species are given the blessing of fertility, to "increase and multiply" (Gen. 8:7) and repopulate the earth. This "ecological covenant,"[27] along with the story of Noah's Ark itself, implicitly recognizes the interdependent relationships of all creatures in their ecosystems. Humans and all other land animals perish together in the flood, and representative remnants of humans and all other land animals are saved together in the Ark. The covenant (9:17) means that "all flesh, all life on the earth, every living being in the millennia of the history of nature and of humanity is preserved in God's affirmation of . . . creation."[28] It is a "covenant of peace," a sign of God's "steadfast love" in one prophetic interpretation (Isa. 54:9-10). It also suggests that the Creator's purpose is to provide living space for all organisms,[29] so that all may share the earth together. The Noachic Covenant is a symbol of the unbreakable bonds among all creatures and with their Creator.

Moreover, the ecological covenant—indeed, every covenant in scripture—assumed responsibilities to future generations of humanity. The covenant is "with you and your offspring forever" (Gen. 13:15). This refrain is frequent in the Old Testament; the "solidarity of the generations" is taken for granted.[30] A transgenerational continuity and set of obligations link past, present, and future. Christianity subsequently embraced this idea, of which the affirmation of the church militant and triumphant is a part. The contemporary value of ecological sustainability finds strong support in the Hebraic-Christian concept of covenant.

This story also provides a symbolic mandate for responsive loyalty to God's ecological fidelity. Though the Noachic Covenant is not typical of other covenants in the Old Testament, it still demands human moral responsibility. The divine promise entails human obligation because faithfulness to God entails loyalty to God's covenants. Similarly, the ecological covenant, which is built into nature's order of interdependence, requires caring and careful responses from humans. Environmental contempt, manifested, for example, in ozone depletion, global warming, and extinctions, is a violation of the Rainbow Covenant and the ecological covenant that it symbolizes. It is, therefore, an attack on

101

the created order itself. It is disloyalty to God, other creatures, other humans, future generations, and ourselves, for we are all bound together with common interests in saving the ecological integrity of our home, the earth.[31] Moreover, respect for relationality will be a sign of the New Covenant, the new ecological and eschatological order, which also is envisioned as inclusive of all creatures in interdependence, but, in addition, will be truly harmonious (Isa. 11:6-9; Hos. 2:18).

DIVINE IMAGE AND DOMINION AS RESPONSIBLE REPRESENTATION

Humans are created, according to Genesis 1:26-28, to be the *image* of God and to exercise *dominion* in relation to all other life forms. The meaning of these two related concepts has been the subject of numerous speculations and debates among exegetes and theologians in Christian history. Rarely, however, has the debate been on center stage. Dominion particularly has been a secondary issue, generally assumed but frequently neglected analytically. Yet, in recent years, dominion particularly has become a major pejorative in the ecological complaint against Christianity. Antidominionism has been a main plank in the platform of those who accuse Christianity of being an antiecological religion. But what do these concepts mean historically? And in the light of recent bludgeonings, can they be revived for our time?

The complaints against the concepts of image and dominion are somewhat surprising in the light of most of Christian history and its Hebraic roots. Both the divine image and human dominion are rare concepts in the Old Testament, and are associated exclusively (except, in the case of dominion, for Ps. 8:5-8) with the P segments of Genesis. Neither apparently had significance in the rest of the Old Testament.[32] The concept of divine image appears ten times in the New Testament, and is used as a means of interpreting Christ or relationships to Christ, and never in an ecological context. Dominion in the sense of Genesis 1 is absent from the New Testament.

In subsequent Christian history, dominion in an ecological sense was widely assumed, but it was certainly not always or generally the dominion of exploitation. In his extensive study of Jewish and Christian interpretations of Genesis 1:28 from biblical antiquity to the Reformation, Jeremy Cohen concludes: "Rarely, if ever, did premodern Jews and Christians construe this verse as a license for the selfish exploitation of the environment. Although most readers of

Genesis casually assumed that God had fashioned the physical world for the benefit of human beings, Genesis 1:28 evoked relatively little concern with the issue of dominion over nature."[33] In the Desert Fathers, the Celtic saints, and Francis of Assisi, for example, dominion was taken for granted, but it was usually the dominion of benevolence, not exploitation, and it was assumed that this benevolence was the normative state of Eden. John Wesley, moreover, like others before him, interpreted dominion as the mediation of divine blessings to nonhuman creatures.[34] In fact, in seventeenth- and eighteenth-century England and elsewhere, a prominent minority of divines—especially among Puritans, Dissenters, and later evangelicals, like Methodists—interpreted dominion as a command *against* tyrannical cruelty or abuse and a mandate for guardianship and benevolence.[35]

Thus for much of Christian history and for many Christians, dominion seems to have been a relatively dormant and often beneficial concept ecologically. Similarly, debates about the image of God have centered not on ecological relationships, but rather predominantly on theological anthropology. In fact, the image has become an extremely valuable grounding for social justice. It has served as a basic affirmation of equal human rights for racial-ethnic minorities, religious groups, women, and the citizens of all nations. In the present theological situation, the image is a secondary issue and dominion is a marginal one, as they have been in most of Christian history. This claim is illustrated by the fact that in the entries of two recent, prominent reference works, *The Westminster Dictionary of Christian Theology*[36] and the *Westminster Dictionary of Christian Ethics*,[37] dominion is listed in neither and the image is discussed briefly and only in the one on ethics.

Still, exploitative interpretations of dominion or functional equivalents have been present in recent Christian history, and at times have been prominent, especially in some Christian-influenced cultures during and after the Enlightenment as "secular" rationalizations for settling (or unsettling) new territories and implementing technological developments. Too frequently and falsely in recent centuries, both the image of God and dominion have been interpreted as the divine grant of a special status making humanity the sole bearer of intrinsic value in creation, or of a special, divine mandate to pollute, plunder, and prey on creation to the point of exhausting its potential.

Contemporary exegesis, however, makes it increasingly clear what the image and dominion in Genesis 1 are *not*. They are not mandates for oppression or sanctions for despotic, totalitarian rule over nature. Approval for the exercise of absolute or unlimited power is alien to

103

Genesis 1 and to the Old Testament as a whole. Humans are creatures; they are always subject to divine dominion. The land is God's; it is entrusted to humanity to "till and keep" (Gen. 2:15) in accord with God's ground rules—which even include a soil conservation mandate to let the land rest every seven years (Lev. 25:3-5; Exod. 23:10-11). In fact, the ecological world over which the images of God have dominion in Genesis 1 is one in which universal vegetarianism is divinely mandated (1:29-30). And even when meat-eating and other destructive acts are permitted after the Flood, these acts are circumscribed by a rule against taking life lightly (9:2-4)—and also by other divine expectations on justice in scripture. The delivery of all animals into humans' hands for food, and the consequent fear and dread of humans by other creatures, is not a license for despotism, but rather appears to be a simple recognition of the ecological reality that humans are comparatively omnivorous and very effective predators.

Anthropocentric oppression of nature, from this perspective, is not a representation but rather a usurpation of divine sovereignty. It is playing God in hubris.[38] It is a distortion of the image and a perversion of dominion. It is a projection rather than a revelation, since it makes God into the image of arrogant humans. Genuine dominion in Genesis 1 and 9, however, as Lloyd Steffen argues, is "a divine counterpoint and judgment on domination."[39] The image and dominion in Genesis, therefore, are not grounds for abuse of nature. The saints who interpreted these concepts as mandates for benevolence appear to have read the texts accurately to this point.

But what are the positive meanings of image and dominion in Genesis? The image of God has been interpreted in remarkably various ways in Christian history. The image has been understood as: rationality, personality, moral agency, moral freedom, immortality, cocreativity, spirituality, relationality with God, accountability to God, and loving capacities.[40] Perhaps all of these overlapping interpretations and more (except for immortality, a foreign concept in the Old Testament) were in the mind of P. However, the text itself is uncomfortably vague.

Most Old Testament scholars agree that the main root of the idea is in the "royal ideology" of the ancient near East, where a statue or viceroy functioned as the symbolic image or representative of the ruler's authority over a territory or people in the ruler's absence.[41] This delegated authority, however, is not unrestricted or oppressive: in the Hebraic mind, the earthly ruler is subject to the rules of God's justice; she/he is the guardian of the good (Ps. 72 especially). Dominion connotes "just governance."[42] Understood in this sense, humans act in the image of God when they are *responsible representatives*, reflecting like governors or ambassadors of antiquity the interests of their Sovereign.[43] The image is not identical with but it includes dominion as a feature of the image.[44] The image incorporates the God-given assignment to exercise dominion or governance *in accord with God's values*. Humans practice dominion properly when they care for God's creation benevolently and justly in accord with the will of the ultimate owner.

The image of God (including dominion), then, is not a special status as the sole bearer of intrinsic value or a special sanction to destroy with impunity, but rather a special role or function—a vocation, calling, task, commission, or assignment. Applied ecologically, the image concept recognizes a basic biological fact: humans alone have evolved the peculiar rational, moral, and, therefore, creative capacities that enable us alone to serve as responsible representatives of God's interests and values, to function as protectors of the ecosphere and self-constrained consumers of the world's goods. The image is as much a responsibility as a right ecologically.

The New Testament understanding of the image of God only enhances this sense of ecological responsibility. Christ is the perfection of the image and, therefore, presumably the paradigm of dominion (II Cor. 4:4; Col. 1:15; Heb. 1:3; John 1:14-18).[45] This concept has ethical implications. Christ is the moral model. Christians are to imitate or mirror the love of Christ (Eph. 5:1-2). Love is the essence of the image, and the assignment of Christians is to reflect that love in relationships with all that God loves. Thus when interpreted in the context of Christ, the realization of the image and the proper expression of dominion are not manifestations of exploitation, but rather *representations of nurturing and serving love*.[46] That is a reason why one of the basic questions for Christian ecological ethics is how to express love, including justice, in an ecological context.

Yet, any contemporary, empirically sensitive reinterpretation of human dominion must be a narrowly defined one. It is important to note, for example, that dominion was neither possible nor necessary until those late-coming moral agents, *Homo sapiens*, with their creative and destructive capacities, entered the evolutionary scene. Until then, the planet thrived biologically without human assistance—and its greatest threats have come recently only as a consequence of human exploitation. God displayed cosmocentric and biocentric values and involvements long before humans arrived, and continues to do so today. Humans have never played any role, and almost certainly never

105

object! Man has done amazing things!! (handwritten, left margin)

will, in the impenetrable stretches of the universe, and have played only very recent roles, and frequently destructive ones, in the evolutionary and geological histories of this planet (though future generations may have good reasons for worrying about the health of this solar system). In this context, the idea that the earth, let alone the whole creation, was made for "man" is not only ludicrous but sinfully arrogant. It is a cultural addendum to the Christian faith, and a violation of the integrity of that faith.

These realities suggest that dominion has narrow implications: it is primarily the protection of the planet and its inhabitants *by* humans *against* human exploitation. Furthermore, these realities suggest that the primary goal of dominion may be to preserve and restore as much as possible, compatible with human physical and cultural needs, the natural systems and dynamics that would prevail without the presence of modern humanity.

None of this denies, however, that humans must "subdue"—yes, trample, conquer, and the other strong connotations of the Hebrew word *kabash* (including in modern slang)—the earth's resistance in order to survive and maintain cultures. Contrary to the romantic view of nature, the much-maligned but realistic writer of Genesis 1:26-28 chose the right word! He probably meant, however, little more than agricultural cultivation, similar to the tilling and keeping in Gen. 2:15.[47] Some degree of domination *of* nature by humans is necessary to prevent the domination of humans *by* nature (which has been the pattern in human history until relatively recently, as plagues, pestilences, and famines testify). The ecosphere is potentially hospitable to human interests, but that hospitality must be coerced by overcoming the earth's manifestations of seeming hostility or neutrality—for instance, predators and parasites or floods and flames. From the beginning, the survival of the human species in relation to the rest of nature has been a nasty, brutish, short, and otherwise Hobbesian struggle for food, clothing, shelter, fuel, health, and other basics. Human ingenuity—manifested in plows, shovels, axes, weapons, medicines, and their modern, sophisticated equivalents—has been a necessity for primitive survival and the construction of civilizations.

The ecological crisis is not a consequence of "kabashing" per se. Survivors in the biophysical world have no choice but to do that. Instead, the ecological crisis is a result of imperialistic overextension—abusing what is divinely intended for use, subduing far beyond the point of necessity, imaging despotism rather than dominion, and failing to nurture benevolently and justly nature's potential hospitality.

It is sin. Whatever tendencies are inherent in the word "subduing" for overreaching human bounds are checked and balanced by the biblical concepts of image and dominion themselves, and by other moral constrictions in scripture and subsequent Christian history.

The original concepts of image and dominion have some rich ecological potential. The Christian church would do well to preserve, revise, and highlight them. Yet, the church is certainly not bound to the words. *Dominion*, after all, is a Latin-derived translation from the Hebrew. It seems to distort the meaning of the original concept, because it often connotes tyrannical domination to many contemporary minds. Other words, probably in combinations, may better convey the original connotations: *Guardian*, *Protector*, *Defender*, and *Preserver*, all of which have been used as titles for the practitioners of just governance in other periods. Thus the Defenders of Wildlife, Friends of the Earth, Worldwatch Institute, and Greenpeace embody in their organizational names parts of the essential meaning of dominion!

I and many others, however, have negative reactions to some descriptions, for instance, *caretaker*, *gardener*, and especially *manager*—all of which have been associated with anthropocentric abuse and the strictly instrumental evaluation of nature. Management is a concept that makes sense contextually, for instance, in agriculture, tree-farming, and wild habitat restoration. But it is a wildly arrogant notion when applied universally to describe human relationships with the whole biosphere. Many things are best left alone. Similarly, some have strong reactions to *conservation* and especially to *steward* and *stewardship*. Though the ethical concept of stewardship justifiably has positive connotations to many Christians, implying love and service, it has negative ones for substantial numbers of environmentalists (including many Christians). Stewardship conveys to them, because of historical associations with Gifford Pinchot and others in this century, the notion of anthropocentric and instrumental management of the biosphere as humanly owned "property" and "resources."[48] In the light of these attitudes, I am ambivalent about the use of the word and the concept of *stewardship* to describe human relationships with and attitudes toward the biosphere.

Yet, perhaps the bottom line is this: the strict constructionists and sectarians who yearn for ideological and verbal purity in the environmental movement do well to pay less attention to words and more to values and commitments. They might find a fair number of allies, including among those "unregenerates" who are content with *conservation, stewardship,* or even *dominion.* My emerging attitude toward these verbal squabbles is the same as Rhett's final words to Scarlett in *Gone with the Wind.*

THE INCARNATION AS COSMIC REPRESENTATION

"The Word became flesh and lived among us" (John 1:14). This simple affirmation of divine incarnation has been the source of more than a little controversy in Christian theology. It has been understood variously, with positions ranging from Chalcedonian literalism (Jesus Christ being the "full substance" of both God and the human) to mythological interpretations. Despite this diversity, however, there is a widespread (though not universal) consensus in Christian theology that God and human essence were definitively associated, and in solidarity, in Jesus of Nazareth. In the life and ministry, humiliation and glorification, of Jesus of Nazareth, the Christian church experienced its decisive encounter with the saving Christ. The fullness of divine grace stooped to enter the human condition, becoming immanent in the material, identifying with the finite, disclosing both the nature of the redemptive God and the character of the redeemed human. This relational mystery of faith has significant ecological implications, and they do not appear to be restricted to a particular interpretation of the Incarnation.

Jesus is not only the Representative of God, in being the decisive reflection of divine love, but also the Representative of Humanity, in being the decisive expression of basic humanness and the fullness of humankind's historical potential for love. In identifying with this Representative of Humanity, however, God entered into solidarity not only with all humanity, but also with the whole biophysical world that humans embody and on which their existence depends. The Representative of Humanity, therefore, is also the Representative of the biosphere, even the ecosphere, indeed, the universe. The Universal Representative is the cosmic Christ, not only as the one who illuminates the love of the Creator of the cosmos, but also as the one who unites all things and holds all things together before God (Eph. 1:10; Col. 1:15-20).

The very nature of being human is to exist as *imago mundi*, a reflection as embodiment of the biophysical world.[49] This idea is hardly new in Christian history. The theme is common in Patristic theology, combined with the assumption that Christ would save all that he embodied. The Greek theologians were fond of saying that humans are the microcosm that represents the macrocosm, past and present—"a microcosm in which all previous creatures are to be found again, a being that can only exist in community with all other created beings and which can only understand itself in that community."[50] Humans exist *in* nature and as *part* of nature. The atoms in human bodies were once part of other creatures, including the original organisms. The chemical and genetic structures of the cells in our bodies are remarkably similar to the cells in all other creatures, including bacteria, grasses, and fish. We have evolved through adaptive interactions, along with all other creatures, from common ancestors, and we continue to exist in symbiotic relationships with all other species. We are embodiments of biotic history on this planet, incorporating all simpler systems in evolution. Through the flora and fauna (including microorganisms), minerals, chemicals, and even radiation that we ingest through the natural processes of eating, drinking, digesting, and breathing, humans embody a representative sampling of all the elements of the ecosphere. We carry within ourselves "the signature of the supernovas and the geology and life history of the Earth."[51] These connections are symbolized in Genesis 2:7 by the formation of humans and other creatures from the same substance, the humus. Humans are representatives of the earth, interdependent parts of nature—and this totality is what God became immersed in through association with the Representative of Humanity in the Incarnation.

The ecological implications of this interpretation of the Incarnation are significant, and have long been recognized in some segments of the Christian church. The Incarnation confers dignity not only on humankind, but on everything and everyone, past and present, with which humankind is united in interdependence—corporeality, materiality, indeed, the whole of the earthly and heavenly. It sanctifies the biophysical world, making all things and kinds meaningful and worthy and valuable in the divine scheme. It justifies "biophilia," the affiliation with and affection for the diversity of life forms.[52] Thus the venerable St. John of Damascus (c. 675–c. 749), in reaction to the neo-Platonic denigration of the material, expresses the appropriate Christian attitude toward the biophysical in response to the Incarnation (as well as to the creation and consummation):

> I do not worship matter. I worship the Creator of matter who became matter for my sake, who willed to take his abode in matter; who worked out my salvation through matter. Never will I cease honouring the matter which wrought my salvation! I honour it, but not as God. . . . Because of this I salute all remaining matter with reverence, because God has filled it with his grace and power. Through it my salvation has come to me.[53]

Nothing then is worthless. Everything has moral value and is worthy of appropriate care and concern. "Spiritual" contempt for the material or earthly, indifference to the fate of other humans and other species, and exclusively anthropocentric valuations in general are rejected—all because the Source of life, matter, and value affiliated in love with the Representative of Humanity and, therefore, with the Representative of the Cosmos.

The Incarnation also sanctions human humility, reminding us of our common roots and connections with other kinds. This recognition of relationships does not diminish human dignity; it enhances it, partly by deflating one of humankind's most unflattering characteristics, the arrogance of exclusivity. It also elevates the status of nonhuman creatures, making them worthy of moral consideration. H. Richard Niebuhr gives a good description of this attitude. He argues that the revelation of God involves a change in the "moral law," so that all creatures and things are "within the network of moral relations,"[54] and subsequently adds: "When the Creator is revealed it is no longer necessary to defend man's place by a reading of history which establishes his superiority to all other creatures. To be a man does not now mean to be a lord of the beasts but a child of God. To know the person [Christ] is to lose all sense of shame because of kinship with the clod and the ape."[55]

This incarnationally-induced humility, however, is constantly resisted through theological devices. The Incarnation, for example, does not mean that the biophysical world has a "derived dignity," in which any dignity or moral status ascribed to the biophysical world is derived from human dignity, since God affiliated with a human.[56] Similar notions occur regularly in Christian history. Yet this perspective seems to be a harmful vestige of anthropocentrism, since it declines to recognize nature's full value in itself. In fact, in the light of evolution and ecology, it is more accurate to say that any dignity ascribed to humanity is derived from our natural history. The intrinsic value or worth of human beings seems to me to be indefensible apart from the intrinsic value or worth of the biophysical world as a whole, of which human beings are descendants and inseparable parts. The Incarnation, however, is not an issue of creaturely derivation or mediation. The Representative of Humanity is *simultaneously and interrelationally* the Representative of the Cosmos, the Cosmic Christ. The incarnated God embraced the whole. The only "derived dignity" is *from* the Creator to *all* creatures.[57]

We are yet a long way from understanding the practical implications of

110

the Incarnation for ecological responsibility, but at least this much can be said with reasonable confidence: When humans destroy life and habitats, as predatorial creatures must to survive in this morally ambiguous world, we should do so sparingly, carefully, and reverently, in recognition of the Incarnation and its consequent duty of respect for our co-evolving kin. Wanton pollution, profligate consumption, and human-induced extinctions are sins from the perspective of the Incarnation.

SACRAMENTAL PRESENCE OF THE SPIRIT

The world is filled with the glory of God (Isa. 6:3; Ps. 19:1; Eph. 4:6). That has been a common Christian claim. The biophysical world provides traces of and testimonies to the mystery and majesty of God. But these "natural" revelations are not simply evidence left behind like clues in a mystery or footprints in the sand; they are also signs, even vehicles, of God's presence. The holy (not wholly) transcendent God is also immanent in the creation. The natural is simultaneously preternatural.

God exists *in* the creation as the Holy Spirit,[58] the Lifegiver in the Nicene Creed. According to various descriptions in Christian theology, this personal, vivifying Presence reconciles, liberates, enlightens, inspires, guides, counsels, comforts, suffers with, nurtures, strengthens, transforms, renews, sanctifies, empowers, and prods created being in its pilgrimage to its destiny disclosed in Christ. As the immanent Spirit, God is intimate with the creation, actively involved, self-revealing, and grace-dispensing, leaving signs and making the divine presence felt in all things—in personal, cultural, and natural histories.

Consequently, the data relevant for faith commitments and theological/philosophical reflections are comprehensive, encompassing the whole of experience—past and present, aesthetic and scientific, mystical and moral, sociological and psychological, subjective and objective, cultural and natural. Indeed, the primary source of faith and the primary data for theological reflection are, as they were in a fair share of scripture and tradition, religious experiences mediated through the sensate. By *religious experiences*, I am referring to the revelatory intimations, intuitions, and illuminations of the divine that come under various names and categories: "witness of the Spirit," the "still, small voice," Buber's I-Thou encounter, the ecstatic visions of the mystics, communion, Schleiermacher's feeling of absolute dependence, Rudolf Otto's *Mysterium Tremendum*, Jonathan Edwards' "sense of the heart," and Peter Berger's "signals of transcendence."[59] These

111

experiences are often so decisively authoritative for the experiencer, so immediate and so compelling, so integrating, so strong a foundation for a vibrant faith, that they may provide an existential argument for the reality of the redeeming God.

No doubt, these experiences are notoriously subjective. They can be—and probably often are—more projection and illusion than revelation. They must be subjected, therefore, to tests of coherence and adequacy. Nonetheless, these experiences cannot be dismissed or excluded. To restrict the database of faith and theology to scripture and tradition (which in themselves are often testimonies from the *past* to "spiritual" encounters), and to exclude general revelation, "natural theology," or mystical experiences, is an arbitrary limitation on the freedom of the Spirit and a denial of God's presence and *present* revelations. This stress on divine immanence breaks down the classical discontinuities between Creator and creation, faith and reason, natural and supernatural, and sacred and secular. It is a revolt against the perception of God as an absentee landlord who enters the premises only for miraculous repairs. It is an affirmation that the hidden, transcendent God is encountered, albeit ambiguously, in the totality of experience through divine immanence.[60]

Thus we live in a "sacramental universe," as William Temple eloquently argued, in which the whole of material existence is essentially holy, because it can be an effective medium of revelation and a vehicle of communion with God, a means of grace. The creation is a sacramental expression of the Creator.[61] Since God dwells in the creation and not in deistic isolation, the world is the bearer of the holy, the temple of the Spirit. For the spiritually receptive, therefore, the cosmos is a complex of sacramental signs that convey the hidden but real presence of the Spirit "in, with, and under" the natural elements. The sacramental presence of the Spirit is the extension of the Incarnation of Christ—and, in fact, the two have often been connected in Christian thought and piety.

The omnipresent God can be encountered anywhere, as countless Christians have testified—in the cathedral and cell, in the community and in solitude, in the faces of people and the faceless silence, in the city and wilderness, in nature and culture. No places are necessarily better than others, and perhaps all are necessary for spiritual wholeness. But different places do appear to have, by association, different characters and consequences. Thus the intuition of the Spirit's presence in power and love in the biophysical world has been a potent force in the development of a human appreciation, admiration, and affection for nature, with both spiritual and ethical consequences.

The natural world has been a prime place for encounters with the grandeur and glory of God. The major reason may be that nature in the raw is relatively unencumbered (though tragically today, decreasingly and almost never totally so) with humanly created artifacts, and, thus, contributes to a feeling of being present in the midst of God's comparatively pure creativity. It arouses a cosmic consciousness, a sense of intimacy, a numinous feeling of creaturely awe in the presence of awe-full majesty that is "beyond apprehension and comprehension."[62] Joseph Wood Krutch, for instance, argued that the desert prompts mystical contemplation and contributed to the emergence of Hebraic religion: "The desert itself seems to brood and to encourage brooding. To the Hebrews the desert spoke of God, and one of the most powerful of all religions was born."[63] This hypothesis is simplistic, but it is worthy of exploration. It is hardly disharmonious with significant portions of Christian history. The desert and other wild or semiwild places have often been viewed as places of contemplation and encounter with God,[64] as witnessed, for example, by the Desert Fathers and perhaps even Jesus' forty days in the wilderness "with the wild beasts" (Mark 1:12-13). The Celtic and other saints saw the natural world as a theophany, which apparently encouraged their affection for the entities that convey the divine presence. Similarly, the Romantic poets who were Christians often displayed an awareness of divine immanence, even though the sacramental scenes that the British representatives celebrated were generally a "humanized nature," domesticated and defanged.[65] Even some contemporary church camps in attractive natural settings appear to have been intended originally to encourage this sacramental consciousness. The theme of sacramental presence in nature, therefore, is a common one in Christian history. Implicitly at least, ecosystems are understood by many as God's primal "holy orders" and places of "holy communion."

Probably most Christians with a vital interest in the dynamics of the biophysical world, and many with far less intense interests, have at least occasionally experienced its sacramentality. Because of the inadequacies of verbalization and the penetrating depth of the intuitions, these experiences both defy and demand descriptions. Generally, these experiences take the form of an acute awareness that the natural world is omnimiraculous, filled with the extraordinary in the midst of the ordinary. Thus the natural growth of a vine becomes more awesome than the magical transformation of water into wine. That is only one of innumerable biological and ecological wonders that surround us, that we normally ignore, and that we often mask with cultural veneers (alleged "improvements"). In a wild or semiwild setting, where humans, as products of culture, are more observers than participants, the numinous sense of the miraculous often arises, and it arouses in the predisposed an awareness and appreciation of the Source.

These sacramental experiences are morally and spiritually regenerative. They are often accompanied by a host of intermixed feelings: gratitude and joy; creaturely humility yet exaltation; solitude yet communion; frequently fear but always awe; a recognition of mystery combined with a feeling of ultimate coherence; pleasure despite the physical demands, discomforts, and sometimes dangers; and a moral yearning to preserve these holy places and subjects from cultural invasions. One senses a sublime beauty surpassing violent origins and ugly details,[66] and a providential order in the midst of apparent chaos.

In its full or at least adequate state, this sacramentality is not romantic or sentimental: it encounters God in the rainbow and the hurricane, in cute critters like Bambi and in the cougar that ambushes and eats Bambi. The sacramental sense, however, is possible for most of us only when one is not fighting to save life or limb, only when one is more an observer of than a participant in the natural struggle for survival, and only when one is the bearer of cultural benefits like proper clothing, tools, and knowledge about natural dynamics. Terror is the normal and proper response to some situations, like being lost amidst the dangers of the desert or confronting an aggressive lion. However, on those occasions when the sacramental sense is a possibility, the experience can be regenerative. Whether stalking an elegant trogon in a southeastern Arizona canyon, or watching an osprey dive for a trout, or a fox pouncing on a mouse, or wandering through a flourishing forest or prairie, or microscopically examining the marvelously intricate and dynamic interactions within an organic cell, or gazing into infinite space at innumerable blazing stars, or exulting with that pious naturalist John Muir over the "wild beauty-making business" of "a noble earthquake" as an "expression of God's love,"[67] numerous men and women have been filled with awe and wonder, moved to humility and contemplation, perplexed by the paradox of holistic order through brutal predation, overpowered by a sense of mystery, and yet strangely grasped by the consciousness of God's loving presence.

This understanding of sacramentality emphatically denies that the Christian faith desacralizes nature. Contrary to a common viewpoint

114 I'm not sure this is due to Christianity but perhaps spirit

among Christian and non-Christian interpreters alike, nature is sacred by association, as the bearer of the sacred. We are standing perpetually on holy ground, because God is present not only in the burning bush but in the nurturing soil and atmosphere, indeed, sharing the joys and agonies of all creatures. The sacramental presence of the Spirit endows all of creation with a sacred value and dignity. Unlike animism and polytheism, which assigned natural objects to different deities or divided nature among competing gods, Christian monotheism provides an integrated, relational world view: "The world is one because God is one. Not only that, but God made the material world one . . . in the sense that all things are made to exist in each other and to be mutually supportive of each other."[68] Christian monotheism, therefore, is not the culprit in desacralization, contrary to Arnold Toynbee. The sacramental presence of the one Spirit does not desacralize but rather sacralizes nature.

Sacramentality also dedivinizes nature: the biophysical world is *not* part of God. Sacramentality is not pantheistic. Perhaps it can instead be described as *pan-en-theistic* in the sense that God is *in all* and all is somehow *in God* without being part of God. The metaphysical problem is how to insure that nothing exists apart from God and still assert that creatures are distinctive entities. The idea of the world as God's "body,"[69] however, suggests a merger of Creator and creation. Most theologians, therefore, have been reluctant to use, or have rigorously opposed, this image. The "body" metaphor seems to compromise divine independence, and deny the distinctive integrity of creation and its creatures. It may contribute to animism and idolatry. It certainly adds nothing to the value and lovableness of nature that is not already accomplished through the traditional affirmation of the sacramental presence of the Spirit. The creation and its creatures are finite and transient; they are not divine and are, therefore, not to be worshiped. Yet they are still to be valued and loved, since they are valued and loved by God as the mode of spiritual presence and residence, God's beloved habitat. Christian sacramentality sacralizes but does not divinize nature.

Nature sacramentality, moreover, is a sensate spirituality. It experiences God in and through the "distractions" of the biophysical world, not by blocking the senses and transcending them. Consequently, it is genuinely mystified by what is technically and now popularly known as "desert spirituality" in contemplative disciplines.[70] In this conception, the term *desert* is often used metaphorically and psychologically, not geographically or ecologically. The so-called desert is any place of solitude, simplicity, and emptiness—a barren wasteland, figuratively—to which one withdraws for undistracted communication with God.[71] One closes one's eyes and blocks out the other senses in order to experience the Spirit with utmost clarity. The process is seemingly transcendental rather than sacramental.

The metaphorical desert, however, is the antithesis of ecological desert, for the latter is rarely barren or a wasteland (except on anthropocentric, especially economic, assumptions); it is usually teeming with interacting life and beautiful distractions. Metaphorical desert spirituality is to ecological desert spirituality as plastic trees are to an ancient redwood forest. The metaphorical type seems to lose the particular feelings of awe, wonder, marvel, gratitude, and ecological sensitivity that arise from associations with the omnimiraculous in wild places. In contrast, the sensate spirituality of the desert opens all the senses—touch, taste, sound, sight, smell—to experience God sacramentally in and through all created being. The biophysical reality of the real desert and other wild ecosystems are not distractions or diversions from God, but rather mediations of the Spirit.

So-called desert spirituality certainly has a valuable place in a total discipline of prayer, but the term is an ecologically insensitive misnomer that may give "aid and comfort" to ecologically insensitive acts. If the spirituality of the desert can be experienced in any isolated, artificial setting, who needs to save the genuine article? Not only should the term be restricted to ecological places of encounter, but the spiritual disciplines should be recognized as truncated without a sensate spirituality associated with real deserts and other wild places.

As the habitation of the Spirit and the context of sacramental presence, the cosmos is a sacred place. Its integrity, therefore, demands moral respect and responsibility. We are created to live together in the fullest possible accord with God's justice and peace, as valued parts of God's beloved habitat, and ours.[72] The diversity, vitality, and beauty of this habitat must be protected, certainly for its own sake, but also for the sake of humanity's physical *and* spiritual well-being.

CHAPTER FIVE

FIRM FOUNDATIONS:

DOCTRINES OF SIN, JUDGMENT, REDEMPTION, AND CHURCH

The ecological relevance of Christian theology is not exhausted by the doctrines of creation, covenant, divine image, incarnation, and spiritual presence. Other less-noted doctrinal affirmations also have important ecological implications. This chapter is a continuation of chapter 4. It focuses on the ecological significance of Christian understandings of sin, judgment, cosmic redemption, and the church. I conclude with a summary of the chief implications of a "reformed" Christian theology for Christian ecological perspectives and responsibilities.

SIN AS AN ECOLOGICAL DISORDER

A perennial problem in Christianity is the tendency to define the meaning of sin too narrowly or even to reduce it to triviality. Sin too often has been functionally limited, for example, to sexual misdeeds, and sometimes to sexual deeds themselves. Instead, the concept of sin is broad and complex in meaning, and is an indispensable element in Christian theology. In our time particularly, the meaning of sin must be properly extended to cover ecological misdeeds, and the human condition underlying them. The ecological crisis and the host of actions contributing to that crisis are best understood in the context of sin. This interpretation alerts us to the powers behind the plunderings and the intimidating obstacles to reform. It shows the seriousness of the disorder and the importance of perpetual public vigilance.

What is sin? Sin is not nearly as easy to define as it is for some to identify. Sin is strictly a human phenomenon, though its effects are universal problems. Even though nature as a whole has not "fallen," it has felt severely the fallout from the Fall of humanity. Sin literally defiles the land. Nature's fate is intimately linked to human acts, like the production of acid rain. Sin is volitional, an avoidable consequence of moral freedom or the power of choice, that only humans possess. It exists only to the extent that humans have freedom to choose (which is limited for all and varies among individuals and cultures). Accountability, therefore, depends on culpability.

Being a bondage of the will, sin is not "original" in the sense of being a genetic condition, but it is dependent on a genetic precondition: the capacities for moral volition inherited through the line of succession from the original parents of the species. Moreover, though sin itself is not an inherited trait from the genes of our forebears, its effects are a feature of our cultural inheritance from them. The results of their sins persist in cultural institutions and patterns, from religious customs to economic systems, limiting our own options and compelling, to some degree, our participation. Every generation benefits from the graces and suffers from the sins of its ancestors. Sin is manifested in both individuals and, in accentuated forms, in social structures. It is not "natural," since sin is not in the exercise of moral freedom per se. But it is ubiquitous in the deliberate, consensual abuse of that freedom. The Fall is perennial, not simply primeval.

Sin is not finitude, but it is rarely separated from finitude. The human capacities for error and evil often team up to exaggerate and exceed human powers. Sin and finitude are frequently encountered as incompetence combined with overconfidence. Sin is generally subtle, possessing remarkable powers to pose as altruism or righteousness, but it is always harmful to relationships. Sin is the condition of alienation between humans and God and all the creatures of God.

Traditionally, the root sin, the condition of sinfulness, has often been interpreted as pride or arrogance, the self-centered lust to dominate and the pretension of self-sufficiency at the expense of other beings.[1] Others have argued, however, that sloth—indifference, apathy, omissions, "deficient participation"[2]—is also a root of sin alongside pride. In my view, pride remains primal. Sloth and other root definitions of sin can be incorporated into pride, for they too reflect self-centered arrogance. I prefer, however, to use the term

118

egoism to describe the root of sin, since it captures the essence of the theological meaning of *pride* and it avoids that word's ambiguity in common usage. Sin, then, makes the self the center of existence, in defiance of divine intentions and in disregard for the interests of other lives. Sin is turning inward, and, thus, turning away from "God, neighbor, and nature."[3] In fact, if love is the core of the gospel, then sin can be seen as its antithesis: egoism is the absence or distortion of love for others in an imperialistic or narcissistic preference for the self (or one's group, from family to nation).

Whatever terms are used to describe the root of sin, there is general agreement on one theological definition that is all-embracing: sin is a declaration of autonomy from the sovereign source of our being. Its essence is rebellion. Whether in omission or commission, sin is the usurpation or rejection of divine authority. That, of course, is a religious interpretation of a broadly verifiable human phenomenon.

On these assumptions, what is the meaning of sin in an ecological framework? What are ecological sins? No single or simple definition will do, because of the complexity and subtlety of relationships between humans and the rest of nature. Several overlapping definitions will give the flavor of ecological sin (and sins). Ecologically, sin is the refusal to act in the image of God, as responsible representatives who value and love the host of interdependent creatures in their ecosystems, which the Creator values and loves. It is injustice, the self-centered human inclination to defy God's covenant of justice by grasping more than our due (as individuals, corporate bodies, nations, and a species) and thereby depriving other individuals, corporate bodies, nations, and species of their due. It is breaking the bonds with God and our comrades in creation. It is acting like the owner of creation with absolute property rights. Ecological sin is expressed as the arrogant denial of the creaturely limitations imposed on human ingenuity and technology, a defiant disrespect or a deficient respect for the interdependent relationships of all creatures and their environments established in the covenant of creation, and an anthropocentric abuse of what God has made for frugal use.

These dynamics of ecological sin are evident in all dimensions of our ecological crisis. Thus, when sin is interpreted in this manner, the miscalculations, foul-ups, high-risk gambles, and negligence surrounding the 1989 "accidental" oil spill from the *Exxon Valdez* into Prince William Sound can properly be called the "sin of *Valdez*."[4]

Descriptions of ecological sin in Christian theological history have been rare until recently. Comparatively few understood sin as having

119

ecological applications. Two descriptions earlier in this century merit some note. One is by the leading voice of the Social Gospel, Walter Rauschenbusch, and the other by the leading reformer of that movement, Reinhold Niebuhr.

In the following description, Rauschenbusch seems to value the natural world primarily for its contributions to human wants—aesthetic, scientific, and economic. He shows some but still little appreciation for the intrinsic value and vibrancy of otherkind in their ecosystems. He represents the Gifford Pinchot-type of conservation common in his era: anthropocentric, utilitarian, and managerial. Nature is "improved" by development for human needs:

> *Human labor beautifies nature.* . . . Science has furnished labor with unparalleled powers to *fashion nature* according to its will and with *wonderful results.* Arid lands have come to teem with life and verdure; dreary swamps have been *redeemed from desolation.* But side by side with this *fertilizing hand* of man goes an influence of devastation.[5]

Rauschenbusch then proceeds to denounce the excesses of capitalistic destruction—the gutted mines, the wasted forests, and dried waterways—because of unsustainable usages:

> Beauty that ages have fashioned and that no skill of man can replace is effaced to enrich a few persons whose enrichment is of little use to anybody. . . . For any long-range care of nature capitalism is almost useless. . . . The avarice induced by our economic system *sacrifices the future of the race* to immediate enrichment. From the point of view of a religious evolutionist that is one of the greatest of all sins. God and nature are always supremely intent on a better future.[6]

As an admirer of Rauschenbusch, I do not find this passage to be pleasant reading. Rauschenbusch can be commended for recognizing the social structure of ecological sin and the ecological havoc caused by unfettered capitalism—a consciousness that was rising in his time. He does not seem to recognize, however, that capitalism is not in itself the cause of the ecological crisis or that every economic system must be ecologically restrained, as contemporary forms of ecologically debilitating socialism well illustrate. Above all, however, Rauschenbusch seems to reflect some of the very ecological sins he condemns. Anthropocentric initiatives to "improve" nature by development and "beautification" have themselves been major causes of ecological disorder. Thus Rauschenbusch is not the best model for helping us to understand ecological sin.

In contrast, Reinhold Niebuhr offers a description of ecological sin that reaches its depths. Humans are insecure in their ambiguous situation of finitude and freedom. So, they seek security against the vicissitudes of nature by pretending to unlimited technological capacities and by exceeding the limits providentially established. Ecological sin is one form of the "pride of power":

> Man's sense of dependence upon nature and his reverent gratitude toward the miracle of nature's perennial abundance is destroyed by his arrogant sense of independence and his greedy effort to overcome the insecurity of nature's rhythms and seasons by garnering her stores with excessive zeal and beyond natural requirements. Greed is in short the expression of man's inordinate ambition to hide his insecurity in nature.[7]

Niebuhr's recognition of ecological sin was somewhat ahead of his time (though his use of sexually exclusive language was not). His description is adequate for alerting us to the seriousness of the problem and the difficulty of finding solutions.

From the perspective of the classical Christian definition of sin, the ecological crisis is not simply a consequence of defective technologies, ideologies, or socioeconomic systems. The importance of these factors, of course, cannot be minimized, as this book testifies. Some technologies, ideologies, and systems *are*, actually or potentially, better than others in controlling or preventing ecological problems. We need personal *and* social repentance and reform. However, no morally flawless New Human will emerge and no ecological tokenism or half-measures will be fitting responses to the persistent source of the problem. The Christian understanding of sin warns us that resolving the ecological crisis demands perpetual vigilance and sufficient reforms. Fortunately, an appropriate Christian understanding of the human potential for good, also a consequence of moral freedom and the empowerment of divine grace, gives some hope that the powers of ecological sin can be contained.

DIVINE JUDGMENTS IN NATURAL HISTORY

The judgments of God beyond history have gotten the bulk of the press in most Christian traditions. Imaginations have worked overtime to provide the gory details of apocalyptic events and literally to scare the hell out of people. But the concern here is with God's judgments *in* history.

Does God exercise judgments in history against ecological sins? Are there "natural" judgments for moral evils? Does the biophysical world communicate divine "wrath" for the exploitation of nature? Is biological unsustainability, for instance, a manifestation of divine punishment for sins against the ecosphere? Contemporary theologians and ethicists often suggest that the answers are in the affirmative. References to the revenge or backlash of nature under the auspices of God are frequent. I generally agree with these assessments, but with qualifications. There can be no doubt that ecological abuses have dire ecological consequences, including for human communities. Moreover, from a Christian perspective, God is actively involved in the processes of cultural and natural history, guiding and judging to redeem. Yet, the attribution of divine judgment to particular natural events is a delicate matter that requires extreme caution.

The association of natural evils with moral evils, the latter causing or contributing to the former, is common in Christian history. The "jeremiads" of seventeenth-century New England preachers, for example, regularly and luridly predicted plagues and other natural disasters, including smallpox epidemics, as judgmental acts of God, unless the people repented and humbled themselves.[8] This association has plenty of scriptural proof-texts for support. Several passages refer explicitly to ecological punishments, like a barren earth or drought, for disobedience to the divine will (Isa. 24:1-7; Jer. 2:7-8; Hos. 4:1-3; Amos 4:6-9; Lev. 26:18-25), or to ecological benefices, like abundant yields, for obedience (Lev. 25:18-19; 26:3-6; Isa. 11:9; 35:1-2). In fact, from some theological perspectives, Adam's Fall had ecological consequences (Cf. Gen. 3:17), even "causing" the fall of nature. It is important to note, though, that the ecological punishments in these biblical passages are *not* the effects of specifically ecological sins. Nature mourns and withers as the device of divine judgment on sins in general, not ecological sins in particular. Because there is no direct causal relationship between ecological abuse and disasters, the use of these texts as bases for sermons or theological reflections on environmental responsibility is at least difficult and often dubious.

In fact, without this causal correlation between actions and effects in ways that are empirically verifiable, the interpretation of natural events as divine judgments is potentially, and usually actually, dangerous and irresponsible. Volcanic eruptions, droughts, floods, and diseases can then be blamed on the alleged moral corruptions of individuals or

or not relevant at all...

communities. These linkages are theologically primitive and were refuted initially in the Book of Job. Certainly, the categories of moral and natural evil are not always discrete.[9] Famines can be caused by both inclement weather and poor agricultural practices. Earthquake damage can be exacerbated by the folly of building major cities on fault lines. Some natural evils are caused directly and solely by moral evils—a nuclear holocaust being an obvious example, and atmospheric ozone depletion being a less obvious one. Nevertheless, if ecological debacles are to be interpreted responsibly as manifestations of divine judgment, the causal connections between moral and natural evils must be empirically verifiable, rather than homiletically irresistible.

James Gustafson suggests a responsible, empirically sensitive way to interpret ecological disorders as divine judgments. He stresses the interdependence of culture and nature. The divine ordering of creation imposes limits on environmental use and mandates the nurturing of nature. Humans must seek empirically to discern proper limits and the duties of care. Divine judgment comes from exceeding the bounds and exercising deficient care: "The religious consciousness confronts the judgment and wrath of God on those occasions when the consequences of our commissions and omissions signal a serious disordering of relationships between persons, in society, in relation to nature."[10]

The biophysical world does "retaliate" for human abuse or negligence, and God is implicated in these natural processes. There is a moral ordering of the world, part of the covenant of creation, and sin is disdainful of the limits and disruptive of the relationships in that order. Theologically interpreted, the natural order sets boundaries to rebellion.[11] Divine judgments, then, are exercised through the natural processes by which humans are compelled to respect biophysical limits—particularly the limits on dynamic ecosystems to survive the stresses of human interventions, the limits on the atmosphere, soil, and waters to absorb toxic wastes, and the limits on the use of renewable and nonrenewable goods. These judgments are "pedagogic," imposing costly effects through which humans are taught to correct their ecological faults. The indiscriminate consequences of these judgments—both the guilty and the innocent, the just and unjust suffer—are reminders of the relationality in both sin and nature; they "show how completely we are members of one another."[12] Thus, in the causal connections between ecological abuse or negligence and ecological disasters with their trains of woes, Christians can perceive the dynamics of ecological sin and divine judgment.

God's natural judgments, however, are not punishments for their own sake. They are the "grace of wrath" (as Old Testament scholar Harrell Beck used to pun) or providence in a stern, disciplinary mode. They are understood as acts of love by those who believe that God is love. The immediate effects are often costly, even deadly, but the intentions are corrective, to preserve the beneficial dynamics of the natural order and to shape human ecological behavior toward wise, beneficent, and just ends. The only appropriate response to God's ecological judgments against ecological sins is, as usual, ecological repentance.

not my idea of loving.

CONSUMMATION AS COSMIC REDEMPTION

bravdo got o!

When John Muir, America's most eloquent voice for wilderness, wandered on a dead bear in Yosemite, he railed against Christian orthodoxies for their "stingy heaven" that had no room in the ultimate inn for this "noble" creature or any other nonhuman kin in creation: "Not content with taking all of earth, they also claim the celestial country as the only ones who possess the kinds of souls for which that imponderable empire was planned." But God's "charity," he added, "is broad enough for bears."[13]

Muir was right: the only Christianity he knew reserved the realm of redemption for human occupants. The predominant characteristic of Western theological traditions, Roman Catholic and Protestant, has been the absence of the hope for the consummation of creation. Heaven is exclusively for humans, who alone have "rational, immortal souls," and generally only for a few of them, who believe the appropriate doctrines and who behave in the proper manner. For most, even the resurrection of the body became the immortality of the soul. The "saved" will sing perpetual praise to their Redeemer in this scene of damnation-like dullness, but not "all God's creatures got a place in the choir." In this ultimate dualism, redemption is the release from nature (including the body), and oblivion is the fate of nature.

really?

This exclusivistic belief has served as a major justification for depreciating the value of creation and destroying its allegedly valueless components. Humans can neglect or abuse what is not redeemable. Since the nonhuman creation is ultimately meaningless or useless, it has no intrinsic value for God, and, therefore, no intrinsic value that should be respected by others. It can be treated as an instrumental value, if it has utility for humans, and without hindrance if it does not—so long as our behavior does not cause harm to humans or dispose us psychologically to cruelty to humans.[14]

124

However, Muir's charge is only partially justified. A strong, minority voice affirming the consummation of all creation has been persistent in Christian history, and it has been an important—in my view, indispensable—grounding for the intrinsic value of creation and other elements of a Christian ecological ethic.

Historical Perspectives

The hope for cosmic redemption is rooted in scripture (Isa. 11:6-9; 65:17, 25; Col. 1:14-20; I Cor. 15:28; Eph. 1:10; Rom. 8:19-22). In the Old Testament, Israel's hope for God's final victory over evil inextricably links humanity with the rest of nature.[15] In the New Testament versions of this view, the cosmic Christ will redeem the whole creation, liberating all creatures from death and reconciling them for harmonious interactions. This minority perspective, however, was not as minor as commonly assumed. Pauline scholar J. Christiaan Beker argues convincingly that for St. Paul, the apocalyptic expectation of cosmic renewal is central. Every creature is destined for resurrected glory, and Jesus' Resurrection is the pledge of that universal salvation. The hope is not for salvation from the body, but rather the redemption of the whole body of creation.[16]

This hope prevailed in the early church. Allan Galloway makes the case that cosmic redemption was "the very heart of the primitive Gospel."[17] It was widely assumed in the Patristic period and was articulated by theologians like Irenaeus, Athanasius, and Augustine. The idea, however, was gradually undermined, partly because of the incorporation of Platonic depreciations of nature into Christian thought. After the Patristic period, cosmic redemption was not featured significantly, if at all, in Western Christian thought.

The cosmic hope, however, was retained and remains intact today in Eastern Orthodoxy, with its passionate loyalty to the Greek Patristic theologians. Timothy Ware (Archimandrite Kallistos) describes this commitment well:

> Not only man's body but the whole of material creation will eventually be transfigured. . . . Redeemed man is not to be snatched away from the rest of creation, but creation is to be saved and glorified along with him. . . . This idea of cosmic redemption is based, like the Orthodox doctrine of icons, upon a right understanding of the Incarnation: Christ took flesh—something from the material order—and so has made possible the redemption and metamorphosis of all creation—not merely the immaterial but the physical.[18]

In Western Christianity, expressions of this hope became relatively rare, largely because it was contrary to official doctrine in its subjection to "spiritualizing" tendencies. The hope of cosmic redemption is not evident, for example, or at least not explicit, in St. Francis, despite his creation-encompassing love.[19] The hope reappeared, however, in the Reformation and Post-Reformation, and was present, though generally not prominently, in the thought of a variety of Western theologians, perhaps partly as a result of scriptural and Greek Patristic studies. Thereafter, however, the cosmic hope was virtually absent from or deemphasized in official Protestant confessions and most theological treatises, to the point that the vast majority of Protestants never knew it existed and probably would have considered it a radical, if not heretical, idea.

Nevertheless, the hope is clearly expressed in Martin Luther, John Calvin,[20] and John Wesley—and that fact makes it almost astonishing that their vision was virtually lost to most of their vast followings. Calvin expressed the hope clearly but circumspectly in a commentary on Romans 8:21:

> Paul does not mean that all creatures will be partakers of the same glory with the Sons of God, but that they will share in their own manner in the better state, because God will restore the present fallen world to perfect condition at the same time as the human race. . . . Let us, therefore be content with this simple doctrine—their constitution will be such, and their order so complete, that no appearance either of deformity or of impermanence will be seen.[21]

Wesley agrees with Calvin, but he is anything but circumspect. He goes into significant detail in an influential sermon defending the redemption of creation.

John Wesley and the Redemption of Creation

Wesley's sermon, "The General Deliverance," based on Romans 8:19-22, first appeared in print in the *Arminian Magazine* in 1782, under the title "Free Thoughts on the Brute Creation."[22] The cosmic hope was certainly not unknown in his time; it was supported by a prominent minority of divines, including the venerable Bishop Joseph Butler in *The Analogy of Religion*.[23] Though not a unique viewpoint, Wesley's sermon is still an exceptional example of this minority perspective. It is theologically imaginative (literally!), ethically sensi-

126

tive, and, to contemporary readers, sometimes charmingly though unintentionally humorous.

Wesley is acutely conscious of the problem of evil in nature and its incompatibility with the goodness of God. A major purpose of the sermon is a defense of divine justice.[24] It is an eschatological theodicy.

In the "original state" of the "brute creation" in Paradise, each creature was "perfect in its kind." But unlike humans, other creatures were not "capable of knowing, loving, or obeying God." They were subject to human dominion: "And as loving obedience to God was the perfection of men, so a loving obedience to man was the perfection of brutes."[25]

Wesley's definition of dominion is intriguing—and perhaps a vanguard of "new discoveries" in our time. It meant that the human is the "governor" of the earth, the "viceregent" of God, and "all the blessings of God flowed through him to the inferior creatures."[26] Though the nonhuman creatures have only the traditional derivative status, dominion is clearly not exploitation, but rather the *conveyance of divine blessings*. In this state, nonhuman creatures were happy, grateful, good, beautiful—and immortal.[27]

The Fall of the original humans changed things dramatically. Nature also fell with the sin of Adam in Wesley's thought, since humans lost the capacities to communicate the blessings of God. The creatures thus were subjected to evil, and suffered severe losses of their physical, mental, and moral powers. They became vicious predators— even the "innocent songsters of the grove." No romantic writes these pages; Wesley seems to enjoy describing the gory details of predation[28] (in fact, he had a serious interest in and a good understanding of the ecological process for his time). Even worse to Wesley, the creatures lost their beauty; they are ugly, "horrid." Wesley here is no great exponent of natural beauty! Worst of all, however, the animals lost their immortality: they are subject to death and its "preparatory evils."[29] The nonhuman creatures are also subject now not to the mediator of original blessings, but rather to their "common enemy," the "violence and cruelty" of the worst predator, the humans:

> And what a dreadful difference is there between what they suffer from their fellow brutes and what they suffer from the tyrant, man! The lion, the tiger, or the shark, give them pain from mere necessity, in order to prolong their own life; and put them out of their pain at once. But the human shark, without any such necessity, torments them of his free choice; and perhaps continues their lingering pain till after months or years death signs their release.[30]

127

Exploitative dominion will find no solace in these lines, which could have been written by a contemporary animal rights activist.

Yet, the "brute creatures" will not remain in this "deplorable condition." They will be "saved"—and Wesley seems to know an indecent number of details. They will be brought to eternal life—with but apparently not through humans, which seems contrary to their original derived dignity. Predation will cease. Their original capacities and joys will be restored and enhanced. They will be beautiful again. Though God values humans far more than the animals, still when humans are made the equals of angels, other creatures may be made equal to what humans are now[31]—a thought suggestive of evolutionary potential in the afterlife.

The bottom line for Wesley, however, is the justice of God. Eternal life is "recompense" for the suffering of sinless creatures.[32] He offers an eschatological solution to the problem of evil:

> The whole brute creation will then undoubtedly be restored, not only to the vigour, strength, and swiftness which they had at their creation, but to a far higher degree of each than they ever enjoyed. They will be restored, not only to that measure of understanding that they had in paradise, but to a degree of it as much higher than that of as the understanding of an elephant is beyond that of a worm. And whatever affections they had in the garden of God will be restored with vast increase. . . . The liberty they then had will be completely restored, and they will be free in all their motions. They will be delivered from all irregular appetites, from all unruly passions, from every disposition that is either evil in itself or has any tendency to evil. No rage will be found in any creature, no fierceness, no cruelty, or thirst for blood. [Quotes Isa. 11:6, 7, 9]
>
> Thus in that day all the "vanity" to which they are now helplessly "subject" will be abolished; they will suffer no more either from within or without; the days of their groaning are ended. At the same time there can be no reasonable doubt but all the horridness of their appearance, and all the deformity of their aspect, will vanish away, and be changed for their primeval beauty. And with their beauty their happiness will return; to which there can then be no obstruction. As there will be nothing within, so there will be nothing without, to give them any uneasiness—no heat or cold, no storm or tempest, but one perennial spring. In the new earth, as well as in the new heavens, there will be nothing to give pain, but everything that the wisdom and goodness of God can create to give happiness. As a recompense for what they once suffered while under "the bondage of corruption" . . . they shall enjoy happiness suited to their state, without alloy, without interruption, and without end.[33]

Wesley subsequently rejects anthropocentric utility as the basis for salvation or present respect, in a rather jolting argument: "If it be objected to all this (as very probably it will): 'But of what use will those creatures be in that future state?' I answer this by another question: 'What use are they of now?' "[34] The point, however, seems to be that God has biocentric and cosmocentric values and intentions that Christians must honor: "Consider this: consider how little we know of even the present designs of God; and then you will not wonder that we know still less of what he designs to do in the new heavens and the new earth."[35] His argument is at least strongly suggestive of the intrinsic value of creation for God.

Finally, Wesley draws from his speculations an important moral conclusion, to which he alluded in his opening paragraph as one of the purposes of the sermon:

> One more excellent end may undoubtedly be answered by the preceding considerations. They may encourage us to imitate him whose mercy is over all his works. They may soften our hearts toward the meaner creatures, knowing that the Lord careth for them. It may enlarge our hearts towards those poor creatures to reflect that, as vile as they appear in our eyes, not one of them is forgotten in the sight of our Father which is in heaven.[36]

Thus Wesley draws an ethical conclusion from an eschatological expectation. This conclusion seems to be a forerunner of theologies of hope and liberation: anticipating the final future now. For Wesley, the cosmic redemption should result in beneficence toward other creatures.

The sermon was subsequently influential in Britain among animal anticruelty campaigners, who included a number of Methodists, and it continues to have an ecologically inspirational power today, despite its excessive speculations and anachronisms. My major regret is that "The General Deliverance" represents a marginal topic in a significant homiletical corpus—another indicator of the marginality of cosmic redemption in historical Christian thought.

Contemporary Revival

Expressions of eschatological hope for creation have become fairly common in the last couple of decades among Protestant theologians, perhaps stirred by the influence of Orthodoxy and probably spurred by ecological consciousness. In fact, the hope seems to be especially evident among ecologically sensitive theologians, including such prominents as Jürgen Moltmann, Carl Braaten, Paul Santmire, Gabriel Fackre, Joseph Sittler, and George Hendry.[37] To them, the promise in Christ is not "redemption *from* the world, it is the redemption *of* the world."[38] Much of this hope seems to be grounded in an awareness of ecological connections. Paul Tillich, for example, stresses that the salvation of humanity apart from nature is "unthinkable": "The interdependence of everything with everything else in the totality of being includes a participation of nature in history and demands a participation of the universe in salvation."[39]

Yet, this hope is still a minority viewpoint. Most traditionalist interpreters appear fixated on strictly human expectations, and many "post-modern" types, substituting abundant life for eternal life, offer only equivocations or denials on the eschatological hope for anyone.[40] The former proclaim an anthropocentric hope, and the latter a de-eschatologized Christianity. The proponents of both an anthropocentric hope and a de-eschatological faith fail, in my view, to recognize that the finality of death for any living being threatens the integrity of the Christian faith. Both the intrinsic value of creatures and the moral character of God are jeopardized.

Death is not a moral issue if life is merely a biological accident in an aimless universe. Yet, mortality is the ultimate problem of morality when God is perceived as beneficent and death is interpreted as conclusive. If conclusive death is inimical to the ultimate good of creatures, then it is hard to see how it can be consistent with a good God who seeks the good of creatures. Arguments from biological necessity—death as a function of the limitation of resources and the condition of new life—do not resolve the problem. They fail to do justice to a fundamental query: why did a good God create a biosphere in which the evil of death is necessary to avoid a greater evil of biological unsustainability?

A non-redemptive God cannot be steadfast love or justice. Any lover who wills or allows the final annihilation of the beloved fails all the tests of love, including the preservation of the loved one's individuality, potentiality, relationships, and sense of ultimate meaning.[41] Similarly, this God cannot be just, since the problems of evil and injustice remain forever unresolved, ending all possibilities of restoration, reformation, and reconciliation for the victims and the perpetrators.[42] A God who saves only by memorializing "has beens" in a flawless memory is not the Suffering Servant, but rather the Supreme Ego who makes all creatures into suffering servants, sacrificed for the sake of God's greater glory. Loyalty to the values of such a God is justification for treating others—including God—as instrumental values; there are no ethically sustaining grounds in ultimate reality for treating others as ends in themselves. Words like *love, justice, fidelity, harmony,* and *reconciliation* are all relational terms that have relevance only in relational contexts. They are inappropriately applied to a God who finally breaks all relationships. It is the ultimate irony, not to mention final incoherence, to be called to love one another and to be agents of reconciliation and liberation by a God who finally snaps forever all the ties that bind.

Thus, in a Christian context, no ultimate loss of the values associated with life, not even of those that we eat or swat or cannot see, can be axiologically irrelevant. No theology that posits a value-conserving God—a God of perfect love and/or justice—can be axiologically adequate or credible unless it also envisions an Isianic hope, a qualitatively New Creation, a cosmic consummation when "the creation itself will be set free from the bondage to decay and obtain the glorious liberty of the children of God" (Rom. 8:21).

From this perspective, the resurrection hope is central to the Christian faith. It need not be—and for some of us, cannot be—taken as literal truth, with an empty tomb, mysterious appearances, bizarre visions, and apocalyptic scenarios, but it must be taken as symbolic truth. The Resurrection is the central symbol of the faith because it points to the basic perception of reality that gives the faith its cosmic integrity and internal consistency: the reality that the One who is Creator and Sustainer is also the Christ, the trustworthy One who defeats death and evil and brings all living creatures to eternal life and love. The point of the resurrection symbol is not that an isolated individual was restored to a new mode of being, but rather that the Representative of Humanity who was, therefore, the Representative of the Cosmos, became the pledge or promise of the full redemption to come (Acts 4:2; John 14:2; Rom. 5:10, 8:10-11; I Cor. 15:12-16; II Cor. 4:14; Col. 1:18; I Thess. 4:14; I Pet. 1:3-5; Rev. 1:5). The Resurrection was the prime sign of the coming Reign; "Jesus Christ is the pledge of God's imminent cosmic triumph."[43] Without this hope, Christian theology and ethics are incoherent. The condition of creation is ultimately tragic and the character of God is ultimately immoral. Only with this hope can the Christian faith maintain its apostolic integrity.

This vision will seem absurd even to many Christians. But it is certainly no greater "absurdity" than an eternal hope for humanity, and it is far more coherent with humanity's evolutionary kinship and ecological interdependence with all creatures than any exclusively human hope. George Hendry makes this point effectively: "If we believe that God will complete his purpose in the creation of us human beings, . . . we may surely believe that he will complete his purpose with the world of nature, of which we are a part."[44] The key issue in the hope for cosmic redemption is the moral character of God in relation to God's valuation of creatures as ends in themselves. If so, the real absurdity is the dual belief in a value-conserving God and the finality of death for any creature of intrinsic value.

We cannot, however, infer reality from hope. Truth may not correspond with meaning; an unbridgeable chasm may exist between aspirations and facts. Cosmic redemption seems essential as a matter of internal consistency in Christianity, but it provides no argument for its external correspondence with reality. Yet, Christians can give reasons for the hope that is in them.

Cosmic redemption, or, of course, an exclusively humanistic redemption, is neither empirically verifiable nor falsifiable. The biological evidence that death decimates body and mind is valid but hardly conclusive in this mystifying creation with possibilities far surpassing the pretensions of scientism. The Christian hope, however, is grounded largely in specifically religious experience, "the witness of the Spirit" (Rom. 8:15-16), the intuitions and the intimations of the character of the God encountered in the totality of life. In the "logic" of hope, eternal life is an inference from divine love,[45] and, circularly, the validation of that love. The promise is inherent in the Presence. The hope of consummation through God is grounded in the experience of communion with God. Hope knows mainly the Who; it knows the what only as deductions and inductions from the character of the Who; it knows nothing about when or how or the details of the what. Despite the hordes of speculations and imaginative descriptions of glory in Christian history, an honest and humble Christianity knows when to keep silent.

Ecological Implications of Cosmic Redemption

The expectation of universal or cosmic redemption is a necessarily vague vision of the consummation of shalom—reconciliation among all creatures (Isa. 11:6-9) and liberation from the bondage to transience (Rom. 8:21). Fundamentally, it is a statement of hope in the goodness and trustworthiness of God. The value-conserving Creator—who embraced all creation in the incarnation and who inhabits all creation through the Spirit—will fulfill the creation, leading it through the process of becoming perfectly good.

Ecologically, this vision gives ultimate meaning and worth to the cosmic ecosphere. It is the confirmation of nature's ultimate value to

God. Nothing is any longer valueless or meaningless or irrelevant. Every living creature counts for itself and for God ultimately. This perspective stands in judgment on anthropocentrism. If the natural world as a whole will participate in God's redemption, then all things must be treated with respect in accordance with divine valuations, and all living creatures must be treated as ends in themselves—not simply as means to human ends. Again, the divine purposes are cosmocentric and biocentric, not simply anthropocentric. Christian ethics must take that fact into account in a process of ecologically-conscious reformation.

This vision of cosmic redemption causes enormous confusion in our current use of ethical language and our understanding of the breadth of ethical obligations. The confusion will not soon end. In general, however, the vision suggests an ethical style for human relationships with the rest of nature. In the midst of the moral ambiguities of creation, we can experience only promising signs—not the full harmony—of the New Creation, the Peaceable Kingdom. The very fact that eschatological visions are necessary precludes romantic illusions about historical possibilities. Nevertheless, the vision represents the ultimate goal to which God is beckoning us. Our moral responsibility, then, is to approximate the harmony of the New Creation to the fullest extent possible under the constricted conditions of the creation. The present task of Christian communities, as I will explain further in the next section, is to anticipate and contribute to the promise of ultimate liberation and reconciliation in human communities and with the rest of nature.[46]

THE CHURCH AS AGENT OF ECOLOGICAL LIBERATION AND RECONCILIATION

Is ecological concern an optional matter for the Christian church, or is it inherent in the nature of the church? The latter seems to be the case. Certainly the church's major affirmations have significant ecological implications that the church ought to embrace in its proclamations and actions. However, Christian ecological responsibilities are also rooted in the nature of the church itself. The very logic of major contemporary ecclesiologies seems to demand that the goal of ecological integrity become a permanent and prominent part of the church's mission.

Understood theologically, the church is a particular kind of caring community. Its members minister to one another, and, in the expansion of love, to all the other communities of which the church is an inherent part. The church is a community of ministers and a constellation of ministries. Ministry is the function of the whole people of God. The *esse* of the church—its divine mandate—is found in the functions of ministry.

The church's ministries, however, are not some set of arbitrary services; instead, they are a response to God as our Minister: "We sought a good to love and were found by a good that loved us. And therewith all our religious ambitions are brought low, all our desires to be ministers of God are humbled; he is our minister."[47] The Christian church, then, is that universal and locally manifested communion of pardoned sinners who have responded gratefully in faith, hope, and love to the creating, sustaining, and redeeming graces of God's all-encompassing ministry. The divine ministry is a mission of love, for it is love that creates, sustains, and saves all creation. The church senses in the experience of divine ministering a beckoning to go and do likewise. Consequently, the church's authentic ministries are manifestations of love.

Moreover, because God's ministries are comprehensive, the church seeks to be "truly catholic"—characterized by wholeness, fullness, universality. The divine ministry offers physical sustenance for all, comforts the afflicted, promises redemption, generates meaning, builds communion, pursues peace, reconciles the alienated, liberates the oppressed, challenges the oppressors, demands the right, and rights the wrong. The church's ministry, consequently, seeks to manifest a similar comprehension. Part of what it means to be the church catholic is to be the full community of Christians seeking to embody the whole gospel for the full needs of all persons and other creatures in all places and times.[48] To do less is to be less than the church catholic, and to envisage less is to display a constricted understanding of the breadth and depth of God's ministry in love. Ecclesiology, then, is grounded not solely in doctrines of Christ or the Spirit, but in the interpenetrating fullness of the divine ministry, which the symbol of the trinity so richly expresses when it is not petrified into platitudinous abstractions.

Because God's ministry of love is universal, and because the church is called to re-present that comprehensiveness of concern, ecological responsibility is an inherent part of being the church catholic. It is not an option, but a mandate that must be incorporated into the whole. It is one of the signs of a valid Christian ministry.

The church's ministries in worship, witness, and work, however, are not simply present functions; they have an ultimate goal, a telos. The church is called to direct its services and design its communal life to be effective expressions of the ultimate goal of God's ministry, the Reign or Commonwealth of God. The church's ministries are acts of confidence in and commitment to the ethos and ethic of God's Reign, which Jesus embodied and proclaimed.

In contemporary theologies of hope and liberation, as well as in the classical social gospel, the church, ideally, is an "interim eschatological community"[49] or "an avant garde of the new creation in a hostile world."[50] This conception reflects a widespread consensus in biblical studies and critical theology that the originating tradition of the church—the apostolic witness in scripture—is thoroughly eschatological in orientation. The essence of the gospel is the good news of the coming Commonwealth: "Eschatology is . . . not just one more element of Christianity, but the very key to understanding the Christian faith."[51] The ministry of Jesus Christ and his Resurrection are promises of the coming Commonwealth. Consequently, communion in Christ must be dedication to Christ's cause, the Reign.[52] Equally, the mission of the Holy Spirit in Paul's writings is focused on the ultimate goal of God: the Spirit is "the power of God driving towards the end of history and carrying us forward to the destiny disclosed and anticipated in the resurrection of Jesus Christ."[53] To be led by the Spirit is to declare and manifest this New Creation.

Thus, if apostolic succession is continuity with the original witnesses, then the church is in that succession when it announces and expresses the eschatological significance of the Resurrection and the expectation of its consummation.[54] This continuity, however, is not in the repetitions of the culture-bound media of the faith in scripture and tradition; it is rather a dynamic continuity that is loyal to the eschatological cause of the originating tradition. This dynamic continuity implies that the church must be truly reforming to be truly evangelical—that is, in conformity with the gospel. The apostolic church, then, is the community of Christians always being reformed, to be in conformity with the divine mission to consummate liberation and reconciliation for the whole creation.

From this perspective, the church is called to be a sign of the Reign, making its vision visible, reflecting Christ's New Creation in personal, social, and ecclesiastical transformations. God's goal is not simply our final destiny; it is also our ethical and ecclesial responsibility. It is a summons to action, to shape the historical present, as the Lord's Prayer suggests, on the model of God's New Heaven and New Earth. The ultimate future is not a mandate for Christian withdrawal from the world or a denigration of personal, social, and ecological responsibility in the present. On the contrary, a valid "otherworldliness" results in a vital worldliness. The church's ethical orientation is "eschatopraxis," doing the final future now.[55] Since God's ultimate goal is the perfection of just and harmonious relationships (shalom) among all living creatures, the church's historical mandate includes the pursuit of justice, peace, and ecological integrity.

These ecclesial responsibilities, however, are more than *anticipations* of the divine Reign. Here the social gospel in North America offers an important corrective to some current eschatological emphases. For Walter Rauschenbusch and the social gospel generally, the symbol of the "Kingdom" (Reign) is the purpose and norm for the life and mission of the church. The church exists for the sake of the Kingdom, but its task is more than an anticipation of the Kingdom; it is the actual but provisional construction or creation of the Kingdom on earth.[56] Certainly, as abundant excoriations of "liberal perfectionism" remind us, the social gospel movement was often naive about historical possibilities for moral transformation. Nevertheless, the social gospel, along with some liberation theologies, understood that ethical and ecclesiastical achievements must be more than anticipations if they are to have eternal significance or meaning. An anticipation of the Reign makes the final future relevant to the present; it does not make present achievements relevant to the final future. Consequently, if our historical existence and moral acts of liberation and reconciliation are to have enduring value, they must in some sense be contributions to, preparations for, and participations in God's final re-creation.

The social gospel rightly recognized that the role of the church is not only to reveal but also to "realize" the Reign, both provisionally in history and as a contribution ultimately.[57] Though this claim must be kept within realistic bounds in history, it does not deny that the New Creation is God's Reign. It is God's design, God's creation of the necessary conditions, God's provision of possibilities, God's re-creations and completions from our fragmentary contributions, and, therefore, God's Reign. This God calls humanity in its moral freedom not to a divine imposition, but rather to participation in creation's deliverance from evil and the growth of the coming Commonwealth.

A commitment to ecological integrity on the part of the church must be understood in the context of the church's eschatological orientation. In this context, ecological responsibility is a sign of the church's apostolicity and catholicity. It is not an option, but an inherent mandate for the church's ministry. It has been one of the serious omissions in the history of the church and is now one of the critical reforms necessary for the integrity of the church. If ultimate catholicity is the consummation of liberation and reconciliation for all creation in the Reign of God, then the church cannot be truly catholic, truly reformed, and truly evangelical unless it anticipates and contributes to this Reign by being a *model* of ecological ministries to the world. What ethos and ethics are implied by this responsibility? What strategies and structures are necessary? What demons must be exorcised in the ecclesia? These are only a few of the questions that the church must confront in becoming an ecological agent of liberation and reconciliation, and in ending the alienation between humanity and the rest of the biosphere.

A SUMMATION

What does a reasonably reformed Christian theology offer as a foundation for ecological integrity? That has been the central question in the two preceding chapters. The following points summarize the main supports for Christian ecological ethics and action.

1. Christian understandings of God as Creator, Spirit, and Redeemer imply that the whole creation and all its creatures are valued and loved by God. Divine valuations appear to be cosmocentric and biocentric, not simply anthropocentric. Since loyalty to God entails loyalty to God's values, Christians are called to practice biophilia. All life forms have intrinsic value, and are to be treated with appropriate care and concern.

2. The Christian faith dedivinizes but also sacralizes nature. No element of the biophysical world is divine; nothing in nature, therefore, is to be worshiped. But all creatures and things are to be treated as sacred subjects and objects, used reverently and respectfully insofar as necessary, and otherwise to be left untouched.

3. The Christian faith is an affirmation of ecological relationality. It recognizes a rational and moral order of interdependence and a theocentric kinship of all creation. Humans are interrelated parts and products of nature. Moral responsibilities for the necessary use of the biophysical world are shaped and limited by these relationships.

4. Humans have "natural" rights to use biophysical goods as resources to satisfy human needs and fulfill our cultural potential, but we also have moral responsibilities to use these resources frugally, fairly, and prudently in respect for our coevolving kin.

5. The biophysical world has an interim goodness in experience and

an ultimate goodness in hope. It is not to be despised, rejected, or transcended, either spiritually or materially.

6. The Christian faith counsels human humility in the light of ultimate mystery, natural limitations, and biological connections.

7. Human dominion (or, preferably, a verbal equivalent) is not a sanction for the exploitation of nature, but a judgment on such exploitation. As a dimension of the image of God, dominion is responsible representation, reflecting the divine love, including justice, in all relationships with humanity and the rest of the biophysical world. It is protecting this planet (and every other planet) from human abuse.

8. All forms of ecological negligence or undue harm—from pollution to profligate consumption—are expressions of sin.

9. In the causal connections between ecological disorders and human violations of the ecological covenant, Christians can perceive God as exercising ecological judgments against ecological sins to call the human community to ecological repentance.

10. Ecological responsibility is an inherent part of the ministry of the church, which is called to re-present God's ministry of love to all creation and to be a sign of God's Reign of love. The church, therefore, should be a model of ecological ministries to the world.

11. The Christian faith provides solid supports for all the ecological virtues outlined in chapter 2—sustainability, adaptability, relationality, frugality, equity, solidarity, biodiversity, humility, and sufficiency. Indeed, even a strictly anthropocentric version of the faith, concerned exclusively with human well-being, provides adequate grounds for most of these virtues.

CHAPTER SIX

LOVING NATURE:

CHRISTIAN LOVE IN AN ECOLOGICAL CONTEXT

Perhaps the most urgent and difficult task in the development of a Christian ecological ethic is an adequate interpretation of Christian love in an ecological context. The task is essential, in my view, because love is the integrating center of the whole of Christian faith and ethics. If so, a Christian ecological ethic is seriously deficient—if even conceivable—unless it is grounded in Christian love.

The task, however, is uncommonly difficult, partly because of the tragic condition of existence in a predatorial biosphere. The state of nature, of which humans are parts and products, is that every species feeds on and struggles against other species in order to survive in a strange system of interdependence. As ecological predators and exploiters—as well as prey and hosts—humans must kill and use other life forms and destroy their habitats if we are to satisfy basic human needs and exercise our peculiar endowments for cultural creativity. This tragic condition of the biophysical world—a mournful awareness of which was the foundation of Albert Schweitzer's ethic of "reverence for life"—can and must be morally restricted, but it cannot be avoided. It is fixed in the "nature of things," and it confronts us with unusual, if not unique, versions of the standard ethical problem of "necessary evil" in dealing with conflicts of values and claims. Christian love seems at first sight to be an alien norm in this context.

The task is further complicated by the fact that the application of Christian love to the biosphere is virtually virgin territory. Casual or general references to the love of nature as a Christian mandate, or to

139

the need for love as a means to protect ecological integrity, are fairly common—for example, in the writings of Schweitzer, Aldo Leopold, Joseph Wood Krutch, John Muir, and such contemporary theologians or ethicists as H. Richard Niebuhr, Robert Shelton, Joseph Allen, Sallie McFague, Douglas John Hall, Jay B. McDaniel, Dorothee Söelle, Loren Wilkinson and his colleagues, Issa J. Khalil,[1] and leading Orthodox theologians.[2] Yet, we have few sustained and systemic explorations, few guidelines, little awareness among Christians that an ethical problem even exists, and no rich dialogue to test our assumptions, remedy our oversights, and correct our errors. The relationship between humans and other forms of life has been perceived, to use Karl Barth's words, as "a marginal problem of ethics"[3]—at best. The issues have been trivialized or bypassed. Consequently, mental misreadings and missteps are almost inevitable on this strange landscape. Yet, these risks must be taken because of the indispensable role of love in defining and shaping Christian ecological responsibility.

I, therefore, must respond to several key questions: What is Christian love? Why is it the basis of Christian ecological ethics? What forms of love are possible and relevant in an ecological context? What does this love require of humans in responsible ecological relationships with one another and to other species and their habitats? The answers I propose only skim the surface, but they may intensify awareness of the problem and prompt deeper probings.

LOVE: THE GROUND OF CHRISTIAN THEOLOGY AND ETHICS

The core affirmations of the Christian faith, I have argued, offer a strong grounding for an ecological ethic. These core affirmations, however, are all expressions of love. Love is the center of the gospel, which everything else radiates from or revolves around. It is the metaethical source of Christian ethics—including, therefore, an ecological ethic.

Christianity affirms that love is the ground and goal of all being. God *is* love—a radical affirmation that Emil Brunner perceived as "the most daring statement that has ever been made in human language," "the very heart of the New Testament, of the Christian Gospel."[4] This claim that God's nature, character, and actions are love has radical implications. If God is love, for instance, the process of creation itself is an act of love. All creatures, human and otherkind, and their habitats are not only gifts of love but also products of love and recipients of ongoing love. Everything then has value imparted by the Source of Value. The value of all beings is objectively and ultimately grounded in Love, and all deserve, therefore, to be treated not merely as means to human ends, but as ends in themselves.

We experience God as love in the mysteries of creation; in the covenants with Israel; in the cause and loyal life-style of Jesus ("the paradigm of God's love"[5]); in the grace evident on the cross and confirmed in the Resurrection; and in the empowering, liberating, and reconciling presence of the Holy Spirit. Christians hope for God's liberation from the travail of creation through love, and eternal life in a new order whose constitution is love. The Reign of God is the rule of love,[6] and, therefore, "the Christian hope is the hope of love."[7]

The story of God's love provides the "basic moral standard,"[8] the "pattern and prototype,"[9] for Christian ethics. The vast majority of Christian ethicists would agree with Paul Ramsey on one fundamental point: "Christian ethics proposes that the basic norm and the distinctive character of the Christian life is Christian love (agape)."[10] And few would deny H. Richard Niebuhr's famous and deceptively simple definition of the church's mission: "No substitute can be found for the goal of the church as the increase among men [and women] of the love of God and neighbor."[11] The Christian life is "faith working through love" (Gal. 5:6), and that is to be "not far" from the Reign (Mark 12:28-34).

From a Christian perspective, encounters with God through diverse human experiences are encounters with the Creator of the moral order. Thus the indicatives of faith contain an "implied imperative"[12] to love. Since fidelity to God implies respect for divine intentions and affections, humans are called to love what God loves, to value what is valued by the Source of Value. Thus, in imitation of Jesus, the exemplar of divine love, and in anticipation of the coming Commonwealth of God, Christians and their communions are called to produce the fruits of justice and generosity, peace and unity, compassion and community, liberation and reconciliation—all of which flow from love. We seek to love as grateful responses to the grace-filled fact that God first loves us (I John 4:7-11, 19; Eph. 5:1). And we are empowered to love, albeit weakly, by God's love working through us. To be in God's image is to be a reflection of the ultimate Lover, to be one who loves *all* that God loves[13]—which covers "all that participates in being."[14]

In essence, therefore, the Christian faith is the confidence that the comprehensive ministries of God to the creatures of God are a mission of love, and Christian ethics and action are loyal efforts to be mirror images of that love.

An ecological ethic that is rooted in the Christian faith is a reasonable extension of love to the whole creation, in order to re-present the all-encompassing affection and care of God. Since God's love is unbounded, loyal Christian love is similarly inclusive or universal. This love resists confinement of any sort. It punctures all forms of ethical parochialism, as a number of interpreters have testified. Albert Schweitzer, for instance, broadened the meaning of love to cover moral responsibility to every organism: "The ethic of Reverence for Life is the ethic of love widened into universality. It is the ethic of Jesus now recognized as a logical consequence of thought."[15] The ecologist Aldo Leopold, knowing the unbreakable connections between life forms and their habitats, broadened the boundaries of love to the whole ecosphere, "the land": "That land is a community is the basic concept of ecology, but that land is to be loved and respected is an extension of ethics."[16] No one, however, has expressed the infinite breadth of love and its transvaluation better than H. Richard Niebuhr in one of his typically tantalizing comments, which seems surprisingly to have had little impact on the formation of Christian ecological ethics:

> The moral law is changed . . . by the revelation of God's self in that its evermore extensive and intensive application becomes necessary. . . . The will of God [cannot now] be interpreted so that it applies within a world of rational beings and not in the world of the unrational, so that men must be treated as ends because they are reasonable but non-human life may be violated in the service of human ends. *Sparrows and sheep and lilies belong within the network of moral relations when God reveals himself; now every killing is a sacrifice.* The line cannot even be drawn at the boundaries of life; the culture of the earth as a garden of the Lord and reverence for the stars as creatures of his intelligence belong to the demands of the universal will . . . [when] the moral law that is a law of God is extended and intensified.[17]

Universality is a central feature of Christian love—indeed, a test for the presence of love. It means that love is not particularistic or exclusive. It is not limited to one's ethnic, social, or ecclesiastical tribe, not even to one's species or biosphere. It is not restricted by criteria of character or conduct, geography or ideology, attractiveness or repulsiveness, consanguinity or utility. Christian love in this sense is indiscriminate. The irony, however, of I John is that at precisely the place where the New Testament peaks in explicitly defining the character of God as love, it also descends to a particularistic application by limiting love to the "brethren" or Christian compatriots (I John 3:14-19; 4:7-12; 5:1-2).[18]

Yet, Christian love in the New Testament is not generally circumscribed. In fact, the "logic" of love in scripture encourages reasonable extensions to universal dimensions. True, explicit statements about love in the New Testament apply only to divine-human or interhuman relationships. However, there is no inherent reason why biblical concepts of love cannot be extended to relationships between humanity and other life forms. Indeed, there are very good reasons why this extension is justified and even necessary—notably, the affirmation that God is unbounded love. This universality is symbolized by the call to love all our neighbors, including our enemies (Luke 6:32-36; Matt. 5:43-48), just as God is "kind to the ungrateful and selfish" (Luke 6:35), making the sun to rise and rain to fall on the evil and good (Matt. 5:45), and just as God cares about the sparrows (Matt. 12:6; Luke 10:29) and the lilies (Matt. 6:28-30; Luke 12:27).

The answer, then, to the question—who is my neighbor?—that prompts the parable of the good Samaritan is: reasonably extended, our neighbors who are to be loved are all God's beloved creatures. The "love of nature" is simply the "love of neighbor" universalized in recognition of our common origins, mutual dependencies, and shared destiny with the whole creation of the God who is all-embracing love. In this context, the task of a Christian ecological ethic is to help us define the character and conduct of the good neighbor, the ecological equivalent of the good Samaritan who shows compassion and heals the wounds of our biotic neighbors in desperate need.

DILEMMAS OF DEFINITION

Once we root Christian ecological ethics in a theology and ethic of love, however, we immediately encounter mental quagmires in defining Christian love and determining its implications for responsible relations in ecological contexts. Vigorous debates abound in Christian ethics about the definitions, types, characteristics, possibilities, demands, and dilemmas of love. Nearly all these earnest and complicated controversies have focused exclusively on divine-human and interhuman relationships. Perplexity and complexity are compounded, however, in ecological situations where damaging and

143

killing are biological necessities for existence (rather than strategic responses to moral evil, as in war), and where human relations with other creatures are between *un*equals.

The ethical debates commence with the definition of Christian love. Christians have no consensus on the meaning of love—and apparently neither does the New Testament.[19] Garth Hallett, for instance, argues that six rival rules of preference or types of love—from self-preference to self-denial—have been represented in Christian history and are within Christian bounds.[20] All are altruistic norms; all can require considerable sacrifice; all can be compatible with the sacrifice of Calvary.[21] But the behavioral differences can sometimes be significant. The most strongly supported, but not the only, norm in the New Testament, claims Hallett, is self-subordination, seeking one's own benefit only on condition that benefits to others are first assured.[22] The problem is obviously complex—and Hallett never deals with the additional moral complications of ecological relations! Love, of course, is an ambiguous word in common parlance. It has multiple meanings, most of which connote amorous sentimentality or drooling passions. The internal Christian problem of definition is not so wide or vague, but it is sufficiently confounding in its own right, especially when love is the basic norm of Christian ethics. It is fair to say that Christian ethics has a nebulous norm.

The problem, moreover, only *begins* with definition; it branches out to cover a broad spectrum of ethical issues. A sampling of the key and overlapping questions indicates the character of the debate and the dilemmas of interpreting Christian love in any context, let alone in an ecological one. What is the nature of agape (the prime Greek word for love in the New Testament) and what are its characteristics? What is the relationship, if any, between agape and eros? Are they antitheses, as Anders Nygren contends?[23] Or can they be synthesized in some way; are eros and other "human loves" incorporated into agape, as D. D. Williams argues?[24] To what degree is love self-sacrificing in relation to goals of self-realization? Is love "equal regard,"[25] "other regard," self-disregard, or some other normative relationship between the self and others? To what degree should Christians be suspicious of egoism, or even of claims to altruism? What role, if any, does mutuality—sharing, reciprocal giving and receiving in a caring community—play in Christian love? What kinds and expressions of love are psychologically and sociologically possible for human beings? What is the relationship between love as disposition and deeds, or attitude and acts? What is the relation of justice to love? What are the "most love-embodying" rules and/or acts[26] in the midst of the tragic choices often associated with conflicting values and claims?

In these complex debates, the starting assumptions about the nature of Christian love obviously will affect the specific applications. Moreover, the meaning of Christian love has been manipulated in a multitude of ways to correspond with self-interest, to reduce the costs to the self of obligations to others. This problem is particularly acute in ecological relationships where humans have exercised a distortion of dominion by denying moral obligations to nonhuman creatures. Excessive self-love is really the root sin of lovelessness, the imperialistic preference for the self and, therefore, the absence or perversion of love for others. It is persistent and imaginative, and constantly corrupts Christian love in practice and dilutes it in theory. The problem is inevitable (even if unnecessary). But an awareness of our human inclinations to whittle away at love may minimize some of its worst effects, like self-deception and self-aggrandizement.

Despite this dissensus in Christian thought, it is still essential and possible to specify some basic implications of Christian love in an ecological context. In what follows, I intentionally have avoided a "radical" definition and opted for a more moderate interpretation of this unfathomable phenomenon we call love. One reason is to enable a wider palatability. Another is the desire to minimize the risks of overstating the case—particularly important in the light of our feeble and vague understandings of love. In effect, I am acknowledging that Christian love may demand more of Christians ecologically, but it certainly demands no less. Even when offered in modest proportions, however, Christian love has an unnervingly demanding quality. Sacrifice of personal interests is an inherent part of love.

By definition, Christian love, as disposition and/or deed, is always at least caring and careful service, self-giving and other-regarding outreach, in response to the needs of others (human and otherkind), out of respect for their God-endowed intrinsic value and in loyal response to the God who is love and who loves all. It seeks the other's good or well-being and, therefore, is always other-regarding (only the degree is up for debate). This love is expressed through kindness, mercy, generosity, compassion, justice, and a variety of other commendable qualities. Love is a relational concept and initiative; it seeks to establish connections and build caring relationships. Its ideal forms are expressed in such terms as *reconciliation, communion, community, harmony,* and *shalom.* These features characterize love in every situation, social and ecological.

145

LOVE AND PREDATION

In reality, love is always compromised, sometimes severely. The human situation is that we are confronted with a host of conflicting, often irreconcilable moral claims that make it impossible to "do no harm," but only to minimize the harm we inevitably do. Moral purity and perfection are illusions; moral ambiguity and selectivity are the normal conditions of ethical decision-making. We must choose the "greater good" or the "lesser evil"—the "best possible"—among sometimes lousy options. War and abortion are two extreme examples of the standard moral dilemma of struggling to love under the conditions of "necessary evil." In ecological relations, the complexities are compounded, because the "necessary evil" is natural and not only moral. The evil is built into the ecosphere (thus, natural or nonmoral evil); it is an inherent tragedy, entailing no human moral blame or sin except insofar as humans normally exacerbate the tragedy by going beyond environmental use to abuse, by exceeding the limits of human abilities and nature's capacities.

To be human is to be initially a *natural predator,* along with all other creatures, in relation to the rest of the biophysical world. I am using the term *predator* broadly to cover not only biological predation per se, but all forms of human destruction and consumption of other life forms and their habitats—both as herbivore and carnivore, both as deliberate and unavoidable acts. Whether in a broad or narrow sense, however, predation is a primary condition of human existence. We are not a special creation, a species segregated from nature. That is bad biology which leads to bad theology and ethics. Humans are totally immersed in and totally dependent on the biophysical world for our being. We cannot talk about humans *and* nature, but only humans *in* nature. We have evolved with all other creatures through adaptive interactions from shared ancestors. We are biologically (and theologically) relatives—albeit remote—of caterpillars, strawberries, the dinosaurs, the oaks, the protozoa, and all other forms of being.

Nevertheless, it is morally imperative that we not romanticize these biological connections, as some "nature lovers" are prone to do. The biophysical creation in which we humans are participants is not a world of "natural harmony" or "biological community" or "familial coopera-tion." These commonly used terms have ethical implications as eschatological concepts, as I will argue later in this chapter. In natural history, however, these terms romanticize and distort reality, hindering our understanding of the moral dilemmas in human

146

relationships with the rest of the biophysical world. That world is a morally ambiguous reality. It is a symbiotic system of predators and prey, edible flora and consuming fauna, parasites and hosts, scavengers and decomposers. The so-called "dynamic equilibrium" of the whole depends upon such primary interactions as lethal competition and amoral mutualism, in which the blood and guts—literally—of deceased creatures provide the nutrients for the generation of new life. In this practically endless recycling of life and death, every member of a species struggles against, uses, and/or feeds on members of other species in order to survive. Euphemisms such as harmony, cooperation, community, or family are hardly fit descriptions of a reality in which species eat and otherwise destroy one another.

Thus, humans are naturally predators—including consumers and self-defenders—in this order. Killing is a biological necessity for existence. We *must* kill and use other life forms and destroy their habitats in order to satisfy human needs (for food, fuel, shelter, etc.), to protect our lives and health from other predators and pathogenic parasites (for which our very bodies are environmental habitats), and to build and maintain the structures of culture. Whatever else human beings may be, we cannot avoid being initially natural predators.

How is it possible, then, to express Christian love in such morally constricted circumstances? Since humans are predators by necessity, is it possible to act as *altruistic predators*—as beings who seek to minimize the ecological harm that we inevitably cause and who consume caringly and frugally to retain and restore the integrity of the ecosphere? Or is altruistic predation a contradiction in terms? The answers to these questions are important, because the development of a Christian ecological ethic depends on the possibility of humans expressing love in an ecological context, on the possibility of humans becoming altruistic predators. Though the answers are by no means easy, they do not appear in principle to be relevantly different from the responses that Christian ethicists generally give to other types of moral dilemmas. Whether the issue is moral evil or natural evil, the ethical problem remains essentially the same: making discriminate judgments to discern the best possible balance, the most love-embodying acts and/or principles under the circumscribed conditions of necessary evil. If the just war theory can provide much of Christian ethics with a means of expressing love in warfare by restricting the conditions and conduct of war, then surely love is relevant in an ecological context—where, unlike human interactions, killing is indisputably necessary—as a means of

147

preventing and restricting environmental despoliation. This chapter and the next are efforts to spell out some of the basic features of altruistic predation.

QUALIFICATIONS OF ECOLOGICAL LOVE

Christian love in an ecological context is not an exact replica of love in an interpersonal or social context. Relevant differences exist between these contexts, and warrant relevant adjustments in the applications of love.

First, even if *interpersonal love* can rightly be defined as "equal regard,"[27] (which I doubt, since this concept seems insufficiently flexible to cover the spectrum of possible forms, from self-sacrifice to self-affirmation, which love ought to take in different situations), this concept seems totally inappropriate as a definition of ecological love. "Equal regard" for others assumes ontological equality of worth between the lover and the loved. That equality, however, is not evident in a comparison of humans with other species. Morally relevant differences exist that justify disparate and preferential treatment for humans.

Humans are more than one among the multitude of natural predators. We are also *the creative predator*—unique, unlike any other creature. This claim does not deny or ignore the fact that nonhuman creatures, probably all in one respect or another, have powers that are superior to those of humans—the speed of the cheetah, the strength of the elephant and the proportionate strength of the ant, the flight of birds and insects, the echolocation of bats, the web-weaving of spiders, the eyesight of raptors, the hearing of owls and deer, and the chemical production of plants, to name only a few. Some species—especially but not exclusively among mammals—display rational and quasi-moral qualities, including courage, compassion, deception, sympathy, grief, joy, fear, mutual aid, and learning abilities.[28] Human superiority over other creatures is restricted and not rigidly demarcated.

Nevertheless, our rational and moral powers, and, therefore, our creative capacities—no matter how weak they may appear in relation to our norms—so radically exceed the powers of any other species that major differences in quantity or degree are legitimately regarded as differences in quality or kind. We can never transcend nature, contrary to that mainstream theological tradition which contrasted nature and spirit. Human psychic-spiritual capacities are not additives to nature, but derivatives from nature. In history, we are inextricably immersed in nature. We can, however, transcend some instinctive necessities and realize some of the rational, moral, and spiritual *potentialities in* nature, far beyond the capacities of any other creature. That apparently is what Paul Tillich meant in describing the human, with slight exaggeration, as "finite freedom" in comparison with the "finite necessity" of other life forms.[29] We are the only creatures with moral agency, that is, relative freedom and rationality to transcend instinct sufficiently in order to define and choose good or evil, right or wrong. We, therefore, are the only creatures who now can be *altruistic predators*—or *profligate predators.*

We are the only creatures capable of intentionally creating and regulating our own environments—and, in fact, destroying every other creature's environment while recognizing the demonic effects of our actions. We are the only species that can create cultures, whether primary or complex, and a multitude of cultural artifacts, from artistic expressions to computer systems, from religious rituals to architectural structures, from moral designs to political orders. Only humans, according to traditional Christian doctrine, have the potential to serve as the image of God and to exercise dominion in creation. Despite historical misinterpretations and abuse, these concepts recognize a basic biological fact: humans alone have evolved peculiar rational, moral, and, therefore, creative capacities that enable us alone to serve as responsible representatives of God's interests and values, to function as protectors of the ecosphere and deliberately constrained consumers of the world's goods. We alone are the *creative predators.* In the light of that fact, it seems unreasonable to put humans on a moral par with other creatures.

Biotic egalitarianism strikes me as a moral absurdity and, in some cases, as an antihuman ideology. The claim of Schweitzer and some "deep ecologists"[30] that the choice of one life form over another, including humans, is "arbitrary and subjective"[31] or "an irrational and arbitrary bias,"[32] cannot be sustained in the light of the unique capacities of humans to experience and create moral, spiritual, intellectual, and aesthetic goods. The value-creating and value-experiencing capacities of humans are morally relevant differences between us and all other species, and justify differential and preferential treatment in conflict situations. I shall have more to say on this problem in the next chapter. In the meantime, it is important to note that while my viewpoint affirms the primacy of human values, it also denies the exclusivity of human values. Other creatures also have

149

intrinsic value—for themselves and for God—which warrants respect from human beings. However, their value is not equal to that of humans. If moral preference for human needs and rights is "speciesism,"[33] I plead guilty, but I think with just cause. Thus, in my view, Christian love in an ecological context is not equal regard, but it must remain at a high level of other regard.

Second, the definition of *Christian love* cannot be restricted to self-sacrifice, especially not in an ecological context of inequality. Reinhold Niebuhr's idea that the essence or highest form of love is self-sacrifice, as symbolized by the cross of Christ,[34] makes sacrificial love into an end in itself, rather than a means to an end. But love is relational. Its ultimate intention is to create and enhance caring and sharing relationships, to unite giving and receiving.[35] It is best described in such relational concepts as reconciliation, harmony, and communion. Sacrificial love, ranging in forms from simple acts of generosity to death on a cross, is a means of advancing the goal of reconciled relationships; it is not the end in itself. In Christian symbols, the instrument of Crucifixion cannot be isolated from its objectives, the reconciling events of the Resurrection, communion, and consummation. The cross is not an end in itself; it is a means to restore broken communion.[36]

Nevertheless, there is an element of self-sacrifice that is an inherent part of every form and context of love. Niebuhr was clearly right on this point: the sacrificial love of the cross stands in judgment on our truncated models of mutuality, and prevents self-regarding motives from pretending to be the ultimate fulfillment of love.[37] Love entails giving up at least some of our own interests and benefits for the sake of the well-being of others in communal relationships. This mandate applies in both human and ecological communities. The agonizing but unavoidable question, then, that Christian love continually poses for us is: what human interests and benefits must be sacrificed in this age of ecological crisis in order to serve the needs of other creatures and to enhance the health of the biotic community of which we and they are interdependent parts?

Third, some dimensions of Christian love appear to be inapplicable in an ecological context. Forgiveness, for example, is a fundamental facet of love in Christian understandings of human relationships with God and with one another. Forgiveness of sins, for example, is the core of Luther's doctrine of justification by faith.[38] But forgiveness is relevant only in interactions between moral agents, parties with moral capacities—to judge right and wrong, to do good or evil, to repent and pardon, to retaliate or return good for evil. Nonhuman creatures, so far as is known in their present evolutionary state, lack moral agency. Forgiveness is irrelevant in direct relationships with creatures that act instinctively or submorally and are incapable of sin or remorse. In fact, an argument for the relevance of forgiveness in this context might be a dangerous anthropomorphism, since it could legitimate a counter-argument for revenge or retribution against nonhuman creatures "guilty" of some "offense" against humans—like biting or attacking. It is best to keep forgiveness and its opposite out of these relationships.

Nevertheless, appeals for divine forgiveness for our sins against the ecosphere and its all-pervasive life forms are essential for a vital Christian piety. Repentance and petitions for pardon for our profligate predation need to be part of ritualized prayer in Christian churches. Karl Barth uncharacteristically said very little about ecological responsibilities, and much of the little he did say seems confused. Yet one point is potent. Barth notes that the killing of animals, which is morally legitimate only under the "pressure of necessity" and only when accompanied by a protest against it, is theologically possible only as "a deeply reverential act of repentance, gratitude and praise on the part of the forgiven sinner in face of the One who is the Creator and Lord of man and beast."[39] That perspective is valid for all dimensions of human ecological consumption.

These three qualifications mean that Christian love in an ecological context will be less rigorous than in human social relations. Relevant differences in the situations justify different levels of moral expectation, just as we hold different standards for family life and international affairs. This fact, however, certainly does not imply that Christian love makes no serious ethical demands upon human beings in ecological interactions. It does! Christian love has many dimensions, and most of them are relevant and relatively rigorous in an ecological context.

ECOLOGICAL DIMENSIONS OF LOVE

A popular and sentimental song from the fifties was called "Love Is a Many-Splendored Thing." Neither the title nor the lyrics deserve any poetic acclaim; still, the title suggests more wisdom than a horde of homilies. The meaning of *Christian love* cannot be encapsulated in simple definitions or a single dimension. Christian love is multidimensional. No single dimension exhausts its meaning; its full brilliance

151

depends upon seeing the multiple facets of love together. My intention, therefore, is to outline several interpenetrating dimensions of Christian love as they apply to ecological relationships.

These dimensions are love as *beneficence, other-esteem, receptivity, humility, understanding, communion,* and *justice.* I shall reserve a discussion of love as justice for the next chapter, because this topic deserves special and extensive treatment.

1. Beneficence (1 aspect of love)

Love as beneficence is looking not only to one's "own interests, but to the interests of others" (Phil. 2:4). It is being "servants to one another" (Gal. 5:13, RSV) by seeking "to do good to one another and to all" (I Thess. 5:15). It is serving Christ by ministering to the hungry, naked, lonely, and incarcerated (Matt. 25:31-46); cf. Isa. 58)—and following the principle of the reasonable extension of love to its uncontainable inclusivity, this mandate for ministry applies to all God's creatures in their natural habitats.

Beneficence means *doing* good, or, realistically, the maximum possible good in the circumstances, rather than merely wanting or willing good.[40] It includes nonmaleficence, doing as little harm or wrong to others (Rom. 13:10) as feasible, and refusing to inflict needless suffering or destruction. It goes beyond that negative duty to a positive quest of the neighbor's good, within the limits imposed by nature. Beneficence is caring and careful service on behalf of the well-being of others, human and otherkind, simply because a need exists, without regard for the earned or instrumental merit of the recipients and without the expectations of *quid pro quos.* Other life forms may have no direct utility for human needs, and most cannot respond to love in kind, but these considerations are irrelevant from the perspective of beneficence or other dimensions of Christian love. Christian love cannot be reduced to beneficence,[41] but it is decrepit without beneficence.

Love as beneficence may be simple acts of kindness to wild creatures, like letting a dead tree stand in the yard as a food source and nesting site for woodpeckers or refraining from too-frequent visits to a fox den. Moreover, love as beneficence can be manifested in every way that Christians and other citizens function as protectors of the biosphere— by preventing, for example, the toxication of the air, water, soil, and stratosphere or by saving the stability and diversity of species in their essential habitats. Lobbying for a clean air act or a pesticide control bill may be an act of beneficence. Similarly, preventing radical reductions and extinctions of species by struggling against deforestation and habitat fragmentation has the character of beneficence. Even human population control is implied by beneficence, since it is necessary, among other reasons, to insure that all species have sufficient living space. Love expressed in the compassionate caring of beneficence is an indispensable element of a Christian ecological ethic.

Distinguishing love as beneficence from love as justice is not always easy, and often it isn't especially useful, except to academic purists. But one thing is clear: beneficence should never be a substitute for justice, as some suggest.[42] In my view, beneficence exceeds the expectations of justice; it begins only when the demands of justice have been satisfied. It is the mercy that tempers justice, the "extra mile" that adds kindness to the calculations of "less and more." In a simple example, ecological justice might allow us to let the mourning dove with the raw, defeathered underwing freeze in the sub-zero temperatures of a New England winter. After all, those are the breaks in the natural struggle for survival. However, beneficence cannot resist feeding and sheltering the bird in the study until the wing heals. In many interpretations, moreover, beneficence has an optional quality, whereas justice is morally mandatory. Again, while beneficence generally connotes doing good, justice deals with the proper distribution of that good. Consequently, it seems important to insist that beneficence should be regarded as a supplement to justice, probably even the primary motivation for justice, but not as a substitute for justice.

2. Other-Esteem

Love as other-esteem "does not insist on its own way" (I Cor. 13:5). It appreciates and celebrates the existence of the other to the empathic point that "if one member suffers, all suffer together with it; if one member is honored, all rejoice together with it" (I Cor. 12:26). Other-esteem values, honors, and respects the integrity of the other, as a precious gift of God. H. Richard Niebuhr has captured the essence of this facet of Christian love:

> Love is reverence. It keeps its distance even as it draws near. It does not seek to absorb the other in the self or want to be absorbed by it; it rejoices in the otherness of the other; it desires the other to be what he is and does not seek to refashion him into a replica of the self or to make him a means to the self's advancement.[43]

Other-esteem is an expression of eros in the classical sense, since it is evoked by the love-worthy qualities or meritorious features in the beloved. But this fact does not disqualify other-esteem for consideration as a form of agape. On the contrary, other-esteem is incorporated into agape, because it values the otherness or distinctiveness of the beloved as a good in itself, and treats the beloved accordingly.

Love as other-esteem speaks forcefully against a variety of forms of ecologically debilitating anthropocentrism. It renounces that anthropocentrism which views the natural world as created for humans, and which values that world only for its contributions to human wants—measuring even ancient forests of sequoias in board feet, evaluating verdant plains and valleys as "worthless" land until "improved" by development, and describing huntable animals as "game" or "trophies" to be "harvested." It rejects that anthropocentrism which treats other creatures kindly only to the extent that they conform to human standards of "beauty" and "civility," and which, therefore, offers bounties on "moral offenders," the "bad" "varmints" like cougars and coyotes.[44] It disdains that anthropocentrism which yearns to transform nature's wild, chaotic order into a Disneyland tameness, with gardens of manicured shrubs, pesticided grass, concrete esplanades, and tender beasts for petting. That anthropocentrism is blind even to the beauty of an untended lawn recuperating from domesticity and overflowing with dandelions.

Other-esteem, in contrast, does not wish to be the manager, gardener, or zoo keeper of the biosphere. It rejects these despotic metaphors for responsible relationships of humans with otherkind. Other-esteem respects the integrity of wild nature—its diversity, relationality, complexity, ambiguity, and even prodigality. It is quite content to let the natural world work out its own adaptations and interactions without "benefit" of human interventions, except insofar as necessary to remedy human harm to nature's integrity and to satisfy vital human interests. Other-esteem groans with the travail of creation, but it also accepts the fact that natural habitats and their inhabitants are generally served best by the absence of human schemes for improvement, beautification, or domestication.

3. Receptivity

Love as receptivity is "not envious or boastful or arrogant or rude" (I Cor. 13:4-5), because it recognizes its dependency. Receptivity is a step beyond love as other-esteem. It too values otherness, but, additionally, it is an acute consciousness that the human community is *receptive to dependance*

incomplete, weakened, and even homicidal apart from others. We need the others, the biotic and abiotic components of the ecosphere. Consequently, receptivity is a yearning for relationship, not only to give to but to *receive from* the treasured others. Like other-esteem, it also is eros. It desires; it longs for the presence and pleasures of the beloved. But it is a self-giving love in the very process of being self-getting, because receptivity gives honor to the gifts of the others by recognizing our deficiencies and our dependencies on the others' gifts.

Receptivity stands in sharp contrast to the self-sufficiency so characteristic of human interactions with the ecosphere. We humans tend to celebrate our uniqueness and completeness in a virtual orgy of anthropocentrism, reminiscent of the competitive rallying boast of "We're Number One"! In our depletion of the ozone layer, our indiscriminate use of pesticides, our destruction of temperate and tropical rain forests, and our indifference to extinctions, we act as if we have no dependence on other parts of the body of earth. Receptivity, however, is a recognition of the intricately interdependent connections between humankind and the rest of the earth and an acknowledgment of our kinship with all earth's elements. It acts caringly to nurture and sustain the vitality, stability, and productivity of the relationship. Receptivity reminds us that love in an ecological context is not a "one night stand"!

Moreover, a full-fledged receptivity desires the raw, unadorned world with a virtually erotic passion. Despite the dangers to life and limb that generate justifiable fears, receptive lovers of nature yearn to be in the presence of the beloved and share in the intimate and omnipresent pleasures. They marvel at the miracles around them. They are filled with awe and humility and mystery. They feel "biophilia." For Christians, receptivity is a celebration of the sacramental presence of the Spirit, discussed in chapter 4. Reflecting my own prejudices, I suspect that many serious ornithologists have experienced these feelings, and probably (though I confess to mystification) so have many herpetologists. Love as receptivity reminds us that the natural world must be protected and nurtured not only for humanity's physical existence, but also for our spiritual well-being. This receptive attitude has aptly been described as "descendentalism," the spiritual appreciation of the earthy,[45] and it has been, as John Muir exemplified, a powerful force in initiating and sustaining the environmental movement. We therefore need to nurture receptivity not only for its inherent value, but also for its dynamic power to promote changes in environmental policy.

155

4. Humility

Love as humility is not thinking of ourselves more highly (or more lowly) than we ought to think (Rom. 12:3. Cf. Matt. 23:11-12; Luke 14:11, 18:9-14). It is a realistic virtue, rejecting both self-depreciation and self-aggrandizement. In response to arrogance, however, humility is other-regarding to the extent that it is self-deflating. It knows the weaknesses in human knowledge and character, and thus, recognizes that we are neither wise enough nor good enough to control the powers we can create or to comprehend the mysterious power that created us. Humility is the counter to hubris, the arrogant denial of creaturely limits on human ingenuity and technology. It is the antidote for triumphalism, the forgetting of our finitude and folly in the midst of celebrating human creativity. It is also a remedy for profligate predation—the excessive production and consumption that strain the limits of nature's capacities and disrespect the intrinsic value of our kin in creation. Humility, therefore, expresses itself as simplicity and frugality—that temperance which undoes self-indulgence.

Humility sits with the lowliest human as an equal (James 2:1-9), and even with unequals in an ecological context, in the manner of the self-emptying God who also sat with ontological unequals by entering and identifying with the human condition (Phil. 2:1-11). It seeks to puncture, therefore, any exaggerations about human powers and any undervaluations of other creatures. It is untroubled by human kinship with all other species. It accepts its relations. Humility recognizes that to be human is to be from the humus and to return to the humus. It regards all creatures as worthy of moral consideration.

Humility is cautious love or careful caring. It thrives in the manifestation of modesty, or choosing restrained, rather than ambitious, means and ends as ways of minimizing the risks of disaster in the light of the virtual inevitability of human error and evil. Undue risks represent the antithesis of humility, since, as that semi-cynical adage notes, if anything can go wrong, it will! Historian Herbert Butterfield spoke forcefully against the arrogance of immodesty:

> The hardest strokes of heaven fall in history upon those who imagine that they can control things in a sovereign manner, as though they were kings of the earth, playing Providence not only for themselves but for the far future—reaching out into the future with the wrong kind of farsightedness, and gambling on a lot of risky calculations in which there must never be a single mistake.[46]

To counteract this arrogance, no virtue will be in greater demand than humility as modesty if we are to avoid ecological catastrophes in the years ahead. The 1989 sludging of Prince William Sound with eleven million gallons of Alaskan crude from the wrecked supertanker *Exxon Valdez* is only one of countless examples of environmental destruction resulting from the sin of immodesty—that exaggerated confidence in human and technical reliability, and the failure to make due allowance for error and evil, the unpredictable and the unknown. Technology, as the contemporary clichés remind us, is both "promise and peril." Technological innovations can provide us with indispensable knowledge and assistance in alleviating some ecological problems. For instance, we would not even know about ozone depletion or be able to reduce toxic emissions without sophisticated technology. Yet, technology also has caused serious ecological damage, and it probably offers no answers to some ecological problems—certainly not to extinctions—to which it has contributed. Moreover, even the most reliable technologies are always subject to breakdowns, technical misuse, and power abuse.[47] Humility as modesty, therefore, cautions us not to be confident, let alone overconfident, in "technological fixes." It warns us that no human plans or techniques are fail-safe, so long as humans are relatively free and definitely finite. It urges us to remember the Achilles' heel of human creativity: the powers to shape the earth contain the powers to destroy it.

The meek or humble may not inherit the earth, but they will dramatically increase the odds that a healthy earth will be there to inherit.

5. *Understanding*

Love as understanding is loving God with our whole mind (Luke 10:27), and therefore loving the created beings that God loves with our whole mind. Not only faith seeks understanding; so does love. Love wants to know everything about the beloved—likes and dislikes, aspirations and anxieties, but above all, the other's needs. In fact, the only way to nurture and serve others adequately is to know their needs. Love requires understanding, or cognitive and emotional comprehension—and that is no less true in an ecological context than in a personal context. In fact, the amount of essential knowledge is far greater ecologically, because of the multitude of creatures in intricate interactions in complex ecosystems.

Knowledge about ecological dynamics is essential for ecological love. A large portion of environmental damage, in both personal and

Know what you're loving

157

corporate settings, is a consequence not of malice but of ignorance[48]—indeed, seemingly invincible ignorance. Too few are aware of even the seemingly obvious ecological effects of their actions. I once talked with a woman who was complaining about the decline of nesting birds in her backyard, and then in the next breath, she indicated that she had tripled the use of pesticides to combat gypsy moths. She did not recognize the linkage, despite Rachel Carson's work and despite widespread publicity about the destructive effects of pesticides like DDT on bald eagles, peregrine falcons, and other wildlife. The problem is magnified many-fold when we are dealing with major corporations dumping massive amounts of diverse pollutants into the air, soil, and water. The ecological effects of industrial and technological wastes on ozone depletion, global warming, acid rain, and species' reductions are difficult to trace. Discovery depends on extensive and expensive technical research. Ecological studies in a number of specialties and subspecialties have expanded dramatically in recent years, but we remain a long way from an adequate understanding of the intricate interdependencies in nature.

Despite the impressive knowledge explosion in the twentieth century, the more impressive fact about the human condition is how little we know. Much of human knowledge about ecology is fragmentary and disconnected. Scientific specialists know only a small percentage of the pieces of the ecological puzzle, and far less about how the pieces fit together in the intricate complexity of ecosystems, not to mention the ecosphere. Not even the number of species is known, and dramatically less is known about how these species depend on one another in the interactions of countless food chains.

One danger in this context is that some human act of negligence combined with ignorance, such as the use of a particular pesticide, could destroy an unrecognized "keystone" species, on which many species in an ecosystem depend directly and indirectly for their survival. The whole ecosystem would then crumble. Such acts of ignorance are commonplace in history, ancient and modern. The great North American ecological disaster of the 1930s, the Dust Bowl, was largely a consequence of agricultural malpractice confronting drought. Ecosystems in the United States have suffered heavy damage from the introduction of exotic aliens, without regard for the absence of natural control mechanisms—from kudzu in the Southeast and feral burros in the Southwest to starlings and house sparrows everywhere! Benjamin Franklin cites an ironic example of ecological ignorance from the eighteenth century, along with a wise warning:

Whenever we attempt to amend the scheme of Providence, and to interfere with the government of the world, we had need to be very circumspect, lest we do more harm than good. In New England they once thought blackbirds useless, and mischievous to the corn. They made efforts to destroy them. The consequence was, the blackbirds were diminished; but a kind of worm, which devoured their grass, and which the blackbirds used to feed on, increased prodigiously; then finding their loss in grass greater than their saving in corn, they wished again for their blackbirds.[49]

Ecological ignorance, then, is hardly bliss; it is a prime ingredient for ecological catastrophes (which may be a single calamity, like an oil spill or, more frequently, an accumulation of abuses that creates a composite calamity, like ozone depletion).

In this context, environmental research and education are important expressions of love. The advancement of ecological understanding is a key responsibility of our educational and ecclesiastical institutions. Knowledge is not virtue, contrary to Socrates, but knowledge is a necessary condition of objectively virtuous behavior in personal and corporate contexts. Knowledge certainly is power. It is power not only to control and manipulate, but also to care and mend. Ecological understanding is essential for acting lovingly.

6. Communion

Love as communion "binds everything together in perfect harmony" (Col. 3:14). It is "the unity of the Spirit in the bond of peace" (Eph. 4:3; cf. 4:15-16), for Christ has broken down all the partitions of alienation (Eph. 2:14). It is the pursuit of "what makes for peace and for mutual upbuilding" in community (Rom. 14:19). Love as communion is the consummation of love; it is the completion of the "drive toward the reunion of the separated."[50] It is the solvent of separation, the adhesive for wholeness and fullness in relations, the final sign of the bonding power of love. Communion is the full extension of love as receptivity and other-esteem. It means that the goal of Christian love is inherently and concretely relational. Communion is not satisfied with the other dimensions of love; it knows that love is incomplete without solidarity, without friendship and partnership in fully interdependent and shared relationships, without the interpenetration of giving *and* receiving. Communion not only wants the loved ones to be in their distinctiveness; it wants them to be *our* loved ones in fully reconciled relationships.[51] Love as communion, then, is reconciliation, harmony, koinonia, shalom. Ultimately, it is

Relational

salvation, for the Reign of God is the consummation of communion or reconciliation.

Such a love, however, is only partially and provisionally known in history. We experience at best precious fragments of this love, which prompt our urges for more. This is especially true in natural history where systemic alienation and predation prevail. The Isaianic vision (Isa. 11:6-9; 65:25) of a lion resting with a lamb, of a child leading a harmonious band of carnivores and herbivores, of a serpent eating only dust, is "unnatural" in history. Indeed, it is a utopian illusion to believe that such possibilities exist in history (except for the ambiguous distortions in domestication). The "peaceable kingdom" is an ultimate ideal or eschatological hope.

Yet, this vision of love as communion is by no means irrelevant to history, human and natural. It functions not only as a judgment on human deficiencies in expressing the demands of love, but also as a goad pressing us to reach out to the limits of love in history. Though we cannot now experience the full harmony of the New Creation, we can approximate it to the fullest extent that the moral ambiguity of this creation makes possible. Historically, for instance, Eastern Christianity found one intriguing way to express the hope for ultimate and comprehensive communion in the relationships between humans and other creatures. Fasting was understood not only as a discipline of piety but also as an exercise of ecological responsibility. For the pious, fasting occupied more than half the days of the year, and involved abstinence from meats, fish, and other animal products, including milk and eggs. But the intentions were a partial recapitulation of an alleged original communion and an anticipation of the consummation of communion:

> Man is thereby reminded that he was a vegetarian when he was placed in the Garden of Eden and was given dominion over the world. . . . So fasting reminds man of his sinfulness as he preys upon the animals for food. In its practice of fasting, the Eastern Christian, in effect, tells the world of nature, especially the animal world, that man will for a period voluntarily abstain from taking life or even living off animal products. . . . Thus, fasting becomes a symbol of the future reconciliation of man and nature in a Transfigured world where the worst predator—man—shall live with the lamb and not hurt it![52]

I cite this example not as a veiled argument for vegetarianism. (I think, however, that a reasonable case can be made for eliminating or at least reducing the consumption of meat, when nutritionally feasible, and eating lower on the food chain, in order to reduce the suffering of animals in factory farms and to increase the supply of vegetable protein for hungry humans.) Rather, my intention is to remind us that Christians are called to embody personal life-styles and advocate cultural patterns that are relevant to present ecological needs and that serve as signs of the Reign of love.

* *
** **

I have only scratched the surface of a major, emerging problem for Christian ethics—but enough, I hope, to reveal some of the dilemmas and possibilities of love in an ecological context, and perhaps enough to encourage others to make deeper scratchings and find fuller meanings.

Love, however, is incomplete without justice. I turn now to that vexing problem of love as justice in an ecological context.

CHAPTER SEVEN

LOVE AS ECOLOGICAL JUSTICE:

RIGHTS AND RESPONSIBILITIES

Look at the beautiful beetle!" I said enthusiastically as I walked with the five-year-old boy along the path to the barn. "Splat" came the sound from his sneakered foot as he exercised a distorted dominion by deliberately—and proudly—squashing the insect. Stunned, my first impulse is best left unmentioned. Instead, I reacted with a harsh reprimand: "That was unjust! You violated that beetle's moral rights without just cause!"

My words surprised even me. And, obviously, my words had no meaning to the puzzled and alarmed child. The more important issue, however, is whether my words can have any moral meaning at all to anyone. Are concepts of justice applicable to beetles—even though God must have had an "inordinate fondness" for beetles, according to the distinguished biologist Lord Haldane, since the Creator made hundreds of thousands of species of them? Can beetles have moral rights? What about indisputably sentient creatures like deer? Or whales or voles? What about allegedly nonsentients like frogs or even plankton? Can we speak meaningfully about justice for spotted owls and snail darters? Do trees have moral standing under the rubric of rights? What about the lilies of the fields or rare louseworts or barely visible flora? Is justice due even to bacteria and other unicellular organisms? What about rocks and rills? Do individual life forms have rights or only species? Where do we draw the line, if at all? Indeed, what about the biophysical world as a whole? Does it make ethical sense to talk about a holistic ethic that emphasizes the rights of nature per se?

162

Many will view these questions as manifestations of the trivialization and excessive complication of ecological ethics. And often these feelings are understandable and reasonable. Yet, I doubt that an adequate Christian ecological ethic can emerge without grappling with these befuddling questions. It is not enough to sputter about stewardship or dominion unless we have a clearer understanding of what moral responsibilities are entailed by these roles, or if, indeed, these roles properly incorporate our responsibilities. This chapter, therefore, struggles with the meaning of love as justice in an ecological context. What is love as justice, and what, if anything, does it involve for human and biotic (or organic) rights as well as human ecological responsibilities? Again, I am treading on territory that is largely unexplored by Christian ethics—and that is as treacherous as it is necessary.

BIBLICAL BASES FOR JUSTICE

Christian responses to ecological problems should be developed in the light of biblical commitments to justice. Justice is a prominent theme in the originating source of Christian norms. Explicit statements about justice, like love in general, in scripture apply only to divine-human and interhuman relationships (though some biblical strictures concerning animals, such as Deut. 4:14, 22:10, 22:6-7 and Exod. 23:12, are clearly suggestive of justice). Again, however, like love in general, there is no inherent reason why biblical concepts of justice cannot be extended to relationships between humanity and other life forms. John Calvin, for instance, in commenting on Deut. 25:4 and Prov. 12:10 and in an effort to highlight the rights of humans, said that humans are "required to practice justice even in dealing with animals." Even animals are "entitled to their food."[1] Moreover, there are good reasons why this extension of justice is justified and maybe even necessary—notably the uncontainable inclusivity of love (including justice) in scripture.

The God portrayed in scripture is the "lover of justice" (Ps. 99:4; cf. Pss. 33:5; 37:28; 11:7; Isa. 30:18; 61:8; Jer. 9:24). In response to the groanings of the enslaved Hebrews in Egypt (Exod. 2:23-24), the God who exercises justice for the oppressed (Ps. 146:7) goaded Moses to become a liberator, smashed the shackles of Pharaoh, and led the people to a new homeland. God's deliverance from Egypt became thereafter the paradigm of justice—and the justification for doing justice—for Israel (as well as for every persecuted group in later Christian-influenced cultures).

163

The covenants between God and the liberated people—which presumably include the Noachic Covenant embracing all creatures (Gen. 9)—were understood in part as God's laws for right relationships. The non-negotiated covenant was a bond of fidelity among the people and with God. It entailed a moral responsibility on the part of the society and its individual members to deal fairly with the participants in the covenant and to provide for the basic needs of all, as an expression of loyalty to their Liberator and as the condition of harmony (shalom) in the community (Isa. 32:17). In the light of the covenant, therefore, to know God is to do justice (Jer. 22:13-16; Mic. 6:8); it is covenant faithfulness. Indeed, justice in the prophetic tradition is a spiritual discipline, an act of worship, without which the values of other spiritual disciplines—prayer, fasting, sacrifices—are negated (Isa. 58:1-12; Amos 5:21-24; Hos. 6:6).

Faithfulness to covenant relationships demands a justice that gives special consideration or a "preferential option" to widows, orphans, aliens, and the poor—in other words, the politically marginalized and excluded, the economically vulnerable and powerless, the communally bruised and bullied (Exod. 23:6-9; Deut. 15:4-11; 24:14-22; Jer. 22:16; Amos 2:6-7; 5:10-12). This tradition of concern for the poor and the weak was embodied in the model of the Jubilee Year (Lev. 25), which prevented concentrations of unjust power and the permanence of poverty by mandating the return of accumulated properties every fifty years; and also in the related Year of Release (Deut. 15:1-18), which provided amnesty for debtors and the liberation from indentured servitude every seven years.

In the diverse strains of the Old Testament (as in the New), the standards of justice are sometimes undeniably parochial and cruel, reflecting their historical and cultural settings. Even the Jubilee is a blemished ideal; it provides, for example, a warrant for holding foreign slaves in perpetuity (Lev. 25:44-46). Standards of justice develop over time as new light breaks forth from the Spirit and misconceptions of God and justice are corrected in the "always-reforming" community of God. Nevertheless, the pervasive commitment to justice, particularly for the poor and powerless, is an enduring guide for the contemporary church.

While justice is a prominent theme in the Old Testament, it is also clearly visible in the New. In fact, contrary to those who hint that the New Testament supersedes and abandons the commitment to justice in the Old Testament, the New Testament writers assume and expand their heritage. Jesus clearly was in the prophetic tradition of Isaiah,

Amos, and Hosea when he denounced those who "tithe mint, dill, and cummin, and have neglected the weightier matters of the law: justice and mercy and faith. It is these you ought to have practiced without neglecting the others" (Matt. 23:23; cf. Luke 11:42). Similarly, Matthew's Gospel reflects the prophetic tradition in its description of divine judgment: Christ comes to us in the form of human need and in the context of the deprivation of rights, soliciting just and compassionate responses. To neglect the deprived is to reject Christ. Individuals and nations will be judged on the basis of their care for the "have-nots" (Matt. 25: 31-46). This concern is also evident in the Epistles, though it is generally restricted for reasons of the cultural situation to the internal Christian communities (II Cor. 8:1-15; Heb. 13:16; James 2:1-14; 5:1-6).

The Reign of God, the central feature of Jesus' preaching, should probably be understood as the fulfillment of the prophetic vision of justice and other dimensions of love (Luke 6:20-31; Matt. 5:3-12; 6:33). The good news of the coming Reign of God, however, is more than an announcement of our ultimate destiny; it is a definition of moral responsibility. We are summoned to shape the present on the model of God's New Heaven and New Earth. That is part of the meaning of the words in the Lord's Prayer: "Your kingdom come, your will be done, *on earth as it is in heaven*" (Matt. 6:10; cf. Luke 11:2). If, however, the Reign of God is understood as the redemption of all God's creatures, then the moral responsibilities that are entailed by that ultimate expectation presumably include justice to all creatures.

Jesus is portrayed in the many stories of the Synoptics as the poor itinerant prophet from a poor family in Nazareth who befriends and defends the dispossessed and the outcastes. The Magnificat of Mary (Luke 1:52-53) and Jesus' reading from Isaiah (61:1-2) in the Temple (Luke 4:16-21) are probably attempts of the primitive church to define the exemplary character of Jesus' ministry and, thus, provide a paradigm for the ministry of the church itself. That ministry emphatically entails the pursuit of justice—including liberation of the oppressed. In fact, the Suffering Servant, with whom the church traditionally has identified Jesus, is the one who *proclaims justice* to the nations (Isa. 42:1-4; Matt. 12:18). Perhaps a good case can be made, as John Haughey argues, that in the New Testament, Jesus is not only the Love but also the Justice of God.[2]

For those whose norms are grounded in scripture, therefore, justice is too close to the core of the biblical message to be ignored or trivialized in the development of an ecological ethic. Justice is not an option for

165

Christians, but a moral imperative. Loyalty to the lover of justice entails a love for justice. That love for justice must be focused especially on securing the needs and rights of the poor and oppressed. There is no inherent reason, however, why the poor and oppressed cannot be extended to include nonhuman creatures—without implying equality of rights or denying human primacy. Nothing hinders the formulation of standards of justice that are applicable to nonhuman life forms, especially since they have been abused by humans acting as profligate predators. The Lover of Justice sets no boundaries on justice. The gospel we are called to incarnate relates to *all* creatures in *all* situations.

LOVE AND JUSTICE

What is the relationship between justice and love? Is the relation of justice to love that of a contrary, a component, a complement, a substitute, or what? This subject has been one of ongoing debate among Christian ethicists, almost rivaling in prominence the exchanges about the extent to which Christian love is sacrificial or mutual.

Reinhold Niebuhr often has been at the center of the love-justice controversy. Niebuhr argued that agape, which he defined as sacrificial love, is symbolized by the cross as the "perfect ethical norm" and the sacrificing Christ as the "perfect norm of human nature." It is the highest form of love. This norm transcends realistic, historical possibilities.[3] It is the "impossible possibility."[4] It is both the fulfillment and the negation of justice and other forms of mutual love. Consequently, this norm prevents any structure of justice or mutuality from claiming that it represents all that love demands.[5] For Niebuhr, the highest good under the limitations of historical ambiguity is mutual love, including justice.[6] Though Niebuhr sometimes contrasts love and justice, he generally claims that the relationship is paradoxical and that mutuality, including justice, is a vital though not final form of Christian love.[7] Niebuhr never denied that love and justice are intimately related—nor have the bulk of his critics.

In the light of this critical debate, it seems reasonable to say at least that love and justice are distinguishable but not separable. Christian love, as I argued earlier, cannot be encapsulated in any single definition or formula. Love is a multidimensional phenomenon; it exceeds by definition the requirements of justice. Whatever the correct relationship might be in detail, love demands more than justice, but it also demands *no less* than justice. Justice is a necessary condition for the existence of love; love incorporates justice. D. D. Williams, following Paul Tillich,[8] rightly argued, "Love without regard for the terms of justice is sentimentality."[9] Love is not present, except as a pretense of piety, without the fair treatment of others and full respect for their rights. Thus, justice seems to be at least "the minimal shape of other-love" or "love in embryonic form."[10] But we can go further in acknowledging the noble values of justice in social—and potentially natural—history, and the indispensable function of justice in completing the meaning of love. Justice is nothing more, but also nothing less, than one indispensable dimension of Christian love. Justice is love when it "rejoices in the right" (I Cor. 13:6). For Christians, the meaning of justice is understood in the context of God's love for creatures and humanity's frail reciprocations.

MEANING OF JUSTICE

What is justice? That question will produce no easy consensus! Justice, like love, is a vague word with multiple meanings and forms. Concepts of justice come in various types[11]—leaving aside the rhetorical definitions at press conferences and pep rallies that translate justice into whatever "our side" wants. My basic concern here is distributive justice, which can be defined as the proper apportionment or allocation of relational benefits and burdens. Other forms of justice, like commutative and retributive, are relevant only in relationships between moral agents. Formally, distributive justice is giving everyone his or her due or fair share. From a Christian perspective, this formal principle is grounded in neighbor-love. We render to others their due because of our loving respect for their inherent dignity or intrinsic value, which is grounded in the "nature of things," God's valuations.

The formal principle of justice is usually based on a distributive principle of impartiality: treat similar cases similarly, and dissimilar cases dissimilarly. That sounds simple, until one thinks of the complications. What criterion or criteria, for instance, should a human community use for determining relevant similarities and dissimilarities? Should it be merit, effort, industry, risk, seniority, sentience, basic needs, special skills, physical size, moral behavior, social status, or some combination of these or others? Common sense tells us that different criteria are relevant in different circumstances, and we often act accordingly. Physical agility, for example, is not a relevant consideration for determining who will graduate from medical schools, but it

167

certainly is for dancing with the Bolshoi or playing for the Packers. Usually, several criteria are relevant for decision-making in particular situations. However, on Christian assumptions, when we are talking about the conditions for due respect in community, basic needs are a prime consideration in the distributive process. In this context, a major task of justice is to insure that the criteria used for the purpose of distributing goods and services are not arbitrary or irrelevant but morally appropriate to given situations,[12] and to prevent any interested party from being deprived of values on the basis of morally irrelevant factors—including, in some cases, not being human.

Treating like cases alike and unlike cases differently also implies that justice is not the equivalent of equality. Equality implies that all cases are to be treated alike in all situations. Justice certainly requires equality in like circumstances. However, equality is not demanded by justice in all cases. Differential treatment is justified when morally relevant differences exist. This distinction between justice and equality can be a delicate one, but it is also essential—as I shall argue—for justice in an ecological context.

On the basis of this interpretation, distributive justice can be defined as love calculating, ordering, differentiating, adjudicating, and balancing dues or interests in the midst of conflicts of claims or interests, in order to provide a proper share of all scarce and essential values and resources for all parties with stakes in the outcome. Since this process rarely starts from ground zero, rarely from some "original position," but rather from a history and context of wrongs, distributive justice is normally redistributive justice.[13] Justice is liberation from deprivation and exclusion—or as Karen Lebacqz argues, restoration, restitution, redress, and reparation.[14] Moreover, humans are not the only relevant parties in the conflicts of interests that love as justice must balance. If nonhuman creatures have intrinsic value and are creations of a loving, value-imparting God, these affirmations seem to imply a claim to treatment respectful of their value. I see no compelling reason why nonhuman organisms should not be included as interested parties in the ongoing process of redistribution.

Justice, moreover, can never be determined in the abstract. It is discovered contextually where relevant similarities and dissimilarities are weighed with discernment, and where injustices are encountered and eliminated. Injustice can be understood as the social form of sin—that self-centered human inclination to defy God's covenant by grasping more than our due and thereby depriving others of their due. If so, justice is love overcoming sin.

168

RIGHTS AND JUSTICE

Justice is generally and properly associated with moral rights—particularly human rights (those moral rights essential for human well-being) and possibly organic or biotic rights (those moral rights essential for the well-being of otherkind). Rights are, in my view, essential to the notion of justice, and are implicit also in biblical concepts of justice.[15] Rights are a way of conceptualizing the basic demands of justice, of giving substance to the formal principles of justice. They are specifications of the *content* of what is due. Justice, then, is rendering to each his or her *rights*, and a just community is one in which everyone's rights are properly rendered—that is, fairly balanced and distributed.[16]

Moral rights are moral entitlements, not privileges, mere conventions, or simply social contracts. As such, they should also be legal entitlements or social rights, recognized and protected by law. Rights are usually expressed in general principles—like freedom of speech or equality under the law—in order to cover an array of circumstances. Yet, if they are to be operative in any society, rights must be defined, delimited, interpreted, and defended in casuistic laws, regulations, and judicial decisions. In this process, the basic rights inevitably and often justifiably will be restricted, in order to minimize conflicts with other rights or other parties' claims to the same rights. Rights are rarely absolute. They exist *prima facie*, which means that we have strong moral reasons for respecting them unless we have stronger moral reasons for not doing so. Rights can be overridden only for compelling moral reasons, like conflicts with other rights, and even then only to the extent necessary. Even the freedom of religion is not absolute. It does not include, for example, the legal legitimation of animal, let alone human, sacrifices! In any case, moral entitlements have substantially reduced social value apart from legal entitlements. That is why environmentalists have been intent on establishing human environmental rights and sometimes biotic rights in law.

In substance, human rights are the prerequisites for creative life in relation to the other members of any society. These rights are the basic necessities—the minimal conditions—to which every member is entitled and which a society should strive to guarantee, in order to enable all to live in accord with their God-given dignity and to participate in social decision-making.[17] These rights have sometimes been categorized as negative or positive—the negative being freedoms from interference, like the human rights of privacy and religious

169

liberty, and the positive being the provision of social goods, like sufficient nutrition and other basic needs. No matter how categorized, however, human rights are justifiable claims on any society for the basic conditions essential for the well-being of its members, God's invaluable creatures. To recognize these rights is to acknowledge others as creatures of God-endowed worth and full members of the society—indeed, full members of the human family. To deny these rights is to regard others as nonmembers or lesser members and, therefore, unworthy of full and equal moral consideration. Presumably, biotic rights would have something of the same character as human rights, with appropriate modifications to reflect different relational settings.

As this conception of rights implies, rights entail correlative responsibilities on the part of communities of moral agents. This correlation does not imply that only moral agents can have rights (which seems quite arbitrary), but rather that only moral agents have responsibilities to respect rights. Nonhuman creatures, therefore, can be rights-bearers without being rights-purveyors, since they lack sufficient capacities for moral decision-making. The correlation simply recognizes that the satisfaction of one's rights depends on others' responsibilities—their recognition of and respect for one's rights. "Rights . . . are expectations regarding responsibilities."[18]

Some argue, however, that responsibilities, not rights, are primary—that in an adequate Christian approach to justice, "justice will reside in responsibilities and duties, not in rights."[19] This argument seems to skew the inseparable and balanced connection between rights and responsibilities. Rights provide an objective moral reference for responsibilities, because we cannot define our duties except in reference to what others are due. Responsibilities to others, in fact, are respect for their rights. An obligation to others exists because these others have just claims on us. If a right exists, it implies a duty on the part of a community of moral agents—any human community—to satisfy this just claim to the fullest extent possible (which might be possible only partially or not at all, depending on the capacities and needs of a community in given circumstances). Without a correlation between rights and responsibilities, human duties may deteriorate to a level of *noblesse oblige* benevolences, which can be taken away as freely as given. With that correlation, however, humans are morally bound to give what is due. That, of course, is an important reason for recognizing environmental and biotic rights.

HUMAN ENVIRONMENTAL RIGHTS

Based on the above interpretation of human rights, do human beings have environmental rights? The only reasonable answer seems to be an emphatic yes! Though environmental rights did not get even an honorable mention in the 1948 United Nations' Universal Declaration of Human Rights, they have received some attention in the following decades. Environmental rights are now emerging as a *cause celebre* in the environmental movement.[20] At this writing, for instance, the National Wildlife Federation is circulating a petition called the "Environmental Quality Amendment" for inclusion in the United States Constitution. Pope John Paul II also joined the chorus in his New Year's Day, 1990 message on the environment: "The right to a safe environment . . . must be included in an updated charter of human rights."[21]

The formation and implementation of environmental rights are imperatives for our time. One of the essential conditions of human well-being is environmental sustainability and integrity. We live in solidarity with all other species of fauna and flora in a shared ecosphere. The satisfaction of basic human needs and expressions of cultural creativity depend totally on the productivity, diversity, and dynamic stability of the natural world. In this context, ecocide is also homicide. Consequently, "all human beings have the fundamental right to an environment adequate for their health and well-being."[22]

This general right can and should be subdivided into several specific environmental rights, including: (1) sustainable productivity and use of regenerative resources, for both present and future generations; (2) protection of the soils, air, waters, and atmosphere from levels of pollution that exceed the safe absorptive capacities of ecological processes; (3) full public disclosure by governments and private enterprises on the practices and risks associated with toxic disposal and other ecologically harmful behavior; (4) equitable shares of natural resources essential for human life; (5) preservation of biodiversity as resources for the human needs of present and future generations; (6) public protection from the social consequences of "private" behavior, particularly unbridled consumption and excessive population; and (7) redress or reparations to victims for violations of their environmental rights. Developing these and other environmental rights is a major challenge to Christian ethics for the nineties.

Moreover, since rights entail duties on the part of human communities to implement these rights, environmental rights can also be expressed as the obligations of governments to protect the environment for the sake

171

of their citizens and those of other governments. Thus the World Commission on Environment and Development has formulated a set of environmental responsibilities for nation-states:

* to maintain ecosystems and related ecological processes essential for the functioning of the biosphere;
* to maintain biological diversity by ensuring the survival and promoting the conservation in their natural habitats of all species of flora and fauna;
* to observe the principle of optimum sustainable yield in the exploitation of living natural resources and ecosystems;
* to prevent or abate significant environmental pollution or harm;
* to establish adequate environmental protection standards;
* to undertake or require prior assessments to ensure that major new policies, projects, and technologies contribute to sustainable development; and
* to make all relevant information public without delay in all cases of harmful or potentially harmful releases of pollutants, especially radioactive releases.[23]

The work of the World Commission on environmental rights and responsibilities is a good start. Yet the process is far from complete—and Christian ethics presumably has a contribution to make to the development and defense of environmental rights and responsibilities.

Moreover, the process is critically important. Since environmental health is essential for human survival and creativity, environmental rights are certainly no less important than social, political, and economic rights. In fact, it is not an exaggeration to say that the possibility of realizing every other human right depends on the realization of environmental rights. Thus, contrary to those advocates who contend that environmental concern detracts from or competes with social justice, the reality is that ecological integrity is a precondition of social justice. Indeed, it is itself a manifestation of social justice. The quest for social justice is truncated without the inclusion of a commitment to environmental rights.

Environmental rights for humans, however, are unabashedly anthropocentric. The assumption is that we ought to take care of the environment so that the environment can take care of us. It is enlightened self-interest or, more specifically, the biological equivalent of supply-side economics. By conserving our natural resources and cleaning up our polluted ecosphere to protect humans, the flora and fauna allegedly will be served by indirect effects. But that trickle-down process is about as effective in protecting species and their habitats as supply-side economics has been in solving the problem of endemic poverty. Economic interests and ecosystemic interests are not always integrated, at least not in the short-run. Economic arguments for protecting a species or ecosystem can be trumped readily by arguments for other, more apparent economic gains, like a hydroelectric dam. Not every life form—not the snail darter in the Tennessee Valley or the spotted owl in the Pacific Northwest or the millions of unclassified plants and insects in tropical forests—is perceived as being beneficial for vital human interests. We can survive, though less richly, without some species. In fact, having exterminated a number of species, we already do! When conflicts occur, and they inevitably do, nonhuman organisms are likely to be the losers—unless there is some reason to respect their existence beyond their instrumental values to humankind. Environmental rights for humans will help but they are no guarantee of ecological integrity. The question then arises about the rights of nature and its biotic components.

[handwritten margin note: Who would you rather die/get killed, a person or tree/animal? How far do we take it?]

BIOTIC RIGHTS

Traditionally, moral rights have been discussed only in the context of human interactions. Ethics has been understood generally as a strictly interhuman concern. But that situation is changing dramatically. A serious debate has emerged over the last couple of decades about the rights of nature.[24] Regrettably, the churches have remained nearly untouched by these controversies, and only a few theologians and ethicists—John Cobb and Jürgen Moltmann being notable exceptions— have thus far entered into the fray. Yet, the Canberra Assembly of the World Council of Churches (February, 1991) called for a Universal Declaration of Human *Obligations* Towards Nature as part of a United Nations' Earth Charter, which will be considered at the 1992 U.N. Conference on Environment and Development.[25] The rights debate is no longer a subject of snickers, especially in philosophical and environmental circles; it has become respectable, a problem worthy of serious reflection, a subject of books and articles in scholarly journals like *Ethics* and *Environmental Ethics*. The basic questions are: Do nonhuman creatures or even their whole ecosystems have rights that humanity should honor? If so, who or what has rights, and what are these rights? The issues are mind-numbing in their complexity.

From a perspective that recognizes the intrinsic value of all God-created being, I affirm the rights of nonhuman creatures—but not without plenty of trepidation and confusion. This position raises some troublesome problems. Four of them deserve preliminary comment.

First, the danger may exist that the recognition of nonhuman rights, including those of microorganisms, will trivialize the very concept of rights and diminish the fundamental importance of human rights. But there is no necessary reason why such trivialization would follow. The cause, if any, would seem to be psychological rather than logical or reasonable, reflecting perhaps human resistance to abandoning a self-designated status of absolute uniqueness. The recognition of rights is not a zero-sum game in which one party's genuine rights are diminished if another party's rights are acknowledged. Rationally, nonhuman rights can coexist comfortably with a strong set of human rights. Indeed, a coherent or seamless garment Christian ethic would seem to require appropriate moral consideration for all levels of being. Moreover, the charge of trivialization is a factual assessment that requires empirical data to defend. It strikes me as a hypothesis with a heavy burden of proof and plenty of counterevidence, including the breadth of concern of some Christian saints and activists.[26]

Second, the assertion of nonhuman rights could lead to a host of absurdities, straining moral sensitivities to the "breaking point."[27] This threat is real, but it is not in itself a refutation of nonhuman rights or of particular formulations of these rights. Nonhuman rights would be absurd if they were construed as equal rights with humans or as the same rights as humans. Yet, nonhuman rights are not identical with human rights where relevant differences exist.[28] No one should be taken seriously, for example, who proposes voting rights for chimpanzees—let alone fair housing rights for parasites in human bodies. Moreover, nonhuman rights can be overridden for lesser reasons, often dramatically lesser, than would be tolerable for human rights.[29] Nonetheless, the *reductio ad absurdum* argument is an important warning that statements about nonhuman rights must be carefully constructed with appropriate qualifications and limitations.

Third, the recognition of nonhuman rights creates countless complications and dilemmas in determining and balancing rights.[30] This claim is true but irrelevant. Nonhuman rights are certainly difficult to formulate, and seemingly intractable dilemmas are inevitable. The same, however, is true of human rights. If nonhuman rights are valid, they cannot be ignored to avoid taxing our mental faculties. The truth cannot be simplified or constricted for the sake of convenience.

Finally, respect for nonhuman rights is often hopelessly impractical, it is argued, whereas valid ethical norms and restraints must be practical, since ought implies can.[31] After all, critics ask, how is it possible or practical to show moral respect for nonhuman rights when the human condition is such that we must destroy many billions of microorganisms simply to do our daily breathing and feeding, not to mention the life-destroying consequences of bulldozers and harvesters? Nonhuman rights seem meaningless in this context. This complaint, then, against nonhuman rights deserves a persistent hearing. But whether or not it is valid may depend on particular definitions of and restrictions on nonhuman rights.

Despite serious difficulties in this embryonic area of thought, the affirmation of the rights of nature cannot be summarily dismissed. Something profound—something coherent with the Christian faith in a creating and redeeming God who is all-encompassing love—is happening in this effort at ethical extension. The stress on nonhuman rights is a way of saying that all life is sacred or intrinsically valuable and worthy of being treated as the subject of human moral consideration. Indeed, the acknowledgment of intrinsic value in nonhuman creatures seems to be implicitly an acknowledgment of their legitimate claims for appropriate treatment from the human community and, therefore, of some level of rights and responsibilities. The underlying concern seems to be human responsibility for nature, and the stress on rights provides an objective moral basis for this responsibility. The assumption—a valid one, I have argued—is that rights and responsibilities are correlative, that a duty to another being exists because the other has a just claim. Advocacy for the rights of nature is the contention that environmental concern is not only an expression of benevolence,[32] but also an obligation of justice—not simply justice to human interests, but also justice to the interests of other creatures. In Western cultures, rights are important; no rights suggest no moral consideration.[33]

This question of the rights of otherkind, however, is not an arbitrary judgment. In fact, it is a means of avoiding arbitrariness. To say that humans have moral rights while other forms of life do not, even though humans are continuous with all other forms of life, is an arbitrary judgment. However, rights are not mere human constructions or attributions. They are recognitions of the moral claims that inhere in living beings.

This viewpoint on nonhuman rights is not so bizarre or so alien to human behavior as it appears to many at first sight. As Joel Feinberg suggests, we functionally recognize the rights of other creatures every time we treat them kindly or avoid treating them cruelly, not simply for aesthetic, scientific, or other human interests but for their own sakes.[34]

175

Whenever, for example, we refrain from trampling an immature robin fallen from a nest or forego plucking a jack-in-the-pulpit in the woods, and do so for reasons relating to the welfare of the creatures themselves, we seem to be implicitly acknowledging some right of theirs. In fact, such rights may also be recognized legally. Some wildlife-related laws in the United States—such as the Wilderness Act, the Marine Mammal Protection Act, and the Endangered Species Act—grant legal rights to nonhumans and may implicitly recognize moral rights.[35]

Admittedly, however, support for nonhuman rights appears to be a minority opinion in philosophical circles. The majority of participants in the rights debate probably would agree that the question of the rights of otherkind is a "bogus issue."[36] This type of charge apparently has prompted some rights-sympathizers to search for alternatives to rights language. Paul Taylor, for example, offers a theory of environmental ethics that he claims does not rely on the idea of nonhuman rights.[37] He argues that moral rights can be applied reasonably to animals and plants, but there are good reasons for not doing so.[38] His reasons are practical or strategic: It is "less confusing" and "less misleading" to forego rights-talk.[39] "By avoiding talk of the moral rights of animals and plants we do not lend aid to those who have no respect for them."[40] Moreover, the idea of rights, he says, are superfluous: they add nothing that cannot be accomplished by means of the central ideas he develops, namely, "respect for nature," the "biocentric outlook," and the possession of "inherent worth."[41]

Nevertheless, perhaps ironically, Taylor provides an impressively strong case for nonhuman rights on philosophical grounds. He uses the concept of rights while shunning the words. His alternatives are really the functional equivalents of moral rights. I doubt, however, that anyone who reads his sophisticated work will be misled by this tactic. Personally, I think it will be less confusing in the long-run to use the language of rights forthrightly. This approach avoids the incoherence of moral dualism or pluralism. It affirms one ethic that is continuous for normative evaluations of both social and ecological relationships, with appropriate adjustments for the different contexts. It reminds us that justice is one, comprehensive, and indivisible.

BOUNDARIES OF BIOTIC RIGHTS

The problems associated with nonhuman rights would be somewhat reduced if we could fix parameters. But where is the boundary to be drawn for inclusion or exclusion from the realm of rights? The usual criteria proposed for determining who or what is in or out are: (1) sentience (the capacity to experience pain and pleasure), (2) reason, (3) moral capacities, (4) moral reciprocity (if no duties, then no rights), (5) consciousness (for instance, the awareness of danger or prey), (6) linguistic communication, and (7) Tom Regan's "subject-of-a-life" (including the presence of desires, perceptions, memories, anticipations, emotions, sentience, psychological identity over time, and so on).[42] None of these criteria, however, seems to be satisfactory, not even in combination. They all appear to be sufficient conditions for the recognition of rights, but they, singly or jointly, are not necessary conditions.

Recognizing this problem, Tom Regan insists that his "subject-of-a-life" criterion does not logically preclude the extension of rights to creatures other than mentally normal mammals of one year or older.[43] He intentionally errs on the side of caution, but urges that other creatures, at least some of them, be given the benefit of the doubt and treated "as if " they are subjects with rights, especially when doing so causes no human harm.[44] Despite this important qualification, however, the various boundary-setting criteria seem arbitrary and anthropocentric; they project human characteristics and values onto the rest of creation and then give or deny moral status on this basis.

So, where do we draw the line? An equally important question, however, may be, why is it necessary or valuable to recognize a boundary at all? That question is especially relevant when the concept of *prima facie* rights, as I shall note later, provides adequate built-in protections against moral absolutes and absurdities. It may be, as H. Richard Niebuhr suggested in his earlier-quoted comments on the extension and intensification of the moral law, that no line is possible or desirable on the basis of Christian norms.[45]

Nonetheless, drawing a line appears to be valuable if rights-talk is to make some practical sense. I have no clear perception, however, about precisely where that line should be drawn. Perhaps the line can be drawn at least at the juncture, insofar as identifiable, where life is distinguishable from nonlife, since nonliving elements—like rocks and gases—have no apparent interests or drives to survive about which rights can be "meaningfully predicated."[46] Even in excluding these elements from coverage under the category of rights, however, humans have no license for abuse, since one must allow for the dependence of all life forms on the abiotic elements in the biosphere. Nonliving elements must be treated with care as instrumental values;

they are the resources and habitations of all creatures. In the biosphere, even rocks and gases are teeming with microorganisms, and the waters of the earth are interpenetrated with organic life. Moreover, even the holistic interactions of biotic and abiotic components in ecosystems and the ecosphere have "systemic values,"[47] on which all life forms are totally dependent and which warrant systemic responsibilities.

Or perhaps we need to draw the line at a higher level, perhaps a much higher level, of species' complexity, if for no other reason than the practical one of avoiding moral absurdities—like campaigns for restricted breathing exercises to minimize injuries to microorganisms, or almost literally, straining at gnats and swallowing camels. Again, however, even here, environmental care is mandated, since all complex organisms and ecosystems are dysfunctional apart from the instrumental benefits of simple organisms. Mutualistic bacteria, for instance, dwell in the human digestive tract and facilitate its functions. Similarly, marine plankton are the foundations of the food pyramid topped by large carnivores, such as eagles, bears, and humans.

My own operational perspective on a rights-boundary is grounded in the criterion of conation—a striving to be and to do. At this point at least, beings may be said to have "interests" in their biological roles *for their own sakes*—a characteristic that is not evident in inanimate objects or probably animate components of members of species. The diverse species of plants and animals, from rudimentary microorganisms to complex organisms, may be good for systemic wholes, like ecosystems. They may be good instrumentally for one another. They may also be good for human interests, whether for scientific, aesthetic, psychological, spiritual, recreational, or economic reasons. Yet, whether they are good or bad for others' interests, *they are good for themselves*—and this claim is the basis for whatever rights ought to be respected by moral agents.

Nonhuman creatures are far more than Cartesian machines. They reproduce their own kind; they interact with their environments with various degrees of indeterminacy; they have inherent powers of mutation to adapt more fittingly to their niches and even to evolve into new and more complex life forms (which, in fact, accounts for the emergence of humankind); and they are defined by a vitality that struggles to fulfill their "reasons for being." They are good for themselves because they possess at least conation—that is, drives or aims, urges or goals, purposes or impulses—whether conscious or unconscious—to be and to do.[48] They are characterized by a volitional and/or instinctive striving to live in order to realize their possibilities, or

178

[Margin note, handwritten:] Not about where to draw it on, who is included but on how much justice is given!

what Albert Schweitzer called, somewhat anthropomorphically, the "will to live."[49] They are "teleological centers of life" that pursue their own good in their own unique ways.[50]

Otherkind have "interests" in their own good. Whether or not these interests exist consciously or subjectively, they exist *objectively*. Otherkind can be helped or hindered by the actions of others in their environment.[51] The important consideration is that a nonhuman creature's interest in its own good is "an objective value concept": a "biologically informed" moral agent in theory can take the standpoint of a plant or animal and judge what is good or bad, beneficial or harmful to that creature from its perspective, and then act empathically to promote this objective interest.[52]

Thus nonhuman organisms—animals and plants—are more than means to others' ends; they are ends for themselves. If so, the conative character of members of all species ought to be respected by all moral agents who honor their biological kinship with all other creatures and who are loyal to the biocentric valuations of an all-loving God. The "will-to-live," according to Schweitzer, should generate a response of "reverence for life." Schweitzer's reverence is a mournful and somewhat mystical empathy with the struggles for survival of all life forms. In defiance of "a ghastly drama of the will-to-live divided against itself," it regards all life as sacred and seeks to prevent any harm beyond the point of necessity.[53] A similar notion, rooted in conative urges, seems to underlie the moral principle of Charles Birch and John Cobb: "All things have a *right* to be treated the way they *ought* to be treated for their own sake."[54] This perspective, or something similar to it, seems to be an essential feature of an adequate Christian ecological ethic.

INDIVIDUALS AND COLLECTIVES

Wherever we choose to fix the boundaries of nature's rights (if we can and must), and whether we do so for practical or more substantive reasons, two polarities must be preserved in creative tension for an adequate ecological ethic. One is moral respect for individuals and the other for collectives or wholes.

At one pole, an adequate Christian ecological ethic must posit respect for individual lives, not simply aggregates like species.

The moral issues in the relationship between species and their individual members are complex, but an adequate answer to these problems seems to require concern for both individual rights and

179

species' rights. The common tendency among rights advocates to endorse one or the other seems incoherent. The two are inseparably linked. Neither a species nor its individual members are simply means to the other; both are means and ends in their interdependence. It is not enough to say that only species have rights, since no species exists without individuals to represent and reproduce it. Equally, it is not enough to say that only individuals have rights, since no individuals exist except as temporary incarnations of a species and carriers of its genetic past and future. A species is much more than a humanly contrived abstraction or classification. It is a genetic lineage that is encoded as the fundamental features of being in every individual and population, inherited from forebears and potentially contributable to successors.[55] The good of a species at any given time is embodied in the good that its living members produce and reproduce.

Certainly, the preservation of viable populations of species is significantly more important ecologically than the fate of individual members, since the extinction of a species or subspecies is the finale for all future generations. Yet, the preservation of a species is unsustainable without sufficient respect for individuals and moral constraints against their destruction. Though a species as an aggregate or a genetic code is not conative in itself, that fact does not contradict a theory of nonhuman rights structured on conation.[56] A species is both the aggregation of conation in individuals and the carrier of potential conation for all future generations. Thus individual rights and species' rights seem to be two sides of the same coin, constitutive of one another. We cannot respect one without respecting the other.

Moreover, on the assumptions that all creatures are good for themselves and good from the perspective of the universal love of God, the individual members of all species seem to have some moral standing as rights-bearers. This is the truth embodied in the life-styles of St. Francis and Albert Schweitzer (even though they lacked adequate principles for making discriminating judgments in conflicts of interest among life forms). Otherwise, it is morally permissible to rip the legs off grasshoppers, shoot frogs or foxes, chop down cherry trees, squash beetles and spiders in natural settings, or pluck rare orchids—all for the fun of it, without just cause, without regard for moral restraints—so long as one does not endanger species or disrupt ecosystems. A holistic ethic, which respects only species and other aggregates, suggests a merciless attitude toward individuals.[57] In its extreme forms, which are often misanthropic, such holism deserves to be branded with Tom Regan's harsh epithet, "environmental fascism."[58] To avoid this moral consequence, it seems important to maintain that all living beings have at least some rights and these rights should be respected by moral agents.

Yet, it also seems important to avoid biotic egalitarianism and to insist on a gradation of value among rights-bearers. Biotic egalitarianism places all species—dandelions and dogs, humans and amoebas, or, in restricted forms, all of a class of species like mammals, from mice to humans—on the same moral plane. The formal theory disallows moral distinctions and preferences among species. In practice, however, most egalitarians have found ways to avoid these impracticalities and rigidities. Some deep ecologists, for instance, claim that biotic equality is true only "in principle," since all species must use others for the sake of survival.[59] In contrast, a graded model claims that all creatures are entitled to "moral consideration," but not all have the same "moral significance."[60] All have intrinsic value, but not equal intrinsic value. In the previous chapter, I argued against biotic egalitarianism that the value-creating and value-experiencing capacities of humans are morally relevant differences between us and all other species, and justify preferential treatment for humans in conflict situations. Here the same criteria are extended to all species, creating an ascending/descending scale of intensity for rights and responsibilities. Among species, the moral significance of rights is proportionate to the value-experiencing and value-creating capacities of their members, and the corresponding responsibilities of moral agents are proportionate to this significance.[61] Other things being equal, sentient creatures, for instance, are to be preferred over nonsentient ones in conflict situations.

This ranking mechanism is often considered "speciesistic," since it gives top moral preference to humans and ranks others descendingly on the basis of the same criteria. Yet the criteria seem reasonable and relevant. Moreover, this speciesism is graded, affirming some level of rights for all organisms, rather than dualistic and absolute, affirming rights for some species and denying them to all others. In this value structure, all life forms, as good for themselves and as valued by the ultimate Valuer, have basic moral rights. These rights are minimalistic in moral significance in the case of microorganisms but rise in moral significance with increases in a species' value-creating and value-experiencing capacities. These rights entitle the bearer to appropriate forms of protection from the human community.

Herman Daly and John Cobb summarize this model well in response to biotic egalitarianism:

181

We do not share this view [biotic egalitarianism]. We believe there is more intrinsic value in a human being than in a mosquito or a virus. We also believe that there is more intrinsic value in a chimpanzee or a porpoise than in an earthworm or a bacterium. This judgment of intrinsic value is quite different from the judgment of the importance of a species to the interrelated whole. The interrelated whole would probably survive the extinction of chimpanzees with little damage, but it would be seriously disturbed by the extinction of some species of bacteria. We believe that distinctions of this sort are important as guides to practical life and economic policy and that the insistence that a deep ecologist refuse to make them is an invitation to deep irrelevance.[62]

Some charge, however, that this model of graded value and rights is the hierarchicalism that has been the source of multiple forms of human oppression, including racism and sexism, as well as domination over nature.[63] This model is indisputably hierarchical. That is its strength; it avoids, for instance, the misanthropic implications of biotic egalitarianism in which humans, other mammals, insects, or flowers presumably deserve equal treatment and rights. But the other charges do not follow. This criticism fails to make the important moral distinction between *intra*-species rights, human rights that apply equally to all humans, and *inter*-species rights, which are not equal and which do not prevent, though they clearly restrict, humans from destroying members of other species.[64] Contemporary Christian ethical thought increasingly provides adequate protections against hierarchical models being applied *within* the human community. For instance, the egalitarian implications of *imago dei* provide important safeguards against hierarchical rankings among human groupings, and thereby oppose racism and sexism.

Nonetheless, graded rankings seem indispensable—even inevitable—in making ethical judgments in conflict situations involving humans and other life forms. Nearly all of us act routinely on hierarchical assumptions in our daily lives, like swatting flies that invade our food or even deciding to eat lower on the food chain. Graded rankings, moreover, are not alternatives to or contradictions of ecological interdependence. Rather, they occur in the context of, and with respect for, relationality.

The question, however, that haunts the individualistic pole of an ecological ethic is: is it practical? The prevailing opinion is that ecological individualism is "practically meaningless" or "hopelessly impractical."[65] But that viewpoint may be too simplistic. An adequate answer depends partly on the particular set of rights and restrictions that are being evaluated. An adequate answer also depends, however, on the exercise of moral discernment, or appropriate moral distinctions.

One important distinction is between those organisms whose individuality can be respected as individuals, and those whose individuality can be respected only collectively. In the former case, it is certainly practical to avoid the deliberate and unnecessary squashing of an individual beetle, the dismemberment of an individual fox, or the felling of a particular tree. In the latter case, however, it simply is not practical to respect the individual rights of the millions of microorganisms that reside in every clod of soil, every bucket of lake water and every breath of air. Nonetheless, even in the latter context, nonhuman rights can be respected in the aggregate by responsible, restrained usage. We can respect the conation of other creatures by protecting the earth from profligate consumption, destruction, and pollution. An individualistic strain, therefore, in ecological ethics causes major complications and confusion, but it does not appear to be totally impractical with the proper exercise of moral discernment. Even in the case of microscopic creatures, individual rights can be respected in the aggregate by following the moral maxim: use sparingly, caringly, reverently. We can thereby minimize harm to individuals. Indeed, if frugal use is the only practical way to respect the rights of simple organisms, we do not need to worry in practice about where we draw the boundaries on nonhuman rights.

In our bizarre biosphere, all species are necessarily instrumental values for other species. Various plant and animals, for instance, provide essential food for human beings. Theologically, these creatures can legitimately be regarded as gifts of God to be used without guilt (but not without a yearning for the Isianic hope!). Yet, these creatures also are ends in themselves and ought to be treated as such. One important way for humans to balance the instrumental and intrinsic values of other creatures is to practice restrained consumption. Frugality is a prime ecological virtue.

At the other pole, an adequate Christian ecological ethic must be holistic, concerned about collective connections.

From my perspective, abiotic elements (like minerals and gases) and ecosystemic wholes cannot be said to have moral rights in any strict sense, since they lack conation. Yet, precisely because conative creatures pervade the biosphere, it still seems legitimate to speak compositely and metaphorically, though not quite literally, about the "rights of nature." Whether or not this claim is defensible, there is no

183

doubt that systemic wholes, composed of diverse biotic and abiotic elements in interaction, are indispensable instruments—systemic values—for the ends of all rights-bearers.

Parasitism and predation, as well as geological and climatic dynamics, mean that the relationships among the parts of ecosystems are ambiguous—harmful and helpful, destructive and creative—for species and their members. The arctic wolf, for example, is a nemesis of the caribou, but this carnivore still contributes to the overall health of the caribou herd by culling the weak and encouraging the survival of the genetically fittest. The wolf also unintentionally promotes a balance between the number of caribou and the carrying capacity of their environment. Similarly, the upheavals of earthquakes and volcanoes create new geographical formations like mountains and islands. The process destroys countless individuals and sometimes even extinguishes whole species; it also prompts the gradual emergence of new species that effectively adapt to the new environments.

Ironically, these ambiguous relationships among the parts are essential for the well-being of the wholes. They contribute to the "common good" of ecosystems and the ecosphere—and reciprocally, the only possibility of good for species and their members depends on the common good of these systems. The common good certainly does not guarantee the survival of individuals or even of particular species. In fact, the very system that sustains individual organisms also eventually destroys them. The same is true of most species. Significantly less than 1 percent of the total number of plant and animal species that have ever existed still exist. Nonetheless, the essential conditions for a species surviving and thriving for a time depend on the common good—ecosystems with maximum diversity of interacting life forms in healthy habitats.

This dependence on the ecological common good is why any ecological ethic must value and nurture ecosystems and the ecosphere as wholes. Thus James Gustafson is right in posing a basic question for Christian ethics: "What is God enabling and requiring us, in the patterns and processes of the interdependence of life in the world, to be and to do?"[66] Unlike most other ethicists, Gustafson is acutely conscious of the fact that a central concern of Christian ethics must be the relationships among parts to wholes, especially responsible human participation in the interdependent systems of the biophysical world.[67] Ethics, especially ecological ethics, must think holistically and relationally.

This concern for relationality also is the fundamental truth in Aldo Leopold's ecocentric "land ethic": "A thing is right when it tends to preserve the integrity, stability, and beauty of the biotic community. It is wrong when it tends otherwise."[68] For Leopold, the "land ethic" is an enlargement of the boundaries of moral concern to include "soils, waters, plants and animals, or collectively: the land."[69] The land is the source of life, "a fountain of [ecological] energy flowing through a circuit of soils, plants, and animals."[70] Its care requires "love, respect, and admiration,"[71] and its components have a "right" to exist.[72] "In short," according to Leopold, "a land ethic changes the role of *Homo sapiens* from conqueror of the land-community to plain member and citizen of it. It implies respect for . . . fellow-members, and also respect for the community as such."[73]

It is unfair to take Leopold's summary maxim of the "land ethic" out of context and accuse him of "environmental fascism," since a respect for individuals is evident in Leopold. Though it is important to avoid environmental fascism, it is equally important to follow Leopold and avoid *nonecological atomism*, which respects individuals in isolation from a holistic context, the ecological common good. Ecological systems are critically important for environmental justice. Indeed, environmental justice is a fantasy without a holistic consciousness and concern, since ecological systems supply the essential conditions for the realization of the rights of all creatures.

The moral problem of individuals and collectives will never be resolved so long as "biocentric individualism" and "ecocentric holism"[74] are seen, as they often are, as competing ideologies or alternative ethical systems. Both perspectives are truncated in isolation. The best hope for resolution, I believe, is in ethical interpretations that regard the two together as a form of the complementary polarities described by Philip Wogaman.[75] They are not mutually exclusive but rather mutually dependent: "Neither pole can continue to exist without some inclusion of the apparent opposite."[76] The two poles must be held in appropriate balance in different situations. Just as humans are social beings for whom the common good is constitutive of the well-being of individuals and vice versa, so all living creatures—including humans—are ecological beings for whom the well-being of wholes is inextricably and reciprocally linked with the well-being of individuals. The individualistic and collectivistic poles—a rights ethic and a land ethic—must be held in tandem, for ultimately they are not two competing ethics, but complementary sides of one ecological ethic.

185

A BILL OF BIOTIC RIGHTS

What are the rights of nonhuman creatures? Thus far, I have concentrated on the complications surrounding this question. Now I must deal with this question directly—and succinctly. My purpose here is best served by simple generalizations accompanied by brief explanations.

Certain caveats, however, are in order. First, in accord with the ecological purpose of this study, my focus is strictly on "wild" nature, the rights of nonhuman creatures in their natural habitats. The human use and abuse of domesticated and other culturally controlled animals, while related, raise special and serious moral problems that are beyond my present purview. Second, the rights listed are not discrete; they overlap, but each adds a dimension to the whole. Better listings will in time overcome this problem. Third, all the rights outlined apply to both *individuals and species.* Fourth, these rights are not absolute for individuals; they can be overridden for moral reasons. Yet, these rights may very well be absolute or near-absolute when applied to nearly all species, as I shall indicate in the next section. Fifth, the nonhuman rights outlined below are considerably different from human rights, since human rights include but far exceed biotic rights. That fact should alleviate some of the major misunderstandings about nonhuman rights. Sixth, the intention behind this catalogue is inclusive rather than exhaustive. In other words, the rights apply to all species, but this does not preclude the possibility of additional rights being recognized for particular species, such as chimpanzees or dogs, because of their greater intrinsic value.

Finally, in articulating the rights of "wild" otherkind, I am in effect defining human responsibilities, since only humans are moral agents capable of respecting rights. These rights, then, are justifiable claims on humans for the basic conditions necessary for the well-being of otherkind. They are specifications of the content of human ecological responsibility.

With these caveats in mind, I propose the following general rights (both freedoms from interference and provisions of essential goods) as the just claims of nonhuman species and their members:

1. *The right to participate in the natural competition for existence.* Biophysical processes do not show much concern for individual lives, human or otherkind. They are ambiguous. That is why ethics cannot simply let nature be its guide. Ethics embodies a dimension of defiance of nature, as Schweitzer well understood. Yet, trophic relationships— members of all species feeding on members of other species—do not

allow for a formal right to life of nonhuman individuals. That claim could lead to moral absurdities, such as preventing "bad" predators from feeding on their prey. In this context, the best way to show moral concern for the welfare of species and the maximum possible number of their members is to respect the integrity of nature, by letting species and their members work out their own interactions and adaptations in the struggle for survival, without unwarranted human protections and interventions. This implies the acceptance of the processes of nature's wild, chaotic order, without, for example, moralistic diatribes against "brutal" carnivores, or "taming" initiatives to organize ecosystems into "kinder and gentler" orders. The moral role of humans is not to protect otherkind from their natural foes, but rather to defend them from injustices, of which humans are the only perpetrators.[77]

2. *The right to satisfaction of their basic needs and the opportunity to perform their individual and/or ecosystemic functions* (whether predator or prey, parasite or host, scavenger or decomposer, oxygen- and protein-producer, or whatever). These are among the essential conditions of the welfare of otherkind, the very core of the concept of rights. This right may simply be a specification of the first; if so, it is an important specification. The intention is to say that human respect for nature implies the preservation of the structures of existence, the sources of survival, for the needs of members of species.

3. *The right to healthy and whole habitats.* This right includes both the general condition of the environment (for instance, a pollution-free atmosphere, without acid rain, global warming, and ozone depletion) and the specialized habitats necessary for the survival of their kind (for instance, large tracts of fire-dependent, immature jack pines in central Michigan for the Kirtland's Warbler). The prevention of dehabitation and the promotion of healthy habitats are probably the most effective means of furthering the good of species and their members.

4. *The right to reproduce their own kind.* Genetic reproduction is a vital function of all species—indeed, seemingly the primary goal or urge of some species. It is, of course, the *sine qua non* of species' preservation. Members of wild species should be free to propagate their own kind, without chemical, radioactive, or bioengineered distortions.

5. *The right to fulfill their evolutionary potential with freedom from human-induced extinctions.* Extinctions have been a "normal" part of the evolutionary process. Human-induced extinctions, however, occurring at an unparalleled and appalling pace, can and should be prevented as a matter of justice. Until the end of a species' natural time, it should be free to propagate and develop its evolutionary potential,

which may include growth in its value-experiencing and -creating capacities, or development through mutations and adaptations into new species.

6. *The right to freedom from human cruelty, flagrant abuse, or frivolous use.* This right provides formal moral protection from such practices as recreational hunting (in contrast to subsistence hunting), destroying elephants to make ivory trinkets from their tusks and umbrella stands from their legs, and trapping fur-bearers to provide decorations for the distastefully opulent. The proper treatment of nonhuman creatures is more than a matter of kindness; it is a demand of justice.

7. *The right to redress through human interventions, to restore a semblance of the natural conditions disrupted by human actions.* Paul Taylor calls this process of compensation or reparations to amend wrongs "the principle of restitutive justice": "The perpetrating of a harm calls for the producing of a benefit. The greater the harm, the larger the benefit needed to fulfill the moral obligation."[78] The duty and costs of restoration are owed by all in modern societies, since all have benefitted from the amenities produced through environmental destruction.[79] This right entails managerial interventions. Under optimum conditions of wildness, it is best to adopt a *laissez faire* strategy, to let nature take its course without the dubious benefit of human managers. Previous human disruptions, however, mean that these optimum conditions frequently do not prevail. Interventions are necessary to enable a return to the closest possible approximation of the original natural interactions. Examples of this redress are clean-ups of polluted rivers and bays, the reintroduction of rare raptors through artificial breeding programs, the restoration of strip mines, the regulation of water in the Everglades, and the use of controlled fires to simulate natural conditions essential for the vitality of certain ecosystems like the California chaparral.

8. *The right to a fair share of the goods necessary for the sustainability of one's species.* This right has been implied by several other rights, but it is worth stating on its own. It is a requirement of distributive justice. Determining a fair share, however, is a mind-boggling task. One important guideline is that no species should be deprived of the resources necessary for the *perpetual* sustainability of a viable population. Perpetuality is a critical qualifier of sustainability. Humans can insure the survival of most endangered species with relative ease for fifty to one hundred years, the typical time lines suggested for how far we need to "think ahead." The real challenge—the one that revolutionizes ecological perspective—is perpetuality, providing spe-

cies with a fair share of the resources necessary to preserve their kind until the end of their natural time. This right is assisted by the maintenance of national and regional parks, wilderness areas, wildlife refuges, and other sanctuaries. The idea of "no net loss" in wetlands and other habitats may be one way to implement this right. In fact, however, we have reached a point in habitat destruction where we must think in terms of net gains to make this right a reality. A "fair share" for all species morally stifles human imperialism.

These rights probably can be supplemented, maybe condensed, and certainly revised. Those outlined here are sufficient, however, to establish my understanding of nonhuman rights and, I hope, to stimulate some profitable debate. If justice is applicable to nonhuman creatures, and if rights are essential to the idea of justice, then Christian ethics has a major task ahead in defining, delineating, and defending biotic rights.

PRIMA FACIE BIOTIC RIGHTS

Rights, however, even human rights generally, are not absolute and inviolable. They are *prima facie* rights, which we have strong reasons for honoring unless we have stronger moral reasons for not doing so. Thus the rights of individual members of species and even large aggregates of them can be overridden when rights conflict and moral claims compete. In rare cases, when no reasonable alternatives exist, and when no disproportionate ecological harm will result, even the deliberate eradication of particular species can be justified to provide vital protections for human health. The case, however, must be exceptionally strong; a "superkilling" requires a "superjustification"[80]—which can and should be made against pathogens and parasites whose basic ecological function is to prey on humans. The guinea worm, the infamous parasite that seriously afflicts millions of Third World residents annually, and against which the World Health Organization has launched a campaign, seems to be a legitimate candidate for this distinction. Several bacteria and viruses also qualify. It must be emphasized, however, that these cases are rare, and require compelling reasons, including the absence of substitute measures. A "nice place for a new mall" will not do.

The relativity of nonhuman rights is critical, because humans, as predatorial consumers in the biosphere, could not survive and exercise their creative potential if nonhuman rights were absolute. In fact, the very concept of nonhuman rights seems absurd unless conceived as *prima facie* in character. As participants in the midst of the natural tragedy of interspecies competition, humans have limited rights to secure their well-being by destroying other forms of life and their habitats.

Though the rights of nonhuman creatures are not inviolable, neither are they violable with impunity. That would make rights meaningless. Biotic rights can be overridden only for clear moral reasons (just causes) and only within the limitations of proportionality and discrimination. Based on my assumption of a hierarchy of rights and values, the degree of justification for an override would rise in intensity from very slight for microorganisms to very significant for complex mammals.

Among the just causes for annulling the rights of nonhuman creatures, or at least some of them for the sake of others, seem to be the following: (1) the satisfaction of basic human needs (for instance, food, clothing, shelter, and medicine); (2) the realization of valuable human benefits (expressions of human creativity and structures of civilization, like means of transportation and centers of economic exchange—but always within the bounds of frugality and sustainability); (3) the exercise of self-defense against crop-destroying insects, harmful bacteria, urban rats, and marauding mosquitoes (Anyone who has ever tried to hike the Snake Bight Trail in the Everglades on a muggy August morn understands this last reference!); (4) the control of the population of prolific species—especially ecological aliens—to prevent them from exceeding the carrying capacities of their environments; (5) the special protection of rare, endangered, or vulnerable species or subspecies from their natural competitors and predators;[81] and (6) the protection of ecologically essential species, including certain soil microorganisms, to maintain, for instance, the viability of given food chains.

Even when a just cause exists, however, other moral constraints are essential to minimize harm to nonhuman creatures. Otherwise, for example, it is possible to justify excessive means for worthwhile ends, like insecticiding or filling a swamp, rather than screening the windows, to provide protection from the nightly nuisance of mosquitoes. Thus the principles of proportionality and discrimination—dominant criteria in the just war theory (conflated here)—are also critical instruments of justice in an ecological context.

Proportionality counsels us that harm to other creatures and their habitats is justified only when necessary (the "last resort," absence of substitutes, or only reasonable alternative), only to the extent necessary (minimal harm or the economic use of destructive means), and only if the values—social and ecological—realized in the achievement of an end outweigh the inevitable losses resulting from destructive means.

The principle of discrimination adds that destructive acts should be focused or targeted on intended objectives, rather than dispersed or generalized, so that harm to "innocent bystanders" or unintended side effects are prevented or minimized. This principle raises serious questions, for example, about the widespread use of chemical pesticides, which frequently are indiscriminate, destroying "beneficial" insects and birds along with the "pests" that are the objects of the attack.

Interpreting nonhuman rights as *prima facie* in character is necessary but precarious. This approach leads to no fixed conclusions when claims conflict. Moral judgments can differ for many legitimate reasons, including disputes about the "facts" or the moral significance of the "facts." Moreover, this approach can sometimes be followed formally to rationalize some ecologically mournful consequences, like destroying the habitat of a species or subspecies for some ignoble or allegedly noble end or private economic gain. That is why the spirit of the laws is what finally counts. And for Christian ethics, the spirit is the total meaning of love in an ecological context. In complex cases, that spirit not only places the burden of proof on the proponents of overrides of nonhuman rights, but it also gives the benefit of the doubt to the rights of nonhuman creatures.

CONCLUSION

A biocentric-ecocentric ethic inevitably will be interpreted by many as an eccentric ethic. Some will see it as excessive sentimentality. I prefer to describe it as essential sensitivity. Yet, after the pejoratives and euphemisms, the bottom line remains: what does Christian love demand of us in defining our responsibilities to and ordering our relationships with our neighbors in nature? I believe that concepts of justice and rights are fundamental elements in answering this question, but I have no illusions that I have resolved the problems or concluded the debate. The question remains as a critical challenge to Christian ethics—one that has potentially revolutionary consequences and one that can no longer be ignored in an age of ecological crisis.

Moral entitlements, however, have comparatively little functional value unless they are also social entitlements—unless they are structured in the ethos, policies, and laws of human communities. What, then, are the implications of the foregoing conceptions of love and justice in an ecological context for new directions in public policies for the nineties and beyond? That is the basic question for the last chapter.

191

CHAPTER EIGHT

POLITICAL DIRECTIONS FOR ECOLOGICAL INTEGRITY

POLITICS IN ETHICAL PERSPECTIVE

F rom an ethical perspective, politics is much more than the art of the possible; it is an essential means for realizing the desirable. In other words, politics is not only about the mastery of the methods of power—though that dimension cannot be dismissed as morally disdainful. More important, politics is about the responsible use of power to bring ethical goals like justice to fruition. Ethically, politics is the way that a pluralistic society ought to govern itself in order to insure that all parties in conflict have a say in decisions, to conciliate rival interests, and to advance social peace and justice. It is a means not only of controlling social evils, but also of promoting the general welfare. The essential moral problem is *not* the *presence* of politics in society, but rather its absence or perversion—when, for instance, the bulk of the people (as in totalitarianism) or particular segments of the populace (as in historic racism and sexism in the United States) are excluded from participation in public decision-making or sharing in social benefits. They are thus pushed into resistance or rebellion, prime signs of the breakdown of politics.[1]

Understood in this sense, politics is an ethical enterprise that no responsible individual or institution can ignore or denigrate. That may be especially true for Christians and their churches. Those Christians who draw a sharp distinction between a personal and social gospel, who argue that the role of the church is the conversion of individuals rather than the reformation of society, imply by their rhetoric and behavior not only that the arena of politics is irrelevant to the concerns of faith

192

but also that the gospel is irrelevant to the decisions of politics. Such an insulation of the Christian religion from politics is theologically indefensible. It is a functional denial of the sovereignty of God in Christ and the ubiquitous involvement of the Spirit.

The gospel relates to *all* creatures and it applies in *all* situations—personal, ecclesial, social, and ecological. The gospel rejects all forms of moral parochialism. The tradition insists that Christ cannot be compartmentalized, locked in some docetic closet. The God known in Christ is central in individual "spiritual" lives, but also is sovereign over the social, economic, and political realms. This God comforts the afflicted, hears prayers, converts minds, and compels proclamation. However, this God is also *political*, blessing the peacemakers, intervening in the affairs of governments and nations, and liberating slaves from the shackles of pharaoh. To be in communion with God the Politician, this "lover of justice" and "Prince of Peace," is to struggle to deliver the community of earth from all manner of evil—private *and* public, personal *and* social, cultural *and* ecological, spiritual *and* material. The sovereign God bans all boundaries on benevolence.

In our complex and technical world, economic and political systems powerfully affect the lives of all of us—too frequently benefiting the "haves" and harming the "have-nots." The regional and national capitals of our world are the scenes where the destinies of billions of humans and millions of species will be determined. Humans are by nature ecological and political animals, inseparably bound together in a web of biological and communal relationships. These entanglements are our true "original position," and they are enhanced in mass societies. Thus, if Christian churches are committed to feeding the hungry, clothing the naked, healing the sick, setting at liberty the oppressed, challenging the powers that be, and exalting those of low degree (all of which characterized the ministry of Jesus and, therefore, ought to characterize the ministry of the apostolic church, according to the Magnificat of Mary and Jesus' reading from Isaiah in the Temple), the churches dare not ignore the political and economic contexts of these concerns. Every political issue that affects biospheric welfare—whether it be the nuclear arms race or the unemployment rate, starvation or pollution, racism or extinctions—is simultaneously a moral and spiritual concern, and, therefore, a challenge to love. If we are to deal with social causes and not merely individual symptoms, these issues in their political settings must be items on the agenda of a truly catholic, evangelical, and reformed church.

The Christian church, therefore, cannot make any theologically phony distinctions between personal rebirth and social reform. It is called to proclaim and live the whole gospel, not some expurgated version of it, in loyalty to the Christ who seeks to minister through all humanity and in all contexts to all the needs and rights of all creatures. Love, therefore, demands the pursuit of justice, peace, and ecological integrity in the realm of politics. Indeed, politics is a critical context for the expression of Christian love.

On these assumptions, this chapter is an effort to spell out some of the major political directions for ecological integrity, directions that are consistent with Christian theology and ethics and that are especially important in the light of the character of the ecological crisis. The emphasis is on the political ends rather than the specific strategies or policies to effect these ends. Some might call these directions "middle axioms," the connecting links between theological-ethical norms and concrete policies like laws and regulations. That term is not wildly popular today, but I think the concept behind it is valid: we need guidelines that embody the somewhat lofty norms of Christian ethics and yet are relevant to the ecological crisis in our time. They are not necessarily absolute, relevant for all times, though they may be. They are not sufficient—specific moral judgments are also important—but they seem necessary. Whatever name is given to these directions, they are not retreats into irrelevant generalities or abstractions.[2] They are *means of guiding us in designing and assessing specific answers to concrete problems* in ways that promote the "best possible" approximation of Christian norms.

Three qualifications of these political directions, however, are necessary.

First, I am concentrating on *political* responsibilities, not only because of my personal interests, but also because these responsibilities often get shortchanged in Christian circles. Value and life-style changes usually receive prime attention. One can find a host of helpful resources on personal changes—50, 75, 101, and 750 things you can do to save our planet.[3] Yet, without political initiatives and reforms, these life-style corrections may serve little more than therapeutic functions, making the practitioners "feel good" or righteous. The political process is the only place where the rules of relationships for a given society are officially established and where sufficient power might be mustered to match the current scale of the ecological crisis. An apolitical posture on contemporary ecological concerns, therefore, is righteous irrelevance.

I am certainly not suggesting, however, that changes in personal values and life-styles and in the social ethos are insignificant or secondary. Ecological conversions of individuals and communities are essential, and they often start with "ecotrivia." In fact, these conversions are generally the root cause of political transformations. Without the prodding, pressuring, and persuading of the official actors in the political process by reform-minded citizens and their organizations, political change is not likely. Moreover, without the voluntary compliance of most citizens on most occasions to laws and regulations perceived as generally reasonable, political decisions would have little public impact.

Equally, however, politically created laws and regulations can have transformative effects, not only on *behavior* through enforcement procedures, but also on public *values* and *attitudes*. Laws against discrimination, for example, have sometimes reduced prejudices. Political changes can even impel technological innovations. When a resistant Detroit was forced in the seventies to comply with stricter auto emission standards, which it argued were economically ruinous and technologically unfeasible, the auto manufacturers somehow managed to produce the catalytic converter and celebrated their new-found commitment to clean air.[4] In effect, laws and regulations themselves can function as catalytic converters of values and behavioral patterns. Thus the relationships between consent and coercion—between personal values and a social ethos, on the one hand, and political mandates, on the other—are complex and dialectical. Both are necessary; neither is sufficient without the other.

Second, my reason for focusing on directions or guidelines is not ideological but strictly practical: I am simply trying to manage an awesome volume of complex concreteness, and not suggesting that Christians and their churches should be similarly restricted in their political advocacy. Legislative and regulatory proposals for ecological protection are abundant, reflecting the breadth and depth of the crisis. For example, *Blueprint for the Environment,* a comprehensive product of twenty major environmental organizations, contains 511 proposals for Federal action alone[5]—and the vast majority of these proposals seems morally important. I could not even contemplate making a moral evaluation of more than a handful of these proposals, and that approach would, in fact, defeat my broader purpose. Yet, political action by Christians and their churches requires involvement in selected specifics.

The process of specificity does entail some risks for the churches. No straight line can be drawn from theology and ethics to public policy.

Too many factual disputes, judgment calls, value conflicts, moral dilemmas, uncomfortable compromises, and unholy alliances block the way. The translation of Christian faith into moral norms and then into prudential laws and regulations is a complex and ambiguous process, and that translation becomes more tenuous with each step toward specificity. Consequently, Christian political activity must be tempered by the realization that no political posture, party, or platform can adequately represent a Christian ideal. On most political issues— though I can never say all, since some stances seem clearly compatible or incompatible with Christian norms—contrary positions among Christians are "ethically possible." Christians, therefore, must be aggressively alert to the dangers of the political captivity of the churches and to the relaxation of the critical tension between religious ideals and their ambiguous embodiments in the necessary compromises of politics.

Nevertheless, Christians and their churches must still take the risks of specificity in order to avoid political ineffectiveness and irrelevance. Specificity is "where the action is" politically. To those who argue that the churches should stick to the articulation of moral principles in order to avoid the risk of tarnishing the image of the faith with error or exceeding the bounds of their competency, Roy Enquist makes a telling response:

> Since the church, at its base, stands or falls on God's willingness to justify the ungodly, it is mistaken to demand that impeccability be a requirement for ethical witness. Perfectionism is no more appropriate in the shaping of social teaching than in any other churchly activity. It is the unwillingness to attempt to speak a concrete Word of the Lord in our time of moral squalor, rather than the inability to do it perfectly, that renders the community's witness suspect.[6]

Thus my focus on political directions is not a tacit counsel for the churches to avoid political specifics, but rather an effort to suggest guidelines for Christians and their churches in structuring and evaluating these specifics.

Finally, this effort to link Christian theology and ethics to public policy does not imply the "Christianization of the social order." I am not suggesting any uniquely Christian solutions to the ecological crisis, let alone any impositions of peculiar Christian moral perspectives on the state. The state is the instrument of society, not an extension of the church. Rather, I am proposing a Christian basis for seeking solutions with others on whatever common moral grounds we can find and in whatever alliances are feasible. That, after all, is the nature of politics. In a pluralistic context (and what modern society isn't?), the church must justify its public stances on public, rational grounds. That raises many complicated questions for Christian ethics that cannot be discussed here.[7] Yet, the evidence seems to indicate that Christians will find—indeed, have found—common grounds for political action with a host of allies. The ecological objectives of many environmental organizations, for example, are usually compatible with Christian theological and ethical formulations—indeed, to a far fuller extent than the positions of the churches themselves have often been. This compatibility should not be greatly surprising. Not only are many "secular" environmentalists proposing solutions that are reasonable responses to the nature of the problems, but they, too, are the beneficiaries of divine proddings. According to classical Christian theology, the Spirit of God pervades the cosmos, renewing, reconciling, and enlightening the peoples of all nations and ultimate convictions.

With these qualifications in mind, what political goals should Christians pursue in their quest for ecological integrity? What features should characterize the legislation, regulations, and policies that Christians support in their efforts to relate Christian theology and ethics to the ecological crisis? The following directions are certainly not exhaustive, but they seem to me to be the most critically important now.

RESOLVING THE ECONOMICS-ECOLOGY DILEMMA

An ecologically sound and morally responsible public policy must continually resolve the economics-ecology dilemma.

The dilemma is real. It is not simply a myth concocted by the greed of robber barons. It is part of an ancient problem, the conflict between the conservation and consumption of resources. Probably every generation and culture of sufficient technical means have faced the dilemma, when human needs and aspirations have exceeded ecological possibilities. It is now a ubiquitous problem of unprecedented proportions as a growing population armed with sophisticated technology creates widespread ecological havoc. As noted in chapter 2, the dilemma is evident in every dimension of the crisis, from the toleration of toxins to the destruction of wild habitats, usually in the name of economic necessity. The northern spotted owl versus the

197

loggers of the Pacific Northwest is an oversimplified symbol—since the issue is saving a whole ecosystem[8]—of a problem that exists in countless locales, from the rain forests in Brazil to the coke ovens in Clairton, Pennsylvania. Economics and ecology cannot be compartmentalized. They interpenetrate and confront us with ethical dilemmas.

Probably every act of ecological protection has some economic consequences, good and bad. The negative effects are usually exaggerated, sometimes wildly exaggerated, by those who will endure economic liabilities. Nonetheless, these effects are often real. It is deceptive, even if politically palatable, to pretend otherwise. The negative effects for particular enterprises may include job losses, profit losses, plant closures, reductions in competitive status, higher costs, technological renovations, and community dislocations—not to mention buffeted politicians. True, for instance, the Clean Air Act of 1990 probably will reduce employment in the higher-sulfur coal industry and increase electricity costs. Protecting old-growth forests may force some loggers to search for alternative jobs, just as the banning of DDT and restrictions against excessive catches by commercial fisheries have had similar effects. But these liabilities may, and often do, have offsetting economic benefits for society. The demand for ecological soundness may stimulate new commercial opportunities, new technologies, and new jobs. Thus environmental protection is expected to be a growth industry in the upcoming decades, and investments are rising in corporations that, for example, specialize in recycling and pollution-prevention devices like coal scrubbers.

These potential consequences must be seen in a broader perspective. The fact is that similar economic disruptions occur daily in market economies as a result of "normal" competitive interactions. They are not peculiar consequences of ecological protection. Technological innovations, for instance, are a main factor in economic change, and their negative effects are generally considered the "price of progress." The advent of the automobile, for instance, certainly had an adverse effect on horsetraders and blacksmiths. Similar economic consequences—good and ill—can be cited for nearly every other technological innovation, from can openers to computers. The argument for destroying ecosystems in order to maintain economic security or expand economic development in a given setting is really an argument for economic inertia, when economic transitions and dislocations are the standard expectations in the ordinary course of modern, particularly market, economies. Ecological protection cannot be dismissed simply as an economic liability. It offers values—including some long-term economic benefits for the whole society—to which economic enterprises must adapt, just as they expect to do to other socioeconomic changes, from child labor laws to technological innovations.

Yet, this argument is not an excuse for doing nothing. Letting the mechanisms of the market take their course is part of the classical callousness of unreconstructed capitalism. Whatever the cause, unemployment can mean physical deprivation and psychological trauma, while mill closures, particularly in one-industry towns, can be destructive of communal ties and public revenues. Whether the cause of the problem is ecological protection or any other economic disruption, government interventions are usually necessary to ease these pains and enable effective transitions. Imaginative and sensitive strategies are critical. These include not only the standardized unemployment insurance, but also counseling, job retraining, employment assistance, economic incentives to attract new enterprises, and regulations to ensure fairness to workers in unavoidable plant closures. These strategies are a part of what it means to resolve the economics-ecology dilemma in microcosmic settings.

The dilemma, however, is also macrocosmic. It is a systemic problem that revolves around the ideology of economic growth. No technical correctives will resolve this dilemma!

Growth-mania is a prime tenet of the North American economic faith. It is a bipartisan commitment, almost an imperative of patriotism. Indeed, internationally, economic growth has become for many nations an obsession that unites capitalism, socialism, and mixed economic ideologies. Allegedly, the perpetual expansion of production and consumption is necessary for progress and prosperity—measured quantitatively in GNP, counting even the losses of ecological "capital" in natural resources as assets, rather than deducting them as liabilities—to satisfy the insatiable wants of consumers, and to provide employment opportunities for an expanding population.

The growth system, however, is morally ambiguous. Just as Edmund Burke did "not know the method of drawing up an indictment against a whole people," so I do not know how to draw up a full-scale indictment against economic growth. But neither can I give a wholesale exoneration. In the North American context, the market method of economic growth offers us a mixed assortment of blessings and curses.

On the positive side, growth has fostered some important—in some cases, indispensable—values: profits as incentives to energize the system; jobs in the tens of millions; a multitude of goods and services;

199

capital for investments and improvements; tax revenues for government programs, including ecological protection; creativity and technological innovations, some of which are environmentally beneficial; and philanthropic benefits that have strengthened voluntary associations, including churches.

Negatively, the capitalistic growth system has some glaring deficiencies. It is not designed to satisfy the needs of the poor and the powerless. Thus millions suffer in the absence of adequate government interventions and assistance. Wealth is severely maldistributed: unemployment and underemployment remain high while the economic elect luxuriate in profligate consumption, capable literally of stifling reform by "buying" elections and votes. Moreover, even the fans of the system agree that it caters to "marketing hedonism," responding to and creating every conceivable desire of people, no matter how "bizarre or ignoble," in order to provide goods and services to meet these demands.[9] "Born to Shop" is the bumper sticker-motto of the human product of this process. The system is generally microcosmically efficient as individual suppliers seek to cut their costs for competitive purposes, but it is macrocosmically inefficient as the total economic product incorporates a wealth of waste and irrelevancies to human welfare.

Most important for our present purposes, economic growth is a major factor in destroying the ecosystems on which the well-being of social and economic systems ultimately depends. Unrestrained production and consumption are key factors in the excessive exploitation and toxication of the renewable and nonrenewable gifts of nature.

The ideology of economic growth tends to assume the indestructibility and inexhaustibility of the products and capacities of nature. This assumption makes this ideology a *utopian illusion!* It ignores the ecological reality of limits and is, therefore, ecologically and economically unrealistic. Unbridled economic growth is eventually destructive of the conditions for economic health. Economic systems—indeed, all social systems—cannot be sustained unless environmental systems are sustained, because human welfare depends on the productivity and integrity of the natural world. Our dilemma is that we want contradictory goals: economic growth and ecological sustainability. Increasingly, it appears that the nations cannot sustain both. One of the "laws of nature" is that human activities must stay within the bounds of nature.

Economic conversion to ecological sustainability, then, appears to be a social, economic, and ecological necessity. Though some forms of economic development are ecologically neutral or "friendly"—various services and "soft" (renewable and decentralized) technologies, for example—and should continue,[10] our nation can neither tolerate nor survive the indiscriminate material development that has character-ized the "American way of life." We need alternatives, and they should be grounded on the ecological virtues outlined in chapter 2. Practically, these alternatives include simpler life-styles, vigorous conservation of energy and other resources, comprehensive recycling, sufficient regulations, polluter-pays penalties, sustainable biodiversity, interna-tional cooperation, and the equitable sharing of economic goods.

One option that needs to be explored seriously is the steady-state economy or "ecological economics"[11] long associated with economist Herman Daly. Daly's complex package, recently restated with John Cobb, emphasizes "sustainable development" as opposed to economic growth, growth in human well-being rather than material productivity, persons-in-community rather than radical individualism, progressive (and "pro-business") taxation, "limited inequality" between rich and poor, "soft" (renewable and decentralized) energy paths, provisions for public control of population, decentralization of political and economic power, relative self-sufficiency of nations and regions rather than competition in the international growth race, and international cooperation.[12]

The steady-state model has been rejected by most conservative and liberal economists, from Julian Simon[13] to Lester Thurow.[14] I personally have serious reservations about some elements of Daly's plan, for instance, the proposals on population control and national self-sufficiency. I doubt that the latter is desirable in a context of globalization; moreover, the extent of decentralization in Daly seems at one point at least to suggest balkanization.[15] Nevertheless, Daly's basic model may be technically feasible, and it seems generally compatible with traditional Christian norms for economic life.

A major issue, however, is whether this model is psychologically and politically possible in the foreseeable future. It is clearly "not possible" now. Resistance would be massive. Yet, unpredictable and critical circumstances can radically shift public attitudes and political behavior, as recent events in Germany, Eastern Europe, and the Soviet republics forcefully remind us. Realism now must allow for potentialities previously declared unrealistic. In any case, some version of the steady-state model seems to be the only potentially realistic means of resolving the economics-ecology dilemma. If so, a major challenge to

So general!!

the churches for the immediate decades will be to form an alternative model to North America's present brand of economic growth. We need a model that enables both the sustainability of a sound and fair economy *and* the integrity of the ecosphere, one that truly represents an "ecological economics."

Yet, the major moral problem with a strategy of economic equilibrium is that it seemingly cannot be applied globally at present. The model fits well the situation of overdeveloped nations with their excessive production and consumption, but it does not fit the situation of impoverished nations. The Third World countries need quantitatively increased material productivity—economic growth—in order to satisfy their citizens' basic needs for food, energy, health care, housing, education, and transportation. Opposition to growth in this context is a formula for the persistence of poverty.

Thus a new concept has emerged from the World Commission for Environment and Development to resolve the economics-ecology dilemma under conditions of mass poverty: "sustainable development."[16] This concept has become the current slogan in some environmental circles. Others, however, see it as vague and contradictory,[17]—and not without plenty of justification, since the World Commission itself seems to equivocate in its perspectives on growth, alternately offering lauds and alarms. Unlike Daly and Cobb, moreover, the Commission does not distinguish between growth and development—the former being quantitative and unsustainable, while the latter may be sustainable, since it is qualitative improvement without necessarily being quantitative.[18]

Yet, the concept of sustainable development still seems to be an accurate reflection of a critical dilemma and an important synthesis of two imperatives in tension. Poor nations need development, and that almost certainly includes sufficient quantitative productivity or economic growth. But they also need sustainability, living within the bounds of the regenerative, absorptive, and carrying capacities of their regions. These twin objectives will require a virtual revolution in energy efficiency, soft energy paths, ecologically suitable technology, pollution controls, recycling, renewable resource stewardship, income redistribution, population controls, and the protection of biodiversity. These are the very same requirements of the First World, but with the added complication of starting from a much lower base. The issue is not economic development per se, but the kind or quality of development.

None of this takes the United States and other affluent nations off the hook. Resolving the economics-ecology dilemma in the Third World will be difficult. But it may be impossible without major economic and technical assistance from the First World, and especially limits on our production, consumption, and accumulation in order to enable the material conditions for sustainable development globally. It would be ecologically disastrous, most environmentalists agree, for the rest of the world to reach our contemporary North American standards of living. Equally, it would be ethically intolerable to argue that they should not do so while we continue to extend our patterns of economic "normalcy." Charges of racism, classism, elitism, parasitism, and whatever else would be justified in this instance. From a Christian perspective of global solidarity and equality of human value, this situation implies limits to growth for the affluent and economic sharing with the poor.

This situation also requires a major redefinition of human needs and wants in relation to "quality of life." As long as humans are defined economically—and often ethically—as the Grand Acquisitors, motivated by insatiable wants, the prospects for frugality and limits on prosperity are not promising. However, this interpretation of human nature corresponds with neither empirical data nor Christian norms. Humans are far more than consumers, and they *do* have the moral capacities to control and distribute consumption. On this assumption, a critical question that the prosperous must ask is: how much is enough in quantity to sustain a high quality of life *and* to ensure that others, present and future, have the same opportunity? With a long though often neglected tradition of preaching frugality, the churches can be helpful in this redefinition of material adequacy.

REGULATORY SUFFICIENCY

An ecologically sound and morally responsible public policy will include public regulations that are sufficient to match social and ecological needs.

Whatever posture on economic growth finally prevails, the resolution of economics-ecology dilemmas will require stronger public regulations and enforcement procedures. This need includes not only regional and national rules, but also, in a context of global interdependence, international treaties and codes of conduct to control, for example, abuses by multinational corporations.

As much as we might wish otherwise, self-regulation and market competition, while indispensably valuable, are insufficient to provide

203

adequate environmental protection. Otherwise, the probability is too high that greed and other economically motivated behavior—even if exhibited only by a small minority—will lead to environmental depradations. In fact, the pressures of competition, which encourage cost-cutting to undersell competitors and maximize profits in market economies, can function as incentives for environmental harm in order to increase competitive advantages. In this context, regulations on both national and international levels can help ensure fair competition, forcing all participants to play by the same rules or pay the penalties.

These rules can take various forms—prohibitions, incentives, consumption and production limits, graduated tax penalties, emission fees, licenses and other user fees. All of these and more exist plenteously now, and the bulk of them we accept as reasonable. In theory, public regulations can cover every aspect of the ecological crisis, from the size of cars to the size of families, from CFC bans to hunting licenses—though certainly not all proposals are wise, enforceable, or just. Public controls establish the boundaries of production, consumption, accumulation, competition, and distribution. They can be important political means of protecting our environmental rights by restraining the self-seeking powers of sin.

Considering the severity of the ecological crisis and the role of many economic enterprises in contributing to that crisis, the persistent voices calling in principle for deregulation or minimal regulation of industry and agriculture seem strangely discordant with reality. These appeals appear to be rooted in classical or neoclassical economic theories that regard economic institutions as almost independent of the social matrix of accountability. In these views, economic enterprises should be generally left alone—so long as minimal rules of fair competition are respected—to fulfill their prime or sole responsibility: the maximization of profits for their owners or stockholders, which will also allegedly maximize the latent social functions of employment and productivity. The trajectory of this economic—as well as ethical—theory is that public regulations are generally bad for business and society. Environmental protection regulations allegedly hinder businesses in pursuing their proper objectives. That's not their department, unless economic incentives are available. The tasks of cleaning up and paying for the externalities belong to other sectors of a segmented society.

It would be grossly unfair to suggest that these ideas are anywhere close to universal among contemporary economic entrepreneurs and theoreticians. The social responsibility of economic institutions is widely proclaimed today, partly from internal values and partly in response to consumer demand. Yet, these classical ideas remain widespread. Many entrepreneurs seem quite content to have economic benefits privatized and the costs socialized.[19] The result is often not capitalism but a corporate welfare system. This dynamic is scandalously evident in the sale—at far below market costs—of water, timber, grazing privileges, and mineral rights on many federal lands in the United States.

Against this almost isolationistic conception of the economy, a social solidarity interpretation argues that economic enterprises, like all other institutions, are part of a complex web of interdependent relationships that constitute a given society. They affect and are affected by every other component. They are dependent on the acceptance of the society for their existence, manner of operations, modes of distributing benefits and costs, and level of profitability, while the rest of the society depends on them for productivity and other material contributions to the well-being of the whole. Businesses, therefore, have social responsibilities precisely because they exist in social relationships that impose broad requirements for order and justice. When businesses fail to fulfill their responsibilities, governments—as the instruments of order and justice for the relevant wholes—have the duty to intervene to protect the common good. These governmental responsibilities may include, if social and ecological needs warrant, bans on products and by-products, limits on production and consumption, mandates on distribution, and appropriate penalties.

Economic enterprises and systems can be evaluated economically on the basis of their productivity and profitability, but they should also be evaluated socially and ecologically on the basis of their contributions and harms to the well-being of humans and other species in our interdependent relationships.

On a social solidarity view, the regulatory function of government should be judged not on some ideologically tainted assumptions that oppose or favor regulations in general. Rather, decisions about particular regulations depend on contextual and prudential considerations (and conflicting values inevitably enter these complex debates). Whether or not "there oughta be a law" depends on questions like the following: Is a regulation valuable or necessary to serve a given social or ecological need? What form should the regulation take? Can the goal be achieved by less coercive means? What are the benefits and liabilities of different types of regulations for all the parties with stakes in the outcome, including nonhuman species? Are the effects economically regressive or otherwise discriminatory toward the poor (like high user fees or consumer taxes)? Does the regulation discriminate unfairly against small or large enterprises? What adjustments or compensations are necessary to eliminate or reduce discriminatory effects? What will be the economic effects, for instance, on inflation, competition, productivity, and employment? Can the regulation be enforced adequately? Will adequate funding for enforcement be available? Are the potential enforcers sufficiently competent and honest, and can they be kept accountable to the public? At what level, branch, or agency of government should the regulatory powers reside?

Obviously, decisions for or against particular regulations are not easy. Errors are inevitable. Some current or proposed regulations are unnecessary and some are plainly wrong, but opposition to public regulations or types of regulations in general or on principle seems to be no less so. I see no compelling reason, for instance, why moral preference should be given to economic incentives over other forms of regulation.[20] That judgment strikes me as rigid or ideological. Economic incentives, like some tax benefits for reducing pollution, can sometimes be unfair to the public, especially to those whose income is insufficient to be benefited.[21] Sometimes bluntly prohibitive and heavily punitive measures are the only tolerable responses to blatant abuses. The necessity, type, and extent of public regulations are best determined contextually and prudentially in moral struggles with the above questions.

Environmental regulations have provided many important protections against ecological abuses. Many more such regulations will almost certainly be necessary in the coming years. The continuing task of environmental advocates will be to insure not only that particular regulations are effective, efficient, and just, but also that the total package of public regulations is sufficient to preserve social and ecological integrity.

RESPONSIBILITIES TO FUTURE GENERATIONS

An ecologically sound and morally responsible public policy will protect the interests of future generations.

The ecological crisis has brought to the fore the question of responsibility to future generations. That is the essence of the virtue of sustainability. The tragedy of the crisis is not only the damage done in the present, but also the harm caused to future generations—if, indeed, our generation will allow them the opportunity to exist. The vital interests of coming generations in a healthy and whole habitat are being sacrificed partly for the present gratifications and glorifications of the affluent. Our age is living beyond its means, receiving dubious benefits from exceeding the regenerative, absorptive, and carrying capacities of the planet, while future generations, if any, will bear most of the human risks and costs. Yet, much of the moral force behind ecological concerns dissipates if the present has no responsibility for the future. Sustainability, for example, ceases to be an ecological virtue unless intergenerational justice is assumed. Ecological ethics and politics, therefore, depend on the moral validity of responsibility to future generations.

"What Has Posterity Ever Done for Me?" Robert Heilbroner asked rhetorically in a famous essay that critiqued and mourned the intergenerational indifference of the Me and Now Generation.[22] This egoistic posture is probably not subject to rational discourse, or maybe even therapy. But more serious questions also have been raised about responsibilities to the future, and these require a response. Some, for example, deny or downgrade responsibilities to future generations mainly on the grounds that we cannot know enough about their needs and preferences to exercise responsibilities, or we can owe no obligation to nonentities that have no interests, and, therefore, no rights.[23] These difficulties seem to me to be exaggerated concerns, reflecting more the inadequacies of ethical conceptualization than dilemmas of allocation.

True, we cannot predict very much about the precise needs and preferences of distant generations, but we can know with reasonable certainty what will in general be beneficial and harmful to them. We can know the functions though not the forms of their needs. Since they will be our biological heirs and relational creatures, their optimal needs will include a healthy biosphere, ample resources, unpoisoned foods, and a sustainable population. The similarities between them and us will far outweigh the differences.[24] Our ignorance about the future is far less than sufficient (and is virtually nonexistent for near generations) to serve as a reason or rationalization for denying ecological responsibilities.

True also, future generations do not yet exist. But they *will* exist, unless human-induced or ecospheric calamities eliminate the conditions necessary for their existence. Their existence can be reasonably anticipated—and any ethic that respects consequences must be structured on the basis of reasonable anticipations. This high probability of their existence is a sufficient ground for affirming rights and responsibilities. Future generations can be said to have *anticipatory rights,* and every present generation, therefore, has *anticipatory obligations.*[25] Though they exist for us only in an anticipatory sense, we certainly "will have existed for them"[26] in a real and dependent sense. They depend on us for their biological and cultural heritage, which they in turn will pass on to their immediate successors. We have obligations to them precisely because what we are and do will have profound effects on them for good or ill. They are part of our moral community because relationships and, therefore, responsibilities extend not only in space but in time, in "a chain of obligation that is passed from one generation to another."[27] We have met the future and it is an extension of us, just as the genetic and cultural heritage of the past, with whatever novelty each generation adds, is perpetuated in the present. On these assumptions, discounting future interests may be a useful device in economics for calculating depreciation, but it is a euphemism for stealing from the future when translated surreptitiously, as it often is, into a moral norm.[28]

These issues have not been controversial ones in Christian theology and ethics. Christianity generally has assumed the legitimacy of intergenerational justice. Just as we have moral duties to strangers in remote lands, so we have similar duties to future strangers in remote times.[29] God's covenant is with you and "your offspring forever" (Gen. 13:15). Moral responsibilities apply not only to our children and grandchildren and not only to the seventh generation, as some contemporary environmentalists argue myopically, since even the problems of plutonium wastes and the potential extinctions of many declining species can be safely ignored if we think only in such short terms. Rather, they apply to the children and grandchildren of every generation in perpetuity, until the end of the age.

Our responsibilities to both present and future generations, however, can lead to some difficult dilemmas. For instance, providing adequate nutrition to a hungry world is a moral necessity, but doing so by methods that increase soil erosion and toxication and thereby decrease long-term productivity will be a moral tragedy for the future. Certainly, the present generation should not be sacrificed for a better future, since we are the only generation that can help the people of our time. Equally, future generations should not be sacrificed for the present one. The real moral challenge is to prevent such intolerable choices. Indeed, the dilemma may often be a false one. In some key respects, behavioral patterns—like sustainability and frugality—that will benefit future generations will also benefit the present one.

What then are some ecological responsibilities to future generations that should be embodied in all contemporary public policies? They can be described in several overlapping rules or principles:

1) Do nothing that could jeopardize the opportunity for future generations to come into being.[30] This rule suggests, for example, the urgency of eliminating nuclear weapons.

2) Do nothing that could deprive future generations of the ecological conditions necessary for their fundamental rights to "a just, sustainable, and participatory society."[31] Inadequate policies for limiting population growth seem to be a serious violation of this responsibility.

3) Leave the ecosphere to its successors in as healthy a state as it was received, so that future generations will have relatively equal opportunities to the present one.[32] This responsibility might require, for instance, major clean-ups of synthetic chemicals, and acid rain, and reduction of carbon dioxide.

4) Going a step further, in the light of the church's role in anticipating the Reign of God, seek not only to maintain the status quo but to enhance the condition of the biosphere by cleaning up even the messes that our forebears left behind. The expansion of wildlife habitat is one possible example of this responsibility.

5) Use no more than our "fair share" of nonrenewable resources like fossil fuels and minerals, or provide reparations. This rule, of course, is dysfunctionally vague, but it is intended as a standard of frugality and redress. Excessive depletions of nonrenewables should be "counterbalanced by the devising of new techniques so that succeeding generations have opportunities matching those of their predecessors."[33] The compulsive overuse of fossil fuels in our generation, then, would seem to require not only a new conservation but also the compensatory development of ecologically friendly technologies, like solar energy.

6) Avoid ecologically irreversible actions. Just as the present generation cannot be sacrificed for a better future, so future generations should not be endangered or deprived irreversibly for the sake of the benefits to some in the present generation.[34] This criterion seems to provide a compelling argument against human-induced extinctions, global warming, ozone depletion,

and nuclear energy. We need to allow room for future generations to remedy our errors.

7) In summary, live sustainably, within the bounds of the regenerative, absorptive, and carrying capacities of the earth, so that all future generations can also do so indefinitely.

In creating and assessing public policy, Christians must be a voice for the unrepresented—future generations. Indeed, Christians should be advocates of an expanded concept of political representation in our time: the constituents of public officials include every generation, past, present, and future. We and our representatives are trustees or stewards for the future. This concept is hardly new in political history. Political communities have nearly always regarded their existence and responsibilities as historically continuous. What is tragically new is a biologically, politically, and culturally indefensible generational isolationism.

THE GUARDIANSHIP OF BIODIVERSITY

An ecologically sound and ethically responsible public policy will provide protection for nonhuman species, ensuring the conditions necessary for their perpetuation and ongoing evolution.

This role of guardian of biodiversity is for Christians an expression of genuine "dominion," in respect for our spiritual and biological kinship and connections with other creatures, in acknowledgment of their intrinsic value, and in fidelity to the biocentric valuations of God. Otherkind are entitled to freedom from the sin of human-induced extinctions and dangerous reductions in numbers and populations. This nonhuman right entails human responsibilities to prevent these consequences to the maximum extent possible. The guardianship of biodiversity is empowered by humility: the whole of nature cannot be defined by human purposes and wants. It has its own integrity under God that defies human arrogance and demands human respect and protection.

What does this role mean in terms of political objectives? Because nonhuman species are threatened by every dimension of the ecological crisis, the political defense of biodiversity must be similarly comprehensive. It means, for instance, provisions for clean air, clean water, and clean soil, as well as the prevention of global warming and ozone depletion. It means controlling the anthropocentric imperialism manifested in human overpopulation and overdevelopment.

The political defense of biodiversity means, moreover, additional controls on bioengineering through public regulations and oversight. Other species are not simply machines to be redesigned. These life forms are the bearers of millions of years of evolutionary adaptations in accord with divine intentions. From a Christian perspective, that reality seems to place a strong burden of proof, a need for compelling justifications, on bioengineering proposals and practices. The value of natural biodiversity is not compatible with the apparent goals of some advocates of bioengineering: the humanization and artificialization of nature. The question of what precise limits are necessary as political controls on bioengineering in its ecological interventions is one with which Christian ethics must struggle in countless contexts in decades to come.[35]

The political defense of biodiversity also requires further controls and bans on the direct overkilling of nonhuman species. The massive driftnets, for example, used widely in commercial fisheries, are not only efficient (perhaps unsustainably so) but also indiscriminate, killing rare and endangered specimens along with the targets. Alternatives should be mandated for this practice and many equivalents.

Recreational hunting, however, raises special problems.[36] Subsistence or "meat" hunting has the moral justification of being a nutritional necessity or asset in the absence of alternatives (or often justice) for poor and indigenous peoples. Indeed, killing in one form or another is a biological necessity. But "bloodsports"—killing animals (including fish) for fun, pleasure, recreation, glory, or even competition (Boone-and-Crockett-Club-style)—are morally dubious at best under my articulation of a biocentric Christian ethic. These "sports" seem to be justifiable only on anthropocentric assumptions that otherkind are only instruments or objects for human wants, including fun and games. The ecological rationalization for sports hunting—for example, "sportsmen" as the functional equivalent of wild predators, culling the herds and flocks of "game" to "save" them from overpopulation and starvation—contains some truth in some circumstances, but it is mostly a romantic illusion. It ignores, for example, the fact that "stocking" of some "game," including alien species, is a widespread practice to remedy overhunting and supply persistent hunting demands; the fact that hunting of wild predators, like wolves and coyotes, has been a major cause of their reduction or elimination in many places; and the fact that nonhuman predation is

211

far more effective than hunting in preserving the "survival of the fittest" among prey species. Even the justification for subsistence hunting could be substantially reduced in many places in this nation if economic justice prevailed. Similar reasoning also raises moral doubts about sports fishing, even if fish are less sentient creatures than mammals and birds. On grounds such as these, I gave up the gun and the rod for the binoculars and camera years ago.

Yet, on strategic grounds, I would not encourage any present efforts to outlaw sports hunting in the United States, except of certain species whose populations are seriously declining. (This exception is already a common game management mandate in theory, though with too many abuses in practice.) Efforts to ban these sports would almost certainly fail miserably and would create antienvironmentalist furies where simple tensions now exist. That is probably one reason why some prominent environmental organizations are neutral on these recreations. More importantly, however, sports hunting and fishing in the United States have served a critical latent function: "sportsmen" have often provided the public pressures and the funds to preserve natural habitats. Most national wildlife refuges, for example, were established to provide breeding, feeding, and resting areas for migratory waterfowl—a prime target of hunters. These valuable habitats—serving also numerous nongame species—might not exist otherwise. Indeed, many organized hunters and fishers are conservationists, strongly committed to preserving species and habitats, the preconditions of their sports. This ambiguous benefit of recreational hunting and fishing seems to me to be sufficient grounds for saying that environmental and some hunting and fishing organizations sometimes should, as they do, make common cause against a common foe, the destruction of natural habitat. Politics, after all, is often about uneasy alliances. Nevertheless, the witness against bloodsports by animal liberationists—despite whatever questions can be raised about some of their tactics and moral assumptions—remains beneficial as a deterrent to destruction and as a catalyst for public debate and cultural transformation.

Yet, the trophy hunters are another story. Many people in high places are willing to pay vast sums to bag prized specimens—the fittest, if possible—of often rare or endangered "big game" species. Leaving aside the questions about the psychology of trophy hunting, the practice warrants shunning and, when possible, banning as a moral offense against biodiversity. The Endangered Species Act and the Convention on International Trade in Endangered Species (CITES)

212

provide some legal protection against these abuses, but many insist that the regulations need to be strengthened.

Above all, the political defense of biodiversity demands the protection and expansion of natural habitat. Expanding human development results in increasing nonhuman dehabitation. That is the process that must be halted if all species are to thrive. Ideally, the political goal should not be simply the preservation of remnant populations of threatened species, but rather the coexistence of humans with viable populations of unthreatened species.

Habitat protection will require new and more effective public restrictions. Restricted use should apply not only to public lands but also to private property, as a new endangered species act in Massachusetts mandates. Many threatened species and habitats are on private property, but property rights are not absolute and do not outweigh the recognized legal responsibility of the state to act, on behalf of the public interest, as trustee or protector of wildlife. It may also be necessary to expand current zoning concepts and to establish "protection and production zones," not only on a national scale but on a virtually global basis,[37] along with more creative efforts to integrate human and nonhuman habitats.[38]

Among the possible guidelines for these political controls, a couple are noteworthy. For instance, since wilderness and other rare or endangered habitats are only a small fraction of their original extent, any further loss to development would be a tragedy and an injustice to otherkind.[39] It would require a heavy burden of proof in accord with the restrictions on rights outlined in chapter 7. Moreover, the rarer, more beautiful, and more fragile an environment, argues Holmes Rolston, the lighter it ought to be treaded.[40] That seems to be a basic rationale, for example, for protecting Alaska's Arctic National Wildlife Refuge, an unmarred and irreplaceable habitat for unusual species, including polar bears and muskoxen, from the irreparable damage of oil and gas drillings. Again, since the *prima facie* evidence indicates that we humans have occupied more than our "fair share" (whatever this vague criterion might require precisely) of inhabitable land in most places, reparations are in order. This criterion suggests, for example, an increase in the number and acreage of wildlife refuges and other sanctuaries (ideally with connecting corridors) and the restoration of degraded lands, like strip mines and overgrazed grasslands. These activities are underway now, but more need to be undertaken.

Though the economics-ecology dilemma is dangerously real, both humans and nonhumans are wronged when human problems of maldistribution are resolved by the sacrifice of nonhuman habitats.[41] These human dilemmas are best solved by frugal and sustainable life-styles, economic efficiency, conservation, population control, and the just redistribution of available resources. For instance, preventing human hunger while preserving natural habitats will require major changes in agricultural land use, including ecosystemic compatibility, improved yields, erosion and pesticide reduction, and land reform.[42]

What kind of rationale for biodiversity is most appropriate in the public sphere? The prevailing view among environmental organizations seems to be that anthropocentric, especially economic, values ought to be highlighted. The impressive *Global Ecology Handbook* of the Global Tomorrow Coalition, for instance, stresses the contributions of biodiversity to medicine, industry, agriculture, recreation, and ecological cycles.[43] The arguments are valid. Yet, arguments from the intrinsic value of biodiversity are virtually ignored, even though most activists in the coalition probably accept an intrinsic value rationale. The apparent assumption, however, is that intrinsic value arguments will be politically ineffective or divisive.

I am not convinced. True, the anthropocentric and biocentric perspectives generally have similar policy objectives; they are complementary, not contradictory.[44] Normally, nothing obstructs political coalitions. Yet, an overemphasis on anthropocentric values to the near-exclusion of biocentric values can have effects that are contrary to intentions. It encourages human arrogance and, by emphasizing "products," aids those committed to the commodification of nature. The arguments also lose force if the utility of a species is only an unknown potential for the remote future or if an artificial substitute seems possible; they can often be outweighed by other economic arguments. Indeed, if the arguments suggest that the primary purpose of biodiversity is to preserve the gene pool for human purposes, much of that goal can be accomplished in zoos and labs![45]

Moreover, I doubt that the anthropocentric rationale is even politically sufficient in itself. An increasing number of contemporaries seems open to biocentric arguments and may be unmoved otherwise. Today, many scientists and government administrators also argue from the intrinsic value or rights of nature.[46] My counsel to Christian and other environmentalists, therefore, is: do not distort or dilute the full rationale for biodiversity on grounds of political strategy. Many are open to a biocentric witness, even if their ultimate grounds differ. Anything less than a full rationale lacks moral validity and may also lack political credibility.

The guardianship of biodiversity, like responsibility to future generations, requires a much broader and more radical concept of political representation than has heretofore prevailed. Christians are called not only to be a voice for voiceless creatures, but to appeal to the public and its officials to perform the same role. Public decision-makers should be understood not only as representatives of an electorate but also as protectors of all the inhabitants of the land, human and otherkind. That will be no easy challenge.[47]

INTERNATIONAL COOPERATION
FOR ECOLOGICAL SECURITY

An ecologically sound and morally responsible public policy will promote international cooperation as an essential means to confront the global ecological crisis.

Ecologically, the world is one and always has been. Though much has been written, and rightly so, about the unitive significance of international communications, transportation, and economic relations in the twentieth century, the planet's perpetual ecological interdependence has been largely neglected until the consciousness of global crisis struck. Now we know that the planet's only ozone layer is being depleted by CFCs floating up from many nations. The climate changes resulting from the excessive production of carbon dioxide in nearly every nation will be globally disastrous. Acid rain has no respect for international boundaries. Neither do the host of toxins, from radiation to pesticides, that float in the world's one atmosphere and interconnected waterways. Migratory species of birds, marine fauna, and other animals are destroyed or dehabitated in lands or seas far from their breeding grounds. Affluence in one nation is linked to poverty and overpopulation in others.

In this setting, national isolationism is impossible; national self-sufficiency is obsolete; and national security is jeopardized apart from ecological security. Thus any concept or vision of globalization that is not finely tuned to the ecological crisis is simply irrelevant, if not harmful, to the resolution of current and emerging dilemmas in the international community.

Many environmental problems, of course, can be solved best by national governments, regional states, local municipalities, voluntary associations, or even families—and often in cooperation, because in our increasingly interdependent societies, the smaller social units often need considerable help from the larger. Consequently, few would debate the classical principle of subsidiarity, which calls for the assignment of a social task to the lowest social unit capable of performing the task adequately. But the ecological crisis confronts us with new realities that compel unprecedented responses. Until recently, most environmental problems were at least perceived as localized and could be corrected locally or regionally. That reality and perception of reality, however, are now changing dramatically, and so are the corresponding proposals for correction.

On the macrocosmic dimensions of the ecological crisis, the social/political units—including nation-states—are simply too parochial jurisdictionally to confront successfully transnational problems: "The traditional forms of national sovereignty are increasingly challenged by the realities of ecological and economic interdependence."[48] No nation can withstand alone the ecological invasions of everyone's sovereign territory; its national security is corrupted by ecological insecurity. Thus Michael Renner is seemingly right in seeing "a fundamental contradiction between the illusion of national sovereignty and the reality of transboundary environmental degradation."[49] In this context, the lowest social/political unit potentially capable of responding effectively to the global ecological crisis is the international community. But that community is mainly tribalistic. It exists as a sufficient political unit only embryonically. Our champion has no armor. That is a major dilemma.

The world is one ecologically, but it is fractured politically. How do we resolve this dilemma? What is required to match solutions and problems? What political transformations are necessary to correspond with ecological realities? These are the questions with which Christian and other environmentalists must struggle today. The prevailing answer, which has become almost hackneyed, is that the crisis requires a high and unprecedented level of international cooperation. Some call for world government. I doubt the present political possibilities or necessities of that solution, though I would welcome particular forms of it. Yet, it seems clear to me that national initiatives, while imperative, will be insufficient. Only international cooperation offers hope of satisfying what I have called the virtue of sufficiency: solutions must be proportionate to the magnitude of the problems. The United Nations and its subsidiary organizations—for example, the Development Program, Food and Agriculture Organization, Population Fund, and Environmental Program—seem to be the logical structures through which this essential cooperation is implemented.

The legal powers of these institutions, however, are now inadequate. They must be enhanced if global ecological security is to be realized. That requires appropriate regulations, funds, and enforcement authority and procedures.[50] The last particularly, while it does not entail a major sacrifice of national sovereignty, certainly means some limitations and controls on sovereignty by voluntary and mutual agreement. In that sense, I am suggesting at least a minimal form of world government.

Are these limitations and controls politically realistic? Very unlikely now. Yet, they do appear to be ecologically essential, and sometimes the widespread consciousness of essential needs can substantially change political possibilities. Indeed, realism can degenerate into an apathetic acceptance of the status quo when it does not allow and press for the extension of the parameters of the politically possible. The situation is not hopeless. Bilateral and multilateral conferences and treaties on the environment are increasing, reflecting a growing political awareness of the problems and the inadequacies of exclusively national solutions. But the situation can only become really hopeful if partisans can make a convincing case.

Flagrant nationalists have often argued that international agreements and institutions are contrary to "national interests." That claim, whatever element of truth it contains, is dissonant with ecological realities, as it has been on nuclear weapons. The global scale of ecological degradation means that every country's vital national interests now depend on global ecological security, which, in turn, depends on international cooperation.[51] Global solidarity is no longer only an ultimate vision; it is fast becoming an ecological and political necessity. The challenge to Christians, whose normative tradition has long been suspicious of narrow national interests and biased in favor of global community,[52] is to help translate these necessities into political realities. That role, however, will demand an intensified and tenacious commitment to Christian unity, for only a church that lives in ecumenical solidarity can be an adequate instrument and effective sign of God's reconciling powers for a human community seeking political solidarity.

LINKING JUSTICE, PEACE, AND ECOLOGY

An ecologically sound and morally responsible public policy will pursue ecological integrity in intimate alliance with the struggles for social peace and justice.

217

This point has been suggested so often in these pages that a complaint of redundancy may be justified. Yet, this linkage is so critical that a final reemphasis on it is warranted.

There can be no ecological integrity apart from social peace and justice!

—There can be no social justice without ecological justice!

—There can be no peace among nations in the absence of peace with nature!

These affirmations are rhetorical exaggerations—slogans, but they highlight the fact, with tolerable validity, that these three prime areas of political concern are interdependent and inseparable. As in the biosphere, so in the political sphere, everything is connected with and has consequences for everything else. Compartmentalization of concerns is malconceived and self-defeating. Holistic and relational strategies are necessary to respond to holistic and relational realities.

This interdependence is the message implied by the biblical concept of *shalom*, by the stress on "ecojustice"[53] among some Christian environmentalists, and by The World Council of Churches' current theme, "Justice, Peace, and the Integrity of Creation" (JPIC). The WCC's linkage initiative reached a peak with the impressive efforts preceding and proceeding from the Faith, Science, and the Future Conference at M.I.T. in 1979. Regrettably, however, the document prepared for the 1990 WCC conference in Seoul, Korea, "Between the Flood and the Rainbow: Covenanting for JPIC," is notable for homiletical exhortations, rather than empirical and ethical analyses. Nevertheless, rigorous and creative work continues in commitees and consultations, and an ongoing commitment to JPIC is evident in the reports of the 1991 WCC Canberra Assembly.[54] These developments remain promising for the future.

Unfortunately, peace, justice, and environmental advocates are still troubled by turf problems, particularly the competition for scarce resources and fears about the diversion of public attention from their respective projects. Much of this is inevitable in the political process, but it is still regrettable. The tensions of the early seventies appear to have subsided but they have not disappeared. Suspicions persist and they periodically pop into public view, prompting shudders at the sometimes silly public and private postures of advocates on all sides. True, a few environmentalists are genuinely misanthropic, speaking as if humans were somehow alien to the biosphere. More are economic elitists, concerned about the perils of ecosystems but indifferent to the plight of the poor. Equally true, some peace and justice activists oppose any rights of nature on the grounds that they will distract from human rights, as if the two are contraries rather than complements. These positions, however, are aberrations, the myopic appeals of partisans. They do not detract from the moral reality of indivisibility among peace, justice, and ecological integrity.

The connections among the three are readily evident in contemporary problems.

Environmental policy can contribute to the advancement or retardation of economic justice. Pollution taxes, for instance, are valuable, but they should be levied in a way that does not cause additional harm to the poor. Similarly, since economic deprivation is a major cause and effect of ecological degradation, ecological problems cannot be resolved unless economic maldistribution is remedied. Otherwise, the people of poor nations are forced to exploit their natural resources beyond the limits of sustainability. Economic equity among nations is as much an issue of ecological ethics as social ethics. Equally, population control is a matter of both social and ecological justice. Environmentalists, therefore, should also be spirited advocates of economic justice. Thankfully, an increasing number are.

Some feminist thinkers have shown the close connections, historically and ideologically, between patriarchalism in gender relations and anthropocentric instrumentalism in ecological relations—between the devaluation and domination of women and the devaluation and domination of nature. Women somehow have been perceived as associated with nature, and both have been treated as objects for male exploitation.[55] I suspect, in fact, that the same case can be made against racism and classism. These linkages suggest at least that environmentalists, feminists (female and male), and other egalitarians should be intimate allies and mutual advocates. Fortunately, more are recognizing an essentially common cause.

Political peace also contributes to ecological integrity, just as war has the opposite effect. War and the preparations for war pose serious threats to ecological health, largely because of the massive consumption of resources and energy, the production of toxic and radioactive wastes, and the destruction of ecosystems through the testing and use of weaponry.[56] Numerous unexploded artillery shells, many containing poison gas, still litter the battlefields of World War I. The ecosystems of Vietnam were seriously damaged—in some respects permanently so—by U.S. defoliants and bombs, to the immediate and long-range detriment of the land's human and nonhuman inhabitants. As a consequence of the Persian Gulf War, "black rain" from the oil well fires in Kuwait created an atmospheric oil slick damaging to crops, water, and human lungs throughout the region. Oil spills in the Gulf have caused irreparable damage to marine life and delicate ecosystems. War wreaks social and ecological havoc long after the fighting stops. Certainly, moreover, nuclear war is the ultimate social *and* ecological threat. The nuclear peril should be seen as "the very center of the ecological crisis," argues Jonathan Schell,[57] because of potential wholesale extinctions, including the human species. "Death," notes Schell, "cuts off life; extinction cuts off birth"—eliminating the possibility of future generations of existing species.[58] Environmentalists, therefore, should logically be passionate peace activists. Happily, many are.

Equally, political peace and social justice are not achievable apart from environmental integrity. A dynamic and diverse ecosphere is a necessary condition of peaceful and just relationships within and among nations, for humans depend upon environmental health to make life possible, productive, and peaceful. The social consequences of an environmental apocalypse, which is our present trajectory, are alarming to contemplate: mass poisonings, accentuated cancer rates, increased poverty and starvation, massive migration of environmental refugees, wars for scarce land and water (especially in the Middle East), conflicts over other resources, systemic economic collapses, political upheavals, and spiritual lamentations. It can't happen, many optimistic technocrats might mutter, but technological fixes cannot correct adequately for global warming, ozone depletion, and a toxicated planet, or restore extinct species and simplified ecosystems. Peace and justice advocates, therefore, should be avid environmentalists. Fortunately, an increasing number are.

Strategically, of course, it is impossible for advocates to focus on all facets of the intertwined social and ecological crises simultaneously. Prudence requires strategic concentration and persistence. Individuals and institutions must pick priorities rationally and deploy resources efficiently in order to be politically effective. The moral mandate to respond holistically and relationally, however, does not require diffusion. Instead, this approach counsels advocates in all spheres to act in ways so that solutions to social or ecological problems do not cause or aggravate other social or ecological problems, and, if possible, contribute to the resolution of them. Obviously, this approach does not reduce moral complexities and ambiguities; it simply reflects the perplexing dilemmas of reality.

As a practical matter, every public policy or political position of the churches on peace and justice concerns should be accompanied by an environmental impact assessment, and every public policy or political position on environmental concerns should be accompanied by a social impact assessment. This same approach should be pressed as standard operating procedure for governments and voluntary organizations. That might help save us from fragmentation. In the final analysis, the integration of peace, justice, and ecological concerns is simply an effort to match ethically and politically the integration that already exists ecologically and socially.

FINALLY

A summary at this point would be absurd. But a note of hope is theologically and politically reasonable.

The multipronged ecological crisis is a persistent and perilous problem, and the essential solutions seem fearfully massive and even presently unrealistic. A revolution in values and policies will not come easy and cheap. The necessary remedial and preventive measures will meet stiff resistance. The environmental clean-up and other costs will be hefty penalties for our sins against the biosphere and each other—though the emerging benefits will be worth the price. In this situation, optimism is not even an option, and pessimism is demoralizing and indefensible.

The best we can do is hustle and hope. We can strive to realize whatever semblances of ecological integrity are maximally possible now. We can also struggle in the confidence that with each step forward, God the Politician and the Lover of life is ever creating new possibilities to realize the integrity of God's—and our—beloved habitat.

NOTES

1. DIMENSIONS AND DILEMMAS OF THE ECOLOGICAL CRISIS: THE POLLUTION COMPLEX

1. John Passmore, *Man's Responsibility for Nature*, 2nd ed. (London: Duckworth, 1980), p. 71.
2. Michael Weisskopf, "EPA Finds Pollution Unacceptably High," *The Washington Post*, April 23, 1989.
3. Hilary F. French, "Clearing the Air," in Worldwatch Institute, *State of the World 1990* (New York-London: W. W. Norton, 1990), pp. 104-10; World Commission on Environment and Development, *Our Common Future* (Oxford-New York: Oxford Univ. Press, 1987), pp. 178-81; Cheryl Simon Silver with Ruth S. DeFries for the National Academy of Sciences, *One Earth, One Future: Our Changing Global Environment* (Washington, D.C.: National Academy Press, 1990), pp. 131-44.
4. Sandra Postel, "Defusing the Toxics Threat: Controlling Pesticides and Industrial Waste," *Worldwatch Paper 79*, September, 1987, pp. 19-20.
5. Ibid., p. 16.
6. Sandra Marquarht, "Thwarting the Circle of Poison," *Christian Social Action*, Sept., 1990, pp. 7-9.
7. *Our Common Future*, p. 228.
8. Holmes Rolston III, *Environmental Ethics* (Philadelphia: Temple University Press, 1988), p. 319.
9. Christopher Flavin, "Reassessing Nuclear Power," in Worldwatch Institute, *State of the World 1987* (New York-London: W. W. Norton, 1987), p. 78.
10. Richard and Val Routley, "Nuclear Energy and Obligations to the Future," in Ernest Partridge, ed., *Responsibilities to Future Generations: Environmental Ethics* (Buffalo, N.Y.: Prometheus Press, 1981), pp. 277-98.
11. Compare Charles Lee, "Toxic Waste in Alabama," *The Egg*, vol. 5, no. 2 (Summer, 1985), pp. 5-6. National Council of Churches, Governing Board, Resolution: "Toxic Pollution in the U.S.A." (Nov. 6, 1986).
12. Ann Leonard, "Brokering Waste," *Christian Social Action*, Sept., 1990, pp. 13-15.
13. *Our Common Future*, p. 221. On "green taxes," see Sandra Postel and Christopher Flavin, "Reshaping the Global Economy," in *State of the World 1991* (New York: W. W. Norton, 1991), pp. 181-85.
14. For sensible criteria on the siting of waste dumps, see Ted Peters, "Not In My Backyard: The Waste Disposal Crisis," *Christian Century*, vol. 106, no. 5 (Feb. 15, 1989), pp. 175-77. Also, Douglas MacLean, "Nuclear Waste Storage: Your Backyard or Mine?" *Philosophy and Public Policy*, vol. 9, no. 2/3 (Spring/Summer 1989), pp. 5-8.

15. Prentiss L. Pemberton and Daniel Rush Finn, *Toward a Christian Economic Ethic* (Minneapolis: Winston Press, 1985), p. 132.
16. On the need and potential for prevention, see, for example, Hilary French, *State of the World 1990*, pp. 110-14.
17. Sandra Postel, *Worldwatch Paper 79*, pp. 25-36.
18. Compare John R. Luoma, "Trash Can Realities," *Audubon*, vol. 92, no. 2 (March, 1990), pp. 86-87. Also, Global Tomorrow Coalition, *Global Ecology Handbook* (Boston: Beacon Press, 1990), pp. 266-285.
19. "Is It All Just Hot Air?" *Newsweek*, Nov. 20, 1989, pp. 64-66. For a restrained discussion on the problem as a whole, see World Resources Institute, *World Resources 1990-91* (New York-Oxford: Oxford University Press, 1990), pp. 11-31, 90-91, 95-98, 109-13, 130-34.
20. William Booth, "Air Pollutant May Counter Global Warming," *The Washington Post*, Sept. 17, 1990.
21. Christopher Flavin, "Slowing Global Warming: A Worldwide Strategy," *Worldwatch Paper 91*, October, 1989, p. 17.
22. Silver and DeFries, *One Earth, One Future*, p. 71. On global warming overall see pp. 63-102.
23. World Resources Institute, *World Resources 1988-89* (New York: Basic Books, 1988), pp. 181, 333-34.
24. Richard A. Houghton and George M. Woodell, "Global Climatic Change," *Scientific American*, vol. 26, no. 4 (April, 1989), pp. 36-44.
25. On the oceanic consequences, see Jodi Jacobson, "Swept Away," *Worldwatch*, Jan.-Feb., 1989, pp. 20-26. Also, *World Resources 1988-89*, pp. 88-89, 181-92.
26. Aug. 7, 1989.
27. *Our Common Future*, p. 168.
28. Christopher Flavin, "Slowing Global Warming," *State of the World 1990*, p. 20.
29. Ibid., pp. 17-38; Lester R. Brown, Christopher Flavin, and Sandra Postel, "Outlining a Global Action Plan," *State of the World 1989*, pp. 175-80; *World Resources 1990–1991*, pp. 24-28; Christopher Flavin and Nicholas Lenssen, "Designing a Sustainable Energy System," *State of the World 1991*, pp. 21-38.
30. Harry P. Gregor, "Alcohol Fuel: The One for the Road," *The Washington Post*, July 9, 1989.
31. Flavin, *State of the World 1990*, pp. 27-28.
32. Resource Policy Dept., U.S. Chamber of Commerce, "Global Climate Change: Cause for Concern, Not Panic," *At Issue*, Feb., 1989.
33. Michael Weisskopf, "Strict Energy-Saving Urged to Combat Global Warming," *The Washington Post*, April 11, 1991.
34. Compare Larry L. Rasmussen, "The Planetary Environment: Challenge on Every Front," *Theology and Public Policy*, vol. 2, no. 1 (Summer 1990), pp. 5-8.
35. Cynthia Pollock Shea, "Protecting the Ozone Layer," *State of the World 1989*, p. 88.
36. William Booth, "Ozone Hole May Harm Marine Life," *The Washington Post*, July 30, 1990.
37. On these questions, compare Shea, *State of the World 1989*, pp. 92-93.

2. DIMENSIONS AND DILEMMAS OF THE ECOLOGICAL CRISIS: EXCEEDING THE LIMITS

1. Loren Wilkinson, ed., *Earthkeeping: Christian Stewardship of Natural Resources* (Grand Rapids: Eerdmans, 1980), p. 51.
2. Ibid., p. 51.
3. Robert Repetto, "No Accounting for Pollution," *The Washington Post*, May 28, 1989.

4. Donnella H. Meadows et al., *The Limits to Growth* (New York: Universe Books, 1972).
5. John Lancaster, "Arctic's Tender Tundra: What Price Oil?" *The Washington Post,* Sept. 17, 1989.
6. Herman E. Daly and John B. Cobb, Jr., *For the Common Good* (Boston: Beacon Press, 1989), p. 406.
7. Charles Birch et al., *Faith, Science and the Future: Preparatory Readings for the 1979 Conference of the World Council of Churches* (Geneva: WCC, 1978), pp. 133-42.
8. Lester R. Brown and John E. Young, "Feeding the World in the 90s," *State of the World 1990,* p. 60.
9. Sandra Postel, "Halting Land Degradation," *State of the World 1989,* p. 23. For a detailed discussion, see *World Resources 1988-89,* pp. 88-89, 215-33.
10. *World Resources 1990-91,* pp. 68-71, 161-74.
11. Ibid., pp. 335-41.
12. Ibid., pp. 101-8.
13. Projections are regularly revised. For instance, the data were dated by the time of publication in *World Resources, 1990-91,* pp. 49-56. Compare Susan Okie, "World Population May Hit 10 Billion by Year 2025," *The Washington Post,* May 17, 1989; Carl Haub (demographer, Population Reference Bureau), "2050: Standing Room Only?" *The Washington Post,* July 8, 1990.
14. *Our Common Future,* pp. 100-101.
15. John Passmore, *Man's Responsibility for Nature,* p. 134.
16. Daly and Cobb, *For the Common Good,* pp. 241-42.
17. For a recent example, see Jacqueline Kasun, *The War Against Population: The Economics and Ideology of Population Control* (San Francisco: Ignatius Press, 1988), esp. pp. 54-57, 206-7. For a refutation of these claims and an excellent analysis of the problem, see Paul R. and Anne H. Ehrlich, *The Population Explosion* (New York: Simon and Schuster, 1990).
18. Compare *World Resources 1990-91,* p. 36.
19. *Our Common Future,* pp. 44, 97, 99, 105.
20. Lester Brown, "Analyzing the Demographic Trap," *State of the World 1987,* pp. 32-36.
21. *Our Common Future,* p. 190.
22. Jodi L. Jacobson, "Abandoning Homelands," *State of the World 1989,* pp. 59-76.
23. William and Paul Paddock, *Famine 1975! America's Decision: Who Will Survive?* (Boston-Toronto: Little, Brown, 1967).
24. Daly and Cobb, pp. 244-46.
25. Compare Paul Abrecht, ed., *Reports and Recommendations,* vol. 2 of *Faith and Science in an Unjust World* (Geneva: WCC, 1980), pp. 83-87.
26. James Gustafson, *Ethics From a Theocentric Perspective,* vol. 2 (Chicago: Univ. of Chicago, 1984), p. 245.
27. "Population and the Dignity of Man," *The Christian Century,* vol. 87, no. 15 (April 15, 1970): p. 448. Italics mine. Compare his *Forced Options* (San Francisco: Harper & Row, 1982), pp. 85-105.
28. *Our Common Future,* pp. 103, 106.
29. Arther J. Dyck, "An Ethical Analysis of Population Policy Alternatives," *The Monist* 60, 1 (Jan., 1977): 43.
30. *Our Common Future,* p. 6.
31. Compare Ingemar Hedström, "Latin America and the Need for a Life-Liberating Theology," in Charles Birch, William Eakin, and Jay B. McDaniel, eds., *Liberating Life* (Maryknoll, N.Y.: Orbis Books, 1990), p. 120.
32. *World Resources 1990-91,* pp. 36-41.
33. Susan Okie, "Health Crisis Confronts 1.3 Billion," *The Washington Post,* Sept. 25, 1989.
34. "Latin America Incomes Continue Decline," *The Washington Post,* April 1, 1990; *World Resources 1990-91,* p. 36.
35. *Our Common Future,* p. 6; Alan B. Durning, "Ending Poverty," *State of the World 1990,* pp. 136-40. I have been informed throughout by this excellent essay.

36. Spencer Rich, "The Eternal Poverty Gap?" *The Washington Post,* June 30, 1989. Also Spencer Rich and Barbara Vobejda, "Poverty Remains High Despite U.S. Expansion," *The Washington Post,* Sept. 27, 1990.
37. Sandra Postel, "Halting Land Degradation," *State of the World 1989,* p. 28.
38. *Our Common Future,* p. 6.
39. *World Resources 1990-91,* p. 39.
40. Alan Durning, *State of the World 1990,* p. 148. On "evironmental racism" see especially the article by Robert Bullard and the interview with Charles Lee in Dana Alston, ed., *We Speak for Ourselves: Social Justice, Race, and Environment* (Washington, D.C.: The Panos Institute, 1990).
41. Ibid., pp. 135-36.
42. (Louisville: Committee on Social Witness Policy, Presbyterian Church USA, 1989), p. 30.
43. Joseph C. Hough, Jr., "Land and People: The Eco-Justice Connection," *The Christian Century,* Oct. 1, 1980, p. 914.
44. Compare M. Douglas Meeks, *God the Economist: The Doctrine of God and Political Economy* (Minneapolis: Augsburg Fortress, 1989), pp. 174-75.
45. Quoted in Bruce C. Birch and Larry L. Rasmussen, *The Predicament of the Prosperous* (Philadelphia: Westminster, 1978), p. 33.
46. Birch et al., *Faith, Science and the Future,* pp. 140-41.
47. Denis Goulet, "The Search for Authentic Development," in Gregory Baum and Robert Ellsberg, eds., *The Logic of Solidarity* (Maryknoll, N.Y.: Orbis Books, 1989), pp. 131-37.
48. Birch and Rasmussen, *The Predicament of the Prosperous,* pp. 12, 39.
49. E. O. Wilson, ed., *BioDiversity* (Washington, D.C.: National Academy Press, 1988), p. 5.
50. Ibid., p. 7.
51. See the classic history, Peter Matthiessen, *Wildlife in America,* rev. ed. (New York: Viking, 1987).
52. On the greenhouse effect, see *World Resources 1990-91,* pp. 130-34.
53. Norman Myers, *The Primary Source: Tropical Forests and Our Future* (New York: W. W. Norton, 1984), pp. 256-59.
54. The subtitle of Norman Myers's *A Wealth of Species* (Boulder, Col.: Westview Press, 1983).
55. *Our Common Future,* pp. 147-68.
56. David Suzuki and Peter Knudtson, *Genethics: The Clash Between the New Genetics and Human Values* (Cambridge: Harvard Univ. Press, 1989), pp. 290-315.
57. Myers, *A Wealth of Species* pp. 195-96. Italics mine.
58. On the dangers of monocultures, see Suzuki and Knudtson, *Genethics,* pp. 290-315.
59. Paul R. Ehrlich, *The Machinery of Nature* (New York: Simon and Schuster, 1986), pp. 236-37.
60. Compare Douglas Meeks, *God the Economist,* pp. 157-180.
61. Compare Bill McKibben, *The End of Nature* (New York: Random House, 1989), pp. 151-70. Also Jeremy Rifkin, *Algeny* (Harmondsworth, England: Penguin, 1984), esp. pp. 252-53.
62. Birch et al., *Faith and Science in an Unjust World,* vol. 2, p. 66.
63. Humility is a powerful theme in Suzuki and Knudtson, *Genethics.*
64. *State of the World 1990,* p. 171; compare *Our Common Future,* p. 43.
65. *Our Common Future,* p. 43.
66. Ibid., pp. 46, 147.
67. Pope John Paul II, *Sollicitudo Rei Socialis* (On Social Concern), Dec. 30, 1987, para. 26.

3. THE ECOLOGICAL COMPLAINT AGAINST CHRISTIANITY

1. *Time,* January 2, 1989, pp. 29-30.
2. Alan W. Watts, *Nature, Man, and Woman* (New York: Random House/Vintage, 1958, 1970), pp. 25-53.

3. Arnold Toynbee, "The Religious Background of the Present Environmental Crisis," in David and Eileen Spring, eds., *Ecology and Religion in History* (New York: Harper & Row, 1974), pp. 137-49.
4. *Science*, vol. 155 (March 10, 1967), pp. 1203-7.
5. Garret De Bell, ed., *The Environmental Handbook* (New York: Ballantine/Friends of the Earth, 1970), pp. 12-26.
6. For qualifications of his thesis, see Lynn White, Jr., "Continuing the Conversation," in Ian G. Barbour, ed., *Western Man and Environmental Ethics* (Reading, Mass.: Addison-Wesley, 1973), pp. 55-64. Thomas Sieger Derr, "Religion's Responsibility for the Ecological Crisis: An Argument Run Amok," *Worldview*, vol. 18, no. 1 (January 1975), p. 44.
7. Donald Worster, *Nature's Economy: The Roots of Ecology* (Garden City, N.Y.: Anchor/Doubleday, 1979), pp. 26-27.
8. Ibid., p. 27.
9. Joseph K. Sheldon, "Twenty-one Years After the Historical Roots of Our Ecologic Crisis: How Has the Church Responded?" *Perspectives on Science and Christian Faith*, vol. 41, no. 3 (September, 1989): 156.
10. See, for instance, Loren Wilkinson et al., *Earthkeeping: Christian Stewardship of Natural Resources* (Grand Rapids: Eerdman's, 1980), pp. 103-4.
11. Arthur O. Lovejoy, *The Great Chain of Being* (Cambridge: Harvard University Press, 1961), pp. 79-85. Compare Paul Santmire, *The Travail of Nature* (Philadelphia: Fortress Press, 1985) pp. 16-26, 45-48, on the spiritual and ecological motifs.
12. Santmire, *The Travail of Nature*, p. 3.
13. Ibid., p. 122.
14. Carolyn Merchant, *The Death of Nature: Women, Ecology and the Scientific Revolution* (San Francisco: Harper & Row, 1980), p. 28. Merchant rightly stresses the historical and ideological connections between the subjugation of nature and the subjugation of women.
15. Ibid., pp. 2-3, 6, 8.
16. Ibid., pp. 29-70.
17. Ibid., pp. 63-68.
18. Ibid., p. 193.
19. Ibid., pp. 164-90. For her intriguing follow-up history of the mechanistic/mastery worldview in the ecological revolution in New England, which compares the Puritans' ethic of subjugation with the Native Americans' ethic of prudent exploitation, including the ambiguities and developments in each, see Merchant's *Ecological Revolutions: Nature, Gender and Science in New England* (Chapel Hill: University of North Carolina Press, 1989).
20. Carolyn Merchant, *Death of Nature* pp. 59, 242-51.
21. Ibid., p. 6.
22. Clarence J. Glacken, *Traces on the Rhodian Shore: Nature and Culture in Western Thought from Ancient Times to the End of the Eighteenth Century* (Berkeley: University of California Press, 1967), pp. 494-95.
23. R. H. Tawney, *Religion and the Rise of Capitalism* (Harmondsworth, England: Pelican, 1938), pp. 28, 92, 237.
24. Ibid., p. 225. Italics mine.
25. Ibid., pp. 119, 244.
26. Glacken, *Traces on the Rhodian Shore*, p. 317.
27. Tawney, *Religion and the Rise of Capitalism*, pp. xiii, 28.
28. Joseph Cullen Ayer, Jr., *A Source Book for Ancient Church History* (New York: Scribner's, 1913), pp. 289, 367-69, 523-28.
29. H. Richard Niebuhr, *Christ and Culture* (New York: Harper and Bros., 1951).
30. William Leiss, *The Domination of Nature* (New York: George Braziller, 1972), pp. 48-57.

31. Roderick Frazier Nash, *Wilderness and the American Mind* (New Haven: Yale University Press, 1967), pp. 23-43.
32. George Williams, *Wilderness and Paradise in Christian Thought* (New York: Harper and Bros., 1962), p. 18.
33. Compare Thomas S. Derr, *Ecology and Human Liberation* (New York: World Student Christian Federation, 1973), p. 18.
34. Roger D. Sorrell, *St. Francis of Assisi and Nature: Tradition and Innovation in Western Christian Attitudes Toward the Environment* (New York: Oxford University Press, 1988), p. 89.
35. Santmire, *The Travail of Nature*, p. 9.
36. Ibid., pp. 128-133.
37. See D. S. Wallace-Hadrill, *The Greek Patristic View of Nature* (Manchester, England: Manchester University Press, 1968).
38. Issa J. Khalil, "The Ecological Crisis: An Eastern Christian Perspective," *St. Vladimir's Theological Quarterly*, vol. 22, no. 4 (1978): 193-211. See also the several substantive articles in *Epiphany Journal*, vol. 10, no. 3 (Spring 1990), and "Orthodox Perspectives on Creation," in Gennadios Limouris, ed., *Justice, Peace, and the Integrity of Creation*, (Geneva: World Council of Churches, 1990), pp. 1-15.
39. Joseph Sittler, *Essays on Nature and Grace* (Philadelphia: Fortress Press, 1972), p. 132n.
40. For a collection of historical readings and prayers, see Andrew Linzey and Tom Regan, eds., *Love the Animals: Meditations and Prayers* (New York: Crossroad, 1989).
41. Saint Hieronymus, "The Histories of the Monks in Egypt," in Ernest A. Wallis Budge, trans., *The Paradise of the Holy Fathers* (London: Chatto and Windus, 1907), p. 352.
42. Ibid., pp. 354-55.
43. Palladius, in Ernest A. Wallis Budge, *The Paradise of the Holy Fathers*, vol 2, pp. 202-3.
44. Rufinus, trans., *History of the Monks of Egypt*, in Helen Waddell, trans. and ed., *The Desert Fathers* (London: Constable, 1936), p. 79.
45. Palladius in Budge, *The Paradise of the Holy Fathers*, vol. 2, pp. 119-24.
46. Ibid., p. 118.
47. Saint Hieronymus, in Budge, pp. 338-39.
48. Count de Montalembert, *The Monks of the West: From St. Benedict to St. Bernard*, vol. II (New York: AMS Press, 1966), pp. 185-237.
49. Eleanor Duckett, *The Wandering Saints* (London: Collins, 1959), p. 72.
50. Ibid., p. 15.
51. Ibid., p. 72.
52. Bede, *Life of Cuthbert*, in J. F. Webb, trans., *Lives of the Saints* (Baltimore: Penguin, 1965), p. 85.
53. *The Voyage of St. Brendan*, in ibid. no. 26.
54. Duckett, *The Wandering Saints*, p. 125.
55. Ibid., p. 16.
56. Ibid., pp. 41-42. Compare Daphne D. C. Pochin Mould, *The Celtic Saints* (New York: Macmillan, 1956), pp. 101-2.
57. Duckett, *The Wandering Saints*, p. 89.
58. Ibid., p. 16.
59. Pochin Mould, *The Celtic Saints*, pp. 44, 102-3. Also Roger Sorrell, *St. Francis of Assisi and Nature*, pp. 26-27, 41; Clarence J. Glacken, *Traces on the Rhodian Shore*, p. 207.
60. Sorrell, *The Celtic Saints*, p. 141.
61. Ibid., p. 16.
62. Edward A. Armstrong, *Saint Francis, Nature Mystic: The Derivation and Significance of the Nature Stories in the Franciscan Legend* (Berkeley and Los Angeles: University of California Press, 1973), pp. 29, 34, 48, 64-65, 210-11. Sorrell claims that the similarities arise from parallel experiences, though the Irish certainly created an ambiance on the continent suitable for the acceptance of Francis. Sorrell, pp. 23-24.
63. Armstrong, pp. 76, 192, 216; Sorrell, pp. 43, 52-54.

64. Armstrong, *Saint Francis, Nature Mystic,* p. 76.
65. Santmire, *The Travail of Nature,* p. 117.
66. Leonardo Boff, *Saint Francis: A Model for Human Liberation,* trans. John W. Diercksmeier (New York: Crossroad, 1982), p. 18.
67. *The Little Flowers of St. Francis,* trans. T. Okey (London: J. M. Dent, 1950, 1910), ch. XXI.
68. *The Mirror of Perfection* (London: J. M. Dent, 1950, 1910), p. 291.
69. *Little Flowers,* ch. XXI.
70. *Little Flowers,* ch. XVI.
71. Armstrong, pp. 11, 16-17, 144-45.
72. G. K. Chesterton, *St. Francis of Assisi* (Garden City, N.Y.: Image Books, 1957), p. 96.
73. St. Bonaventure, *Life of St. Francis,* trans. E. Gurney Satter (London: J. M. Dent, 1950), ch. VIII, no. 9.
74. Ibid.
75. *Mirror of Perfection,* pp. 293-94.
76. For a collection that illustrates this extraordinary influence, see Roy M. Gasnick, O.F.M., ed., *The Francis Book: 800 Years with the Saint from Assisi* (New York-London: Collier/Macmillan, 1980).
77. See Matthew Fox, *Original Blessing: A Primer in Creation Spirituality* (Santa Fe, N.M.: Bear and Co., 1983).
78. T. H. White, trans. and ed., *The Bestiary: A Book of Beasts* (New York: G. P. Putnam's Sons/Capricorn Books, 1960), p. 247.
79. Keith Thomas, *Man and the Natural World: A History of the Modern Sensibility* (New York: Pantheon, 1983), pp. 154-59.
80. Gerald Carson, *Men, Beasts, and Gods: A History of Cruelty and Kindness to Animals* (New York: Charles Scribner's Sons, 1972), pp. 41-42, 47; James Turner, *Reckoning with the Beast: Animals, Pain and Humanity in the Victorian Mind* (Baltimore and London: Johns Hopkins University Press, 1980), pp. 12, 15, 17, 35.
81. James Turner, *Reckoning with the Beast,* pp. 9-12. For excerpts from Primatt's work, see Andrew Linzey and Tom Regan, eds., *Animals and Christianity* (New York: Crossroad, 1988), pp. 127-30.
82. James Turner, *Reckoning with the Beast,* p. 17.
83. Gerald Carson, *Men, Beasts and Gods,* p. 49.
84. H. J. Massingham, ed., *The Essential Gilbert White of Selborne* (London: Breslich and Foss, 1983); Donald Worster, *Nature's Economy,* pp. 3-11. Apparently, nature lovers were numerous in a Christian-influenced culture. For some names of other parson-naturalists, see Keith Thomas, pp. 280-81.
85. James Turner, p. 124.
86. George H. Williams, p. 117.
87. See the chapter "The Greening of Religion" in Roderick Nash, *The Rights of Nature: A History of Environmental Ethics* (Madison: University of Wisconsin Press, 1989), pp. 87-120.
88. Derr, *Ecology and Human Liberation,* p. 19.
89. "Religious Responsibility for the Ecological Crisis: An Argument Run Amok," *Worldview,* vol. 18, no. 1 (January, 1975), p. 43.
90. Compare Rene Dubos, "Franciscan Conservation versus Benedictine Stewardship," in David and Eileen Spring, eds., *Ecology and Religion* (New York: Harper, 1974), pp. 114-136. Also Ron Elsdon, *Bent World: A Christian Response to the Environmental Crisis* (Downers Grove, Ill.: Intervarsity Press, 1981), p. 13.
91. Lewis W. Moncrief, "The Cultural Basis of Our Environmental Crisis," in Ian G. Barbour, ed., *Western Man and Environmental Ethics: Attitudes Toward Nature and Technology* (Reading, Mass.: Addison-Wesley, 1973), pp. 39-40.
92. Peter Farb, *Ecology* (New York: Time-Life Books, 1970), p. 164. Rene Dubos makes the same point about population growth and technological means in "Franciscan

Conservation versus Benedictine Stewardship," in David and Eileen Spring, eds., *Ecology and Religion*, p. 123.

93. Compare Sean McDonagh, *To Care for the Earth: A Call to a New Theology* (Santa Fe, N.M.: Bear and Co., 1986), pp. 143-153.

94. Tom Regan, "Environmental Ethics and the Ambiguity of the Native American's Relationship with Nature," in *All That Dwell Therein: Animal Rights and Environmental Ethics* (Berkeley and Los Angeles: University of California, 1982), pp. 207, 233.

95. Compare ibid., p. 235. For a romantic account, in my view, of the Native American's ecological life-styles, see Thomas Berry, *The Dream of the Earth* (San Francisco: Sierra Club, 1988), pp. 180-193. For a very favorable but nonromantic view, see J. Baird Callicott, *In Defense of the Land Ethic* (Albany: State Univ. of New York Press, 1989), pp. 177-219.

4. FIRM FOUNDATIONS: DOCTRINES OF CREATION, COVENANT, DIVINE IMAGE, INCARNATION, AND SPIRITUAL PRESENCE

1. Certainly philosophical ethics can be, should be, independent of particular religious assumptions, values, and institutions. Yet it is hard to see how this discipline can be detached from some "religious" or metaphysical assumptions and values, some ultimate though tacit convictions about the nature of reality. Indeed, from a theistic perspective, even though philosophical ethics can be independent of "religion" (whatever that vague word means), it cannot be independent of God, the Ground of value and obligation, the Source of the rational and moral order. Compare Walter G. Muelder, *Moral Law in Christian Social Ethics* (Richmond, Va.: John Knox, 1966), pp. 148-51. The Ultimate Is is also the ultimate Ought. God is the Good, and the source of all knowledge of the good and duties to realize it.

2. William R. Hutchinson, *The Modernist Impulse in American Protestantism* (Cambridge: Harvard Univ. Press, 1976), p. 87. Compare Tom F. Driver, *Christ in a Changing World: Toward an Ethical Christology* (New York: Crossroad, 1981).

3. Joseph Sittler, *Essays on Nature and Grace* (Philadelphia: Fortress Press, 1972), pp. 76-77.

4. Ibid., p. 88.

5. Ibid., p. 74.

6. Ibid., pp. 82, 86, 2, 8-9. Compare George Hendry, *A Theology of Nature* (Philadelphia: Westminster, 1980), p. 116. For a review of historical and contemporary intrepretations of nature and grace, with an emphasis like Sittler's on the "grace of nature," see James A. Carpenter, *Nature and Grace* (New York: Crossroad, 1988).

7. Compare Jonathan Helfand, "The Earth is the Lord's: Judaism and Environmental Ethics," in Eugene C. Hargrove, ed., *Religion and Environmental Crisis* (Athens, Ga. and London: Univ. of Georgia Press, 1986), p. 42.

8. Conrad Hyers, *The Meaning of Creation: Genesis and Modern Science* (Atlanta: John Knox, 1984), p. 47.

9. Langdon Gilkey, *Maker of Heaven and Earth* (Garden City, N.J., Doubleday, 1959), pp. 47-51.

10. Claus Westermann, *Genesis 1–11: A Commentary*, trans. John J. Scullion, S.J. (Minneapolis: Augsburg, 1984), pp. 46, 108-9.

11. Walter Brueggemann, *Genesis: Interpretation* (Atlanta: John Knox Press, 1982), pp. 29-30.

12. Gilkey, *Maker of Heaven and Earth*, pp. 65-66.

13. Westermann, *Genesis 1–11*, pp. 173-74.

14. Ibid., pp. 64-65, 584, 597.

15. Gilkey, *Maker of Heaven and Earth*, p. 43.

16. Hyers, *The Meaning of Creation*, p. 30. Compare Brueggemann, *Genesis*, p. 26.

17. Bernard W. Anderson, "Introduction: Mythopoetic and Theological Dimensions of Biblical Creation Faith," in Anderson ed., *Creation in the Old Testament* (Philadelphia and London: Fortress/SPCK, 1984), p. 3.
18. Brueggemann, *Genesis*, p. 17.
19. Hyers, *The Meaning of Creation,* pp. 9-35.
20. Bernard W. Anderson, "Creation and the Noachic Covenant," in Philip N. Joranson and Ken Butigan, eds., *Cry of the Environment* (Santa Fe, N.M.: Bear and Co., 1984), p. 49.
21. Quoted in Robin Attfield, *The Ethics of Environmental Concern* (New York: Columbia Univ. Press, 1983), p. 35.
22. St. Bonaventure, "The Life of St. Francis," in Andrew Linzey and Tom Regan, eds., *Animals and Christianity: A Book of Readings* (New York: Crossroad, 1988), p. 28.
23. Westermann, *Genesis 1–11*, pp. 113, 166.
24. Hyers, *The Meaning of Creation,* pp. 165-193.
25. H. Richard Niebuhr, *The Meaning of Revelation* (New York: Macmillan, 1962, 1941), p. 172.
26. Westermann, *Genesis 1–11*, p. 176. Italics mine.
27. Bernard W. Anderson, "Creation and the Noachic Covenant," in Philip N. Joranson and Ken Butigan, eds., *Cry of the Environment* pp. 50-51.
28. Westermann, *Genesis 1–11*, p. 474.
29. Bernard W. Anderson, "Introduction," in *Cry of the Environment* p. 48.
30. Thomas Sieger Derr, *Ecology and Human Liberation* (New York: World Student Christian Federation, 1973), pp. 65-66.
31. Charles S. McCoy, "Covenant, Creation, and Ethics: A Federal Vision of Humanity and the Environment," in Joranson and Butigan, eds., *Cry of the Environment*, pp. 357, 369-70.
32. Westermann, *Genesis 1–11*, p. 148.
33. Jeremy Cohen, *"Be Fertile and Increase: Fill the Earth and Master It": The Ancient and Medieval Career of a Biblical Text* (Ithaca, N.Y.: Cornell University Press, 1989), p. 5. See also pp. 268, 309-14.
34. "The General Deliverance," in Albert C. Outler, ed., *The Works of John Wesley*, vol. 2, *Sermons II*: 33-70 (Nashville: Abingdon, 1985), pp. 436-50. Compare Paulos Gregorios, *The Human Presence: An Orthodox View of Nature* (Geneva: WCC, 1978), pp. 63-66, 73, 85.
35. Keith Thomas, *Man and the Natural World: A History of the Modern Sensibility* (New York: Pantheon, 1983), pp. 149-181.
36. Alan Richardson and John Bowden, eds. (Philadelphia: Westminster, 1983).
37. James F. Childress and John Macquarrie, eds. (Philadelphia: Westminster Press, 1983).
38. George M. Landes, "Creation and Liberation," in Bernard Anderson, ed., p. 146.
39. "In Defense of Dominion" (paper presented at Annual Meeting, Society of Christian Ethics, January, 1990), pp. 18-22.
40. Compare John Reumann, "Introduction" to C. F. D. Moule, *Man and Nature in the New Testament: Some Reflections on Biblical Ecology* (Philadelphia: Fortress Press, 1964), pp. ix-xi; Westermann, pp. 148-54; Douglas John Hall, *Imaging God: Dominion as Stewardship* (Grand Rapids: Eerdmans, 1987), pp. 88-108.
41. Westermann, pp. 38-39, 146, 153-54. Compare Brueggemann, p. 132.
42. Steffen, "In Defense of Dominion," p. 5.
43. Compare Susan Power Bratton, "Christian Ecotheology and the Old Testament," in Eugene C. Hargrove, ed., *Religion and Environmental Crisis* (Athens, Ga., and London: University of Georgia Press, 1986), pp. 62-63; B. Anderson in Joranson and Butigan, eds., p. 33; B. Anderson, "Creation and Ecology," in Anderson, ed., p. 163; Hall, pp. 61-87. Note the idea of "God's proxy" and "justice of the peace" in Jürgen Moltmann, *God in Creation* (San Francisco; Harper & Row, 1985), pp. 188-89.
44. Westermann, *Genesis 1–11*, p. 155.

45. Compare Moltmann, *God in Creation*, pp. 225-28; Reumann in Moule, *Man and Nature in the New Testament*, pp. xii-xv; Hall, *Imaging God*, pp. 76-87.
46. Hall, *Imaging God*, pp. 107-8, 113-28, 184-87; compare Loren Wilkinson, ed., *Earthkeeping: Christian Stewardship of Natural Resources* (Grand Rapids: Eerdmans, 1980), pp. 130, 214-16.
47. James Barr, "Man and Nature: Ecological Controversy and the Old Testament," in David and Eileen Spring, eds., *Ecology and Religion in History* (New York: Harper & Row, 1974), pp. 63-64.
48. Roderick Nash, *The Rights of Nature: A History of Environmental Ethics*, pp. 96, 107, 111. But compare Hall, pp. 175, 184-87.
49. Jürgen Moltmann, *God in Creation*, pp. 50-51.
50. Ibid., pp. 186-90. Compare D. S. Wallace-Hadrill, *The Greek Patristic View of Nature* (Manchester, England: Manchester Univ. Press, 1968), pp. 76-77; Archimandrite Kallistos Ware, "The Value of the Material Creation," *Sobornost*, series 6, no. 3 (Summer 1971), p. 158.
51. Sean McDonagh, *To Care for the Earth* (Santa Fe, N.M.: Bear and Co., 1986), pp. 118-19.
52. Edward O. Wilson, *Biophilia* (Cambridge: Harvard Univ. Press, 1984), p. 85.
53. St. John of Damascus, *On the Divine Images* I:16. Quoted in Myroslaw Tataryn, "The Eastern Tradition and the Cosmos," *Sobornost*, vol. 11, nos. 1-2 (1989), p. 49.
54. *The Meaning of Revelation* (New York: Macmillan, 1962, 1941), p. 167. Compare *Radical Monotheism and Western Culture* (New York: Harper & Row, 1970), pp. 32-38, 126. For Niebuhr, whatever has being is valuable and worthy of love, since in radical monotheism, God is the source of being and value.
55. Ibid., p. 173.
56. Ted F. Peters, "Creation, Consummation and the Ethical Imagination," in Joranson and Butigan, eds., pp. 422-23.
57. Gabriel Fackre, "Ecology and Theology," in Ian G. Barbour, ed., *Western Man and Environmental Ethics* (Reading, Mass.: Addison-Wesley, 1973), p. 121.
58. Jürgen Moltmann, *God in Creation*, pp. ii, xii-xiii, 14-15, 63-64, 98-100.
59. *A Rumor of Angels* (New York: Doubleday/Anchor, 1969), pp. 52-75.
60. For a fuller exposition of this position, see my "Christian Liberalism: Ambiguous Legacy, Enduring Ethos," *The Unitarian Universalist Christian*, vol. 41, no. 1 (Spring 1986), pp. 12-18.
61. William Temple, *Nature, Man and God* (London: Macmillan, 1934), pp. 482-495. On *finitum capax infiniti* (the finite bears the infinite) in Luther, see Larry Rasmussen, "Returning to Our Senses: The Theology of the Cross as a Theology for Ecojustice" (unpublished paper, 1990). Contrary to some ecclesiastical sacramentalists, however, I fail to see the significance for the love of nature in the elements of the Eucharist. The wine and bread are products of culture, signifying the gifts of labor in the human transformation of nature. That is a critical rite for the church, but nature sacramentality values nature in the raw.
62. Rudolf Otto, *The Idea of the Holy*, 2nd ed. (London, Oxford, New York: Oxford University Press, 1958), esp. pp. 12-20, 28, 52-53; Holmes Rolston, III, *Environmental Ethics* (Philadelphia: Temple Univ. Press, 1988), pp. 25-27. Compare S. Paul Santmire, *Brother Earth* (New York-Camden: Thomas Nelson, 1970), pp. 151-61.
63. *The Voice of the Desert: A Naturalist's Interpretation* (New York: William Sloan Associates, 1972), p. 220. His point should not be dismissed casually. After all, what should we make of the fact that the biblical authors of Job, Jeremiah, II Isaiah, and Psalm 104 seemed to be acute nature observers?
64. Compare George Williams, *Wilderness and Paradise in Christian Thought* (New York: Harper, 1962), pp. 5, 17.
65. W. H. Auden and Norman Holmes Pearson, eds., *Romantic Poets: Blake to Poe* (New York: Viking Press, 1950), p. xxiii.

66. Holmes Rolston III, pp. 241-45. Compare Richard Cartwright Austin, *Beauty of the Lord: Awakening the Senses* (Atlanta: John Knox, 1988). Austin emphasizes natural beauty, but by romanticizing, in my view, natural evil. He perceptively sees, however, the moral effects of encounters with natural beauty (pp. 16, 20-21, 135, 148, 172-90).

67. Edwin Way Teale, ed., *The Wilderness World of John Muir* (Boston: Houghton-Mifflin, 1954), pp. 166-169.

68. Issa J. Khalil, "The Ecological Crisis: An Eastern Christian Perspective," *St. Vladimir's Theological Quarterly*, vol. 22, no. 4 (1978), p. 203.

69. Charles Hartshorne, *Beyond Humanism* (Chicago/New York: Willett, Clark, 1937), pp. 5, 76, 315-16. Sallie McFague, *Models of God: Theology for an Ecological, Nuclear Age* (Philadelphia: Fortress Press, 1987), pp. 69-77. For a "relational panentheism" grounded in process theology, see Jay B. McDaniel, *Of God and Pelicans: A Theology of Reverence for Life* (Louisville: Westminster/John Knox, 1989), pp. 26-31, and *Earth, Sky, Gods and Mortals* (Mystic, Conn.: Twenty Third Publications, 1990), pp. 50-57, 102-6. McFague uses the body image cautiously and restrictively, with clear awareness of its pitfalls. I sense, however, that some of her qualifications of the metaphor may serve as disqualifications of its value (e.g., God's love of God's body seems narcissistic!), and I doubt that these qualifications will be widely respected in common usage. I prefer, therefore, a safer, more ecological metaphor, namely, *the world as the Spirit's beloved habitat.* This image preserves the "otherness" of the world and God, and yet is compatible with McFague's models of God as mother (and father), lover, and friend. Similar images have equivalent benefits, for example, the world as God's homeland, home, or household—the divine "oikos." Compare Douglas Meeks, *God the Economist* (Minneapolis: Augsburg Fortress, 1989), pp. 33-36,75-97.

70. On the history, see George Williams, *Wilderness and Paradise in Christian Thought*, pp. 4, 46-55.

71. Henri J. M. Nouwen, *The Way of the Heart: Desert Spirituality and Contemporary Ministry* (New York: Seabury, 1981), pp. 14-15, 24, 30-32, 57; Kenneth Leech, *True Prayer: An Invitation to Christian Spirituality* (San Francisco: Harper & Row, 1980), pp. 175-77.

72. Compare Meeks, *God the Economist*, pp. 75-97.

5. FIRM FOUNDATIONS: DOCTRINES OF SIN, JUDGMENT, REDEMPTION, AND CHURCH

1. Reinhold Niebuhr, *The Nature and Destiny of Man*, vol. I (New York: Charles Scribner's Sons, 1949), pp. 182-90.

2. James Gustafson, *Ethics from a Theocentric Perspective*, vol. 1 (Chicago: Univ. of Chicago Press, 1981), pp. 242-47.

3. Gabriel Fackre, *The Christian Story* (Grand Rapids: Eerdmans, 1978), pp. 72; 72-74, 78. Fackre has long been sensitive to ecological sins.

4. See my "The Sin of *Valdez*," in *Impact: Environmental Stewardship* (July, 1989), pp. 2-3.

5. Walter Rauschenbusch, *Christianizing the Social Order* (New York: Macmillan, 1912), pp. 25-53. Italics mine.

6. Ibid., pp. 253-54. Italics mine.

7. Reinhold Niebuhr, *Nature and Destiny*, I, pp. 190-91.

8. Perry Miller, *The New England Mind: From Colony to Province*, vol. II (Boston: Beacon Press, 1961, 1953).

9. L. Harold DeWolf, *A Theology of the Living Church*, rev. (New York: Harper, 1960), pp. 139-40.

10. James Gustafson, *Theocentric Ethics*, vol. I (Chicago: Univ. of Chicago Press, 1981), pp. 246, 242-47. Gustafson's "God" is a nonconscious and nonmoral ordering power without intention, volition, or cognition. This power sustains the universe, apparently unintentionally, but lacks the purposive, benevolent, or redemptive qualities to seek the good of individuals, the human species, otherkind, or the whole

cosmos. See pp. 106, 183-84, 248-50, 270-73. This perspective seems close to atheism or pantheism. Yet, many of his empirically grounded characterizations of God are eminently helpful.

11. Gabriel Fackre, *The Christian Story*, p. 80.

12. DeWolf, *A Theology of the Living Church*, pp. 284-85.

13. Edwin Way Teale, ed., *The Wilderness World of John Muir* (Boston: Houghton-Mifflin, 1954), pp. 313-17.

14. Compare the selections from St. Thomas Aquinas, *Summa Theologica*, I, Q XCVI, Q LXIV, Art. 1 and Q LXV, Art. 3 in Andrew Linzey and Tom Regan, eds., *Animals and Christianity: A Book of Readings* (New York: Crossroad, 1988), pp. 17-20, 124-27; and from Joseph Rickaby, *Moral Philosophy* (1901), and Immanuel Kant, *Lectures on Ethics*, in Tom Regan and Peter Singer, eds., *Animal Rights and Human Obligations* (Englewood Cliffs, N.J.: Prentice-Hall, 1976), pp. 179-80, 122-23.

15. Donald E. Gowan, *Eschatology in the Old Testament* (Philadelphia: Fortress Press, 1986), pp. 97-120.

16. J. Christiaan Beker, *Paul the Apostle: The Triumph of God in Life and Thought* (Philadelphia: Fortress Press, 1980), pp. ix, 149-81, 269-70, 351-52. Compare Richard Hiers on Jesus' message, *Jesus and the Future: Unresolved Questions for Eschatology* (Atlanta: John Knox, 1981), pp. 87, 104.

17. Allan D. Galloway, *The Cosmic Christ* (New York: Harper, 1951), p. x.

18. *The Orthodox Church* (Harmondsworth, England: Penguin, 1963), pp. 239-40. Compare "Orthodox Perspectives on Creation" in Gennadios Limouris, ed., *Justice, Peace, and the Integrity of Creation* (Geneva: WCC Publications, 1990), p. 9; Vladimir Lossky, *The Mystical Theology of the Eastern Church* (London: James Clark, 1957), pp. 101, 110-13, 235.

19. I disagree with Santmire's interpretation of Francis on this point. See Paul Santmire, *The Travail of Nature* (Philadelphia: Fortress Press, 1985), pp. 113-17.

20. On Calvin and Luther, see ibid., pp. 122-131.

21. Excerpt in Andrew Linzey and Tom Regan, eds., *Animals and Christianity: A Book of Readings* (New York: Crossroad, 1988), p. 100. Compare *Institutes*, III, XXV, 2.

22. "The General Deliverance," in Albert C. Outler, ed., *The Works of John Wesley*, vol. 2, *Sermons II*: 34-70 (Nashville: Abingdon Press, 1985), Sermon 60, pp. 436-50.

23. Keith Thomas, *Man and the Natural World: A History of the Modern Sensibility* (New York: Pantheon, 1983), pp. 137-42, 154-80; James Turner, *Reckoning with the Beast*, pp. 8, 146n. Also, on John Bradford, royal chaplain under Edward and martyr under Mary, see George Williams, *Wilderness and Paradise*, pp. 83-84.

24. "The General Deliverance," pp. 437-38.

25. Ibid., pp. 440-41.

26. Ibid., p. 440.

27. Ibid., p. 441.

28. Ibid., pp. 442-44.

29. Ibid., p. 444.

30. Ibid., pp. 444-45.

31. Ibid., pp. 446, 448.

32. Ibid., pp. 447, 449.

33. Ibid., pp. 446-47.

34. Ibid., p. 448.

35. Ibid.

36. Ibid., p. 449. Compare 437.

37. Jürgen Moltmann, *Future of Creation* (Philadelphia: Fortress, 1979), p. 98; *God in Creation*, pp. 93-94, 276-78; Carl Braaten, *Ethics and Eschatology* (Minneapolis: Augsburg, 1974), pp. 68-70; Paul Santmire, *Travail of Nature*, pp. 171-73, 210-18; Gabriel Frackre, *The Christian Story*, p. 224; Joseph Sittler, *Essays on Nature and Grace*, pp. 110-11; George Hendry, *Theology of Nature* (Philadelphia: Westminster, 1980), pp. 11, 172, 189, 200, 206, 220-21.

38. Hendry, *Theology of Nature*, p. 172.
39. Paul Tillich, *Systematic Theology*, vol. II (Chicago: Univ. of Chicago Press, 1957), pp. 95-96. Compare vol. III (1963), pp. 406-9.
40. James Gustafson, *Theocentric Ethics*, I (Chicago: Univ. of Chicago Press, 1981), pp. 89, 182-84, 202-3, 268-72, 310; Gordon D. Kaufmann, *Systematic Theology: An Historicist Perspective* (New York: Charles Scribner's Sons, 1968), pp. 459n, 462-64, 469-70; Charles Hartshorne, *Reality as Social Process* (Glencoe, Ill.: Free Press, 1953), pp. 42, 208-11; Schubert Ogden, *Reality of God and Other Essays* (New York: Harper & Row, 1966), pp. 36, 65, 179, 186, 206-30; *Faith and Freedom: Toward a Theology of Liberation* (Nashville: Abingdon Press, 1979), pp. 56, 83-85; Norman Pittenger, *After Death: Life in God* (New York: Seabury/Crossroad, 1980), pp. 31-35, 47-80.
41. Compare Gabriel Marcel, *Homo Viator: Introduction to a Metaphysic of Hope*, trans. Emma Craufurd (Chicago: Henry Reynery Co., 1951), pp. 47, 49, 66, 147, 152; John Baillie, *And the Life Everlasting* (New York: Charles Scribner's Sons, 1933), pp. 62-65; W. E. Hocking, *The Meaning of Immortality in Human Experience* (New York: Harper & Row, 1957), pp. 6-7, 247.
42. Compare S. Paul Schilling, *God and Human Anguish* (Nashville: Abingdon Press, 1977), pp. 169-73; John Hick, *Death and Eternal Life* (San Francisco, Harper & Row, 1976), p. 159.
43. Beker, *Paul the Apostle*, pp. 269, 270.
44. Hendry, *Theology of Nature*, p. 221.
45. Compare John Baillie, *And the Life Everlasting*, pp. 196, 229-33; Hendrikus Berkhof, *Christian Faith* (Grand Rapids: Eerdmans, 1979), pp. 521-22; John Macquairre, *The Christian Hope* (New York: Seabury, 1978), p. 75; Langdon Gilkey, *Message and Existence* (New York: Seabury, 1981), pp. 251-55.
46. Compare Carl Braaten, *Eschatology and Ethics*, p. 182.
47. H. Richard Niebuhr, *The Meaning of Revelation*, p. 189.
48. Compare J. Robert Nelson's exposition of the four-fold definition of catholicity in Cyril of Jerusalem (347 A.D.), *The Realm of Redemption* (Chicago: Wilcox and Follett, 1951), pp. 206-8.
49. Beker, *Paul the Apostle*, pp. 303-4.
50. Ibid., p. 155.
51. Gustavo Gutiérrez, *Theology of Liberation* (Maryknoll, N.Y.: Orbis/Maryknoll, 1973), p. 162.
52. Wolfhart Pannenberg, *Theology and the Kingdom of God* (Philadelphia: Westminster, 1969), pp. 76-78.
53. Alisdair I. C. Heron, *The Holy Spirit* (Philadelphia: Westminster, 1983), p. 51.
54. Compare Jürgen Moltmann, *Theology of Hope* (New York: Harper, 1975), p. 302, and *The Church in the Power of the Spirit* (New York: Harper & Row, 1977), p. 357; Wolfhart Pannenberg, *The Church* (Philadelphia: Westminster, 1983), pp. 44-68.
55. Carl Braaten, *Ethics and Eschatology*, pp. 121-22, 141.
56. Walter Rauschenbusch, *A Theology for the Social Gospel* (Nashville: Abingdon, 1917), pp. 143-44.
57. Compare Gutiérrez, *Theology of Liberation*, pp. 217-18, 231-32.

6. LOVING NATURE: CHRISTIAN LOVE IN AN ECOLOGICAL CONTEXT

1. Albert Schweitzer, *Out of My Life and Thought* (New York: Mentor ed., 1953), p. 180; Aldo Leopold, *Sand County Almanac* (New York: Ballantine Books ed., 1970), pp. xix, 239; Joseph Wood Krutch, *The Voice of The Desert: A Naturalist's Interpretation* (New York: William Sloane Associates, 1955), pp. 193, 201-202; Edwin Way Teale, ed.,

The Wilderness World of John Muir (Boston: Houghton-Mifflin, 1954), p. 313; H. Richard Niebuhr et al., *The Purpose of the Church and Its Ministry* (New York: Harper & Row, 1956), p. 38; Robert Shelton, *Loving Relationships* (Elgin, Ill.: Brethren Press, 1987), pp. 103-113; Joseph Allen, *Love and Conflict: A Covenantal Model of Christian Ethics* (Nashville: Abingdon Press, 1984), pp. 66-69, 78; Sallie McFague, *Models of God: Theology for an Ecological, Nuclear Age* (Philadelphia: Fortress Press, 1986), pp. 125-155; Douglas John Hall, *Imaging God: Dominion as Stewardship* (Grand Rapids: Eerdmans, 1986), pp. 128-132; Jay B. McDaniel, *Earth, Sky, Gods and Mortals* (Mystic, Conn.: Twenty Third Publications, 1990), pp. 44-45, 68-70 and *Of God and Pelicans* (Louisville: Westminster/John Knox, 1989), pp. 21-26; Dorothee Söelle, *To Work and to Love: A Theology of Creation* (Philadelphia: Fortress, 1984), pp. 3, 16, 32; Loren Wilkinson, ed., *Earthkeeping: Christian Stewardship of Natural Resources* (Grand Rapids: Eerdmans, 1980), pp. 215-223; Issa Khalil, "For the Transfiguration of Nature: Ecology and Theology," *Epiphany Journal*, Vol. 10, No. 3 (Spring, 1990), pp. 19-36.

2. "For the Transfiguration of Nature: On Orthodox Responsibility for the Creation," *Epiphany Journal*, vol. 10, no. 3 (Spring 1990), p. 74. This statement emerged from the 1989 Symposium on Orthodoxy and Ecology. The love of nature has deep historical roots in Orthodoxy.

3. Karl Barth, *Church Dogmatics*, vol. III, pt. 4, "The Doctrine of Creation" (Edinburgh: T. and T. Clark, 1961), p. 333.

4. Emil Brunner, *Dogmatics*, vol. I, *The Christian Doctrine of God* (Philadelphia: The Westminster Press, 1950), pp. 183, 185, 199.

5. Hall, *Imaging God*, p. 136.

6. Compare Victor Furnish, "Love of Neighbor in the New Testament," *The Journal of Religious Ethics* vol. 10, no. 2 (Fall 1982), p. 329.

7. George M. Newlands, *Theology of the Love of God* (Atlanta: John Knox Press, 1980), pp. 20, 201.

8. Allen, *Love and Conflict*, pp. 49, 52-53.

9. Gene Outka, *Agape: An Ethical Analysis* (New Haven and London: Yale University Press, 1972), pp. 149, 155.

10. Paul Ramsey, *Deeds and Rules in Christian Ethics* (New York: Charles Scribner's Sons, 1967), p. 2.

11. H. Richard Niebuhr, *The Purpose of the Church and Its Ministry*, p. 31.

12. Compare John P. Crossley, Jr., "Theological Ethics and the Naturalistic Fallacy," *The Journal of Religious Ethics*, vol. 6, no. 1 (Spring 1978), pp. 126-27, 132.

13. Hall, *Imaging God*, pp. 185-86, 198-99.

14. H. Richard Niebuhr, *The Purpose of the Church and Its Ministry*, p. 38.

15. Schweitzer, *Out of My Life and Thought*, p. 180.

16. Leopold, *Sand County Almanac*, p. 239.

17. H. Richard Niebuhr, *The Meaning of Revelation* (New York: Macmillan, 1962, 1941), p. 167. Italics mine.

18. For a discussion of this irony, see Anders Nygren, *Agape and Eros*, vol. I, rev. and retrans. ed. (London: SPCK, 1953), pp. 147-54.

19. Victor Furnish, "Love of Neighbor in the New Testament," pp. 328-29.

20. Garth L. Hallett, *Christian Neighbor-Love: An Assessment of Six Rival Versions* (Washington: Georgetown Univ. Press, 1989), pp. 2-10.

21. Ibid., pp. 48, 14.

22. Ibid., pp. 47, 53, 110.

23. *Agape and Eros.*

24. D. D. Williams, *The Spirit and the Forms of Love* (New York: Harper and Row, 1968), pp. 3, 5, 13, 49, 202-12.

25. Outka, *Agape*, p. 12.

26. Paul Ramsey, *Deeds and Rules*, p. 5.

27. Outka, *Agape*.

28. Susan Armstrong-Buck, "Non-Human Experience: A Whiteheadian Analysis," *Process Studies*, vol. 18, no. 1 (Spring, 1989), pp. 1-18. Also, on sentient creatures, see Tom Regan, *The Case for Animal Rights* (Berkeley/Los Angeles: University of California Press, 1983), pp. 1-81.

29. Paul Tillich, *Systematic Theology*, vol. II (Chicago: Univ. of Chicago Press, 1957), pp. 31, 41-42.

30. Compare Roderick Nash, *The Rights of Nature* (Madison: Univ. of Wisconsin, 1989), pp. 146-60. See also George Sessions, "Ecological Consciousness and Paradigm Change," pp. 28-44, and Arne Naess, "Identification as a Source of Deep Ecological Attitudes," pp. 256-70, in Michael Tobias, ed., *Deep Ecology*, rev. (San Marcos, Calif.: Avant Books, 1988).

31. Schweitzer, *Out of My Life and Thought*, p. 181.

32. Paul Taylor, *Respect for Nature: A Theory of Environmental Ethics* (Princeton, N.J.: Princeton Univ. Press, 1986), p. 260.

33. According to Peter Singer, the coiner of the term, my preference is not speciesism, since relevant differences justify unequal treatment and rights. See *Animal Liberation: A New Ethic for Our Treatment of Animals* (New York: Avon, 1975), pp. 2-3, 6-8, 20-22, 251.

34. Reinhold Niebuhr, *The Nature and Destiny of Man*, vol. II (New York: Charles Scribner's Sons, 1949), pp. 68-70.

35. Compare J. Philip Wogaman, *Christian Moral Judgment* (Louisville, Ky.: Westminster/John Knox, 1989), p. 84.

36. Stephen Post, "Communion and True Self-Love," *Journal of Religious Ethics*, vol. 16, no. 2 (Fall 1988), pp. 351-52. Compare Christine E. Gudorf, "Parenting, Mutual Love, and Sacrifice," in Barbara Hilkert Andolsen et al., *Women's Consciousness, Women's Conscience* (San Francisco: Harper & Row, 1985), pp. 175-91.

37. Compare Reinhold Niebuhr, *The Nature and Destiny*, vol. II, pp. 70, 82, 86, 96.

38. Jaroslav Pelikan, *The Christian Tradition*, vol. 4: *Reformation of Church Doctrine (1300-1700)* (Chicago: Univ. of Chicago Press, 1984), pp. 149-50.

39. Barth, *Church Dogmatics*, vol. III, pt. 4, "Doctrine of Creation," p. 355.

40. This distinction is in William K. Frankena, *Ethics*, 2nd ed. (New York: Prentice-Hall, 1973), pp. 45, 47.

41. Frankena makes this reduction. Ibid., p. 58. For a criticism, see Frederick S. Carney, "On Frankena and Religious Ethics," *The Journal of Religious Ethics*, vol. 3, no. 1 (Spring 1975), pp. 18-22. In this same issue, see Frankena's response, "Conversations with Carney and Hauerwas," pp. 58-60.

42. Compare William Blackstone, "The Search for an Environmental Ethic," in Tom Regan, ed., *Matters of Life and Death: New Introductory Essays in Moral Philosophy* (New York: Random House, 1980), pp. 309-11.

43. H. Richard Niebuhr, *Purpose of the Church and Its Ministry*, pp. 35-36.

44. See Donald Worster, *Nature's Economy: The Roots of Ecology* (Garden City, N.Y.: Anchor/Doubleday, 1979), pp. 260-61.

45. David Oates, "Descendentalism: The Thoreavian Inscape of the Environmental Movement: Some Texts, Some Remarks: or, The Spirituality of Shit," *Contemporary Philosophy*, vol. 12, no. 11 (Sept./Oct., 1989), pp. 33-36.

46. Herbert Butterfield, *Christianity and History* (London and Glasgow: Collins/Fontana Books, 1957), p. 137.

47. For a good discussion of the ambiguities of technology, see Lester W. Milbrath, *Envisioning a Sustainable Society* (Albany: State University of New York, 1989), pp. 232-73.

48. On corporate ignorance, see, for example, Barbara Bramble and Sheila Hartz, "Environmental Concerns Associated with Multilateral Bank Activity," in W. Michael Hoffman et al., eds., *Ethics and the Multinational Corporation* (Lanham, Md.: University Press of America, 1986), pp. 239-47.

49. Quoted in Robert Cahn, *Footprints on the Planet: A Search for An Environmental Ethic* (New York: Universe Books, 1978), p. 200.
50. Paul Tillich, *Systematic Theology*, vol. III, pp. 134, 137, 156-57. Compare D. D. Williams, *The Spirit and the Forms of Love*, pp. 14, 130.
51. Compare John Giles Milhaven, "Response to Pure Love by Robert Merihew Adams," *The Journal of Religious Ethics*, vol. 8, no. 1 (Spring, 1980), pp. 101, 103-4.
52. Issa J. Khalil, "The Ecological Crisis: An Eastern Christian Perspective," *St. Vladimir's Theological Quarterly*, vol. 22, no. 4 (1978), pp. 210-11.

7. LOVE AS ECOLOGICAL JUSTICE: RIGHTS AND RESPONSIBILITIES

1. Joseph Haroutunian, trans. and ed., *Calvin: Commentaries* vol. 23, Library of Christian Classics (Philadelphia: Westminster Press, 1958), p. 32.
2. John C. Haughey, S.J., "Jesus as the Justice of God," in Haughey, ed., *The Faith That Does Justice* (New York: Paulist Press, 1977), pp. 264-90. In this volume, see also John R. Donahue, "Biblical Perspectives on Justice," pp. 68-112.
3. *The Nature and Destiny of Man*, vol. II (New York: Charles Scribner's Sons, 1949), pp. 68-76.
4. Ibid., II, p. 76.
5. Ibid., I, p. 295; II, p. 74.
6. Ibid., II, pp. 68-69, 81, 88.
7. Ibid., II, pp. 70, 78, 81-82.
8. Paul Tillich, *Systematic Theology*, vol. II (Chicago: Univ. of Chicago Press, 1963), pp. 172, 174.
9. D. D. Williams, *The Spirit and the Forms of Love* (New York: Harper & Row, 1968), pp. 250, 260.
10. Daniel C. Maguire, *The Moral Choice* (Minneapolis: Winston Press, 1978), pp. 94-95.
11. For examples of typologies, see Otto A. Bird, *The Idea of Justice* (New York: Praeger, 1967); Karen Lebacqz, *Six Theories of Justice: Perspectives from Philosophical and Theological Ethics* (Minneapolis: Augsburg Press, 1986).
12. Joseph L. Allen, *Love and Conflict: A Covenantal Model of Christian Ethics* (Nashville: Abingdon Press, 1984), p. 164.
13. Karen Lebacqz, *Justice in an Unjust World: Foundations for a Christian Approach to Justice* (Minneapolis: Augsburg Press, 1987), p. 128. Compare Stephen Charles Mott, *Biblical Ethics and Social Change* (New York: Oxford University Press, 1982), pp. 67-71.
14. Karen Lebacqz, *Justice in an Unjust World*, pp. 103-120.
15. Mott, *Bibilical Ethics and Social Change*, pp 52-53.
16. Allen, *Love and Conflict*, pp. 153-55.
17. Similar understandings of human rights are common in contemporary Christian ethics. In addition to Allen, see also David Hollenbach, *Justice, Peace, and Human Rights: American Catholic Social Ethics in a Pluralistic Context* (New York: Crossroad, 1988); Lisa Soule Cahill, "Toward a Christian Theory of Human Rights," *Journal of Religious Ethics*, vol. 8, no. 2 (Fall 1980), pp. 277-301; Joseph Allen, "Catholic and Protestant Theories of Human Rights," *Religious Studies Review*, vol. 14, no. 4 (October, 1988), pp. 347-53; National Conference of Catholic Bishops, *Economic Justice for All: Pastoral Letter on Catholic Social Teaching and the U.S. Economy* (Washington: National Conference of Catholic Bishops, 1986), paragraphs 61-95; and Mott, pp. 59-81.
18. Arthur J. Dyck, "Grounding Human Rights: Autonomy vs. Interdependence," in Alan B. Anderson, ed., *The Annual: Society of Christian Ethics, 1986* (Washington: Georgetown Univ. Press, 1987), p. 80.

19. Karen Lebacqz, *Justice in an Unjust World*, pp. 155, 106.
20. See, for example, Alexander S. Timoshenko, "International Environmental Law and the Concept of Ecological Security," *Breakthrough*, vol. 10, no. 4/vol. 11, no. 1 (Summer/Fall, 1989), pp. 22-24. Also, in this same issue, Edith Brown Weiss, "Passing It On: Climate Change, Intergenerational Equity and International Law," pp. 25-27.
21. Pope John Paul II, "Peace with God the Creator, Peace with all of Creation," *Origins*, vol. 19, no. 28 (Dec. 14, 1989), p. 467.
22. World Commission on Environment and Development, *Our Common Future* (New York: Oxford Univ. Press, 1987), Annexe I, p. 348.
23. Ibid. p. 331. Also see Annexe I, pp. 348-51.
24. For an historical overview, see Roderick Nash, *The Rights of Nature: A History of Environmental Ethics* (Madison: Univ. of Wisconsin Press, 1989), esp. pp. 6, 8, 127, 132, 155 171-76.
25. See especially the Canberra Assembly statement, "Giver of Life, Sustain Your Creation" (unpublished at this writing), which followed the recommendations from a preassembly consultation in Kuala Lumpur, Malaysia (May 1990). See also the report of the WCC, Church and Society consultation in Annecy, France, 1988, "Liberating Life: A Report to the World Council of Churches," in Charles Birch, William Eakin, and Jay B. McDaniel, eds., *Liberating Life* (Maryknoll, N.Y.: Orbis, 1990) pp. 273-90.
26. Compare Stephen R. L. Clark, *The Moral Status of Animals* (Oxford: Clarendon Press, 1977), p. 197.
27. K. E. Goodpaster, "From Egoism to Environmentalism," in K.E. Goodpaster and K. M. Sayre, eds., *Ethics and Problems of the 21st Century* (Notre Dame, Ind.: Univ. of Notre Dame Press, 1979), p. 29. Compare J. Baird Callicott, "The Search for an Environmental Ethic," in Tom Regan, ed., *Matters of Life and Death: New Introductory Essays in Moral Philosophy*, 2nd ed. (New York: Random House, 1986), pp. 402-3.
28. R. and V. Routley, "Against the Inevitability of Human Chauvinism," in Goodpaster and Sayre, eds, *Ethics and Problems of the 21st Century*, p. 56.
29. See discussion in Mary Anne Warren, "The Rights of the Non-Human World," in Robert Elliot and Arran Gare, eds., *Environmental Philosophy* (University Park: Pennsylvania State Univ. Press, 1983), pp. 109-20.
30. "All these life-based approaches [moral rights and intrinsic values for all life-forms] encounter the same problem: they produce overwhelming conflicts and incoherence, and thereby reduce to absurdity." Jack Weir, "Species Extinction and the Concho Water Snake: A Case Study in Environmental Ethics," *Contemporary Philosophy*, vol. 12, no. 7 (Jan., 1989), p. 3.
31. Compare Callicott in Tom Regan, ed. *Matters of Life and Death*, 2nd ed., pp. 402-3.
32. Compare William Blackstone, "The Search for an Environmental Ethic," in Tom Regan, ed., *Matters of Life and Death*, pp. 309-11.
33. Mary Midgley, *Animals and Why They Matter: A Journey Around the Species' Barrier* (Hammondsworth, England: Penguin Books, 1983), pp. 62-63, and Midgley in Elliot and Gare, eds., *Environmental Philosophy*, p. 171. Also, Andrew Linzey, *Christianity and the Rights of Animals* (New York: Crossroad, 1987), pp. 96-97.
34. Joel Feinberg, "Can Animals Have Rights?," in Tom Regan and Peter Singer, eds., *Animal Rights and Human Obligations* (Englewood Cliffs, N.J.: Prentice-Hall, 1976), p. 196.
35. Roderick Nash, *The Rights of Nature*, pp. 6, 8, 127, 132, 155, 171-76.
36. Michael Fox, " 'Animal Liberation': A Critique," *Ethics*, vol. 88, no. 2 (January, 1978), p. 107.
37. Paul W. Taylor, *Respect for Nature: A Theory of Environmental Ethics* (Princeton: Princeton Univ. Press, 1986), p. 219.
38. Ibid., pp. 224-25.
39. Ibid., p. 254.

40. Ibid., p. 226.
41. Ibid., pp. 254, 226.
42. Tom Regan, *The Case for Animal Rights* (Berkeley and Los Angeles, Univ. of California Press, 1983), pp. 243-45.
43. Ibid., p. 246.
44. Ibid., pp. 367, 391, 398.
45. H. Richard Niebuhr, *The Meaning of Revelation*, p. 167.
46. Compare Feinberg in Regan and Singer, eds., pp. 190-191, 195.
47. Holmes Rolston III, *Environmental Ethics: Duties to and Values in the Natural World* (Philadelphia: Temple Univ. Press, 1988), pp. 188-89. Compare Andrew Brennan, *Thinking About Nature* (Athens, Ga.: Univ. of Georgia, 1988), pp. 150-56.
48. Compare Feinberg in Regan and Singer, eds., pp. 195-96.
49. Albert Schweitzer, *Civilization and Ethics,* 2nd ed. (London: A. and C. Black, 1929), pp. 247-58.
50. Taylor, *Respect for Nature,* p. 100.
51. Meredith Williams, "Rights, Interests and Moral Equality," *Environmental Ethics,* vol. 2, no. 2 (Summer 1980), pp. 152-53, 156. In contrast, see Lawrence Haworth, "Rights, Wrongs, and Animals," *Ethics,* vol. 88, no. 1 (Jan., 1978), pp. 98-99.
52. Taylor, *Respect for Nature,* pp. 65-68.
53. Schweitzer, *Civilization and Ethics,* pp. 247-58.
54. Charles Birch and John B. Cobb, Jr., *The Liberation of Life: From the Cell to the Community* (Cambridge-New York: Cambridge University Press, 1981), p. 170.
55. Compare Rolston's discussion, *Environmental Ethics,* pp. 135-36, 144, 147.
56. Contrary to J. Baird Callicott, *In Defense of the Land Ethic* (Albany: State Univ. of New York Press, 1989), p. 115.
57. Robin Attfield, *The Ethics of Environmental Concern* (New York: Columbia Univ. Press, 1983), pp. 156-60, 179-82; compare Callicott in Regan, ed., *Matters of Life and Death,* 2nd ed., p. 410.
58. Regan, *The Case for Animal Rights,* pp. 361-363.
59. Bill Devall and George Sessions, *Deep Ecology: Living as if Nature Mattered* (Salt Lake City: Peregrine Smith Books, 1985), p. 67. For deep ecology principles, see pp. 70-76.
60. Robin Attfield, pp. 140, 154-55.
61. Compare Birch and Cobb, pp. 152-72, 205; Also, John B. Cobb, Jr. and David Ray Griffin, *Process Theology: An Introductory Exposition* (Philadelphia: The Westminster Press, 1976), pp. 76-79. For a helpful discussion from a process perspective of theoretical and practical problems in degrees of moral consideration, see Jay B. McDaniel, *Of God and Pelicans* (Louisville: Westminster/John Knox, 1989), pp. 69, 75-84, and *Earth, Sky, Gods, and Mortals* (Mystic, Conn.: Twenty Third Publications, 1990), pp. 65-68, 86-93.
62. Herman E. Daly and John B. Cobb, Jr., *For the Common Good: Redirecting the Economy Toward Community, the Environment, and a Sustainable Future* (Boston: Beacon Press, 1989), p. 378.
63. Elizabeth Dodson Gray, *Green Paradise Lost* (Wellesley, Mass.: Roundtable Press, 1979, 1981), pp. 5-6, 12, 19-20, 74-76, 148-49.
64. Callicott makes this distinction in a critique of Tom Regan and other ethical "extensionists." He, however, denies organic rights. Callicott in Regan, ed., *Matters of Life and Death,* 2nd ed., pp. 412-13.
65. Callicott in Regan, ed., *Matters of Life and Death,* pp. 402-3.
66. *Ethics from a Theocentric Perspective,* vol. II (Chicago: Univ. of Chicago Press, 1984), p. 146.
67. Ibid., pp. 16-19, 239-40, 290. vol. I (Chicago: University of Chicago Press, 1981), pp. 99-101, 209-11.
68. Aldo Leopold, *A Sand County Almanac* (New York: Ballantine, 1970), p. 262. For the

best contemporary exposition of the land ethic, see J. Baird Callicott, *In Defense of the Land Ethic* (Albany: State University of New York, 1989), esp. ch. 5, "The Conceptual Foundations of the Land Ethic." Leopold's "land ethic" should not be confused with the biblical concept of "the land." Each, however, may have some relevance for the other, and these possible connections need to be explored. For a study which draws some broad ecological implications from the Biblical concept of the land, see Geoffrey R. Lilburne, *A Sense of Place* (Nashville: Abingdon Press, 1989).

69. Leopold, *A Sand County Almanac,* p. 239.
70. Ibid., p. 253.
71. Ibid., p. 261.
72. Ibid., p. 240.
73. Ibid.
74. Wenz's terms. See Peter Wenz, *Environmental Justice* (Albany: State Univ. of New York Press, 1988).
75. J. Philip Wogaman, *Christian Moral Judgment* (Louisville, Ky.: Westminster/John Knox, 1989), pp. 116-21.
76. Ibid., pp. 116..
77. Compare the discussion in Dale Jamison, "Rights, Justice, and Duties to Provide Assistance," *Ethics,* vol. 100, no. 2 (January, 1990), pp. 349-62.
78. Taylor, *Respect for Nature,* pp. 191, 292, 304-6.
79. Ibid., p. 191.
80. Rolston, *Environmental Ethics,* p. 310.
81. Robert E. Goodin, "Ethical Principles for Environmental Protection," in Elliot and Gare, eds., p. 11.

8. POLITICAL DIRECTIONS FOR ECOLOGICAL INTEGRITY

1. Compare Bernard Crick, *In Defence of Politics,* rev. ed. (Harmondsworth, England: Pelican, 1964).
2. Ralph B. Potter, "The Logic of Moral Argument," in Paul K. Deats, Jr., ed., *Toward a Discipline of Social Ethics* (Boston: Boston University Press, 1972), p. 100.
3. For a valuable review of some of these resources, see Alan Durning, "Ecology Starts at Home," *World Watch* (March-April, 1990), pp. 39-40.
4. Michael Weisskopf, "Auto Pollution Debate Has Ring of the Past," *The Washington Post,* March 26, 1990.
5. T. Allan Comp, ed., *Blueprint for the Environment: A Plan for Federal Action* (Salt Lake City: Howe Bros., 1989).
6. Roy J. Enquist, "A Paraclete in the Public Square: Toward a Theology of Advocacy," *Theology and Public Policy,* vol. 2, no. 2 (Fall, 1990), p. 27.
7. For one example of this discussion, see Robin Lovin, ed., *Religion and American Public Life* (New York-Mahwah: Paulist Press, 1986).
8. For a good account of the dilemma, see John G. Mitchell, "War in the Woods: West Side Story," *Audubon* 92, no. 1, (January, 1990), pp. 82-121.
9. Robert Benne, *The Ethics of Democratic Capitalism: A Moral Reassessment* (Philadelphia: Fortress, 1981), pp. 251-54.
10. For a discussion, see Robert L. Stivers, *Hunger, Technology and Limits to Growth* (Minneapolis: Augsburg, 1984), pp. 14-24, 127-29.
11. The title of a new international journal that explores ecology-economics integration and for which Herman Daly is an associate editor.
12. Herman E. Daly and John B. Cobb, Jr., *For the Common Good* (Boston: Beacon Press, 1989).
13. Julian Simon and Herman Kahn, eds., *The Resourceful Earth: A Response to Global 2000* (Oxford-New York: Basil Blackwell, 1984), pp. 1-48.

14. *The Zero-Sum Society* (New York: Penguin, 1981), pp. 106-20.
15. Daly and Cobb, p. 349.
16. *Our Common Future*, p. 43.
17. See, for example, the comments in *Earth Ethics*, vol. 2, no. 1 (Fall 1990).
18. Daly and Cobb, pp. 72, 75.
19. Ibid., p. 231.
20. Compare Robert Benne, *The Ethics of Democratic Capitalism*, p. 191. He does allow, seemingly reluctantly, for other forms of regulation.
21. Beverly Wildung Harrison, *Making the Connections: Essays in Feminist Social Ethics* (Boston: Beacon Press, 1985), p. 186.
22. Reprinted in Ernest Partridge, ed., *Responsibilities to Future Generations: Environmental Ethics* (Buffalo: Prometheus Books, 1981), pp. 191-94.
23. Richard T. DeGeorge, "The Environment, Rights and Future Generations," in K. E. Goodpaster and K. M. Sayre, eds., *Ethics and Problems of the 21st Century* (Notre Dame: Univ. of Notre Dame Press, 1979), pp. 94-98. See also the essays in Robert I. Sikora and Brian Barry, eds., *Obligations to Future Generations* (Philadelphia: Temple University Press, 1978), esp. the essays by Thomas Schwartz and Brian Barry.
24. Thomas Derr, "The Obligation to the Future," in Partridge, ed., p. 41.
25. Compare Daniel Callahan, "What Obligation Do We Have to Future Generations?" in Partridge, ed., *Responsibilities to Future Generations*, pp. 81-83, 73-74.
26. Ibid., p. 73.
27. Ibid., p. 84.
28. Daly and Cobb, *For the Common Good*, pp. 152-58; compare Peter Wenz, *Environmental Justice* (Albany: State Univ. of New York, 1988), pp. 332-33.
29. Robin Attfield, *The Ethics of Environmental Concern* (New York: Columbia University Press, 1983), pp. 89-91.
30. Callahan in Partridge, ed., *Responsibilities to Future Generations*, p. 83.
31. The quoted words are an earlier theme of the World Council of Churches. Compare Ibid., p. 84.
32. Attfield, *The Ethics of Environmental Concern*, pp. 109, 136.
33. Ibid., p. 187.
34. "National Council of Churches' Energy Document: The Ethical Implications of Energy Production and Use," in Dieter T. Hessel, ed., *Energy Ethics: A Christian Response* (New York: Friendship Press, 1979), pp. 122-24.
35. For a recent example of this process, see The United Methodist Church, Genetic Science Task Force, "Draft Report to Annual and Central Conferences, December, 1990," *Christian Social Action* vol. 41, no. 1 (January, 1991), pp. 17-27.
36. For a fascinating and fair portrayal of hunting in the United States, which grasps the ambiguities and often absurdities of this "sport," see John G. Mitchell, *The Hunt* (Harmondsworth, England: Penguin, 1980). Also, Marti Kheel, "Ecofeminism and Deep Ecology: Reflection on Identity and Differences," in Carol S. Robb and Carl J. Casebolt, eds., *Covenant for a New Creation* (Maryknoll, N.Y.: Orbis Books, 1991), pp. 151-60.
37. Bill Devall and George Sessions, *Deep Ecology: Living as If Nature Mattered* (Salt Lake City: Peregrine Smith Books, 1985), p. 124.
38. Compare J. Baird Callicott, "Genesis and John Muir," in Robb and Casebolt, eds., *Covenant for a New Creation*, pp. 129-35.
39. Rolston, *Environmental Ethics*, pp. 261-62, 268-70.
40. Ibid., pp. 304-7.
41. Ibid., pp. 281-82.
42. Global Tomorrow Coalition, *Global Ecology Handbook* (Boston: Beacon Press, 1990), pp. 82-83. For the effective argument that these objectives can be acheived best by public encouragement of owner-operated farms, see Carol S. Robb, "The Rights of Farmers, the Common Good, and Feminist Questions," in Robb and Casebolt, eds., *Covenant for a New Creation*, pp. 277-78, 283. For a reformed agriculture that stresses

ecosystemic compatibility and the enhancement of rural community, see Wes Jackson, *Alters of Unhewn Stone: Science and Nature* (San Francisco: North Point Press, 1987).

43. Ibid., pp. 100-12, 116-32.
44. Bryan G. Norton, *Why Preserve Natural Diversity?* (Princeton: Princeton Univ. Press, 1987), pp. 237-39.
45. For an extensive and useful discussion, see ibid., pp. 124-26, 232-71.
46. For example, see Report of the Science Advisory Board, Relative Risk Reduction Strategies Committee, *Reducing Risk: Setting Priorities and Strategies for Environmental Protection* (Washington: EPA, 1990), p. 9. Also, note the World Charter for Nature adopted by the U. N. General Assembly, 1982.
47. Compare Larry L. Rasmussen, "The Planetary Environment: Challenge on Every Front," *Theology and Public Policy*, vol. II, no. 1 (Summer 1990), pp. 7-8.
48. World Commission on Environment and Development, *Our Common Future*, p. 261.
49. "Enhancing Global Security," *State of the World, 1989* (New York: W. W. Norton, 1988), pp. 141-42.
50. *Our Common Future*, pp. 308-47.
51. Ibid., p. 19.
52. J. Philip Wogaman, *Christian Perspectives on Politics* (Philadelphia: Fortress Press, 1988), pp. 263-65.
53. On ecojustice, see especially *The Egg*, a valuable periodical from the Center for Religion, Ethics, and Social Policy at Cornell.
54. The *Ecumenical Review*, a WCC periodical, regularly contains analyses, reports, and updates on JPIC. Volume 41, no. 4 (October, 1989) was devoted to the topic. See also Janice Love "JPIC and the Future of the Ecumenical Movement," pp. 107-19, and Wesley Granberg Michaelson, "An Ethic for Sustainability," pp. 120-30, both in *Ecumenical Review* 43, no. 1 (January 1991).
55. See Carolyn Merchant, *The Death of Nature: Women, Ecology, and the Scientific Revolution* (San Francisco: Harper & Row, 1980) and *Ecological Revolutions: Nature, Gender, and Science in New England* (Chapel Hill and London: Univ. of North Carolina Press, 1989); Rosemary Radford Ruether, *New Woman/New Earth* (New York: Seabury, 1975), pp. 186-96 and *To Change the World* (New York: Crossroad, 1981), pp. 57-70; Elizabeth Dodson Gray, *Green Paradise Lost* (Wellesley, Mass.: Roundtable Press, 1981); Margaret A. Farley, "Feminist Theology and Bioethics," and Joan L. Griscom, "On Healing the Nature/History Split in Feminist Thought," in Barbara Hilkert Andolsen, Christine E. Gudorf, and Mary Pellauer, eds., *Women's Consciousness, Women's Conscience* (San Francisco: Harper & Row, 1985); Marjorie Casebier McCoy, "Feminist Consciousness in Creation," in Philip N. Joranson and Ken Butigan, eds., *Cry of the Environment* (Santa Fe, N.M.: Bear and Co., 1984), pp. 132-47; Lois K. Daly, "Ecofeminism, Reverence for Life, and Feminist Theological Ethics," in Birch, Eakin, and McDaniel, *Liberating Life*, pp. 87-92.
56. On the relation between ecology and weaponry, see *Global Ecology Handbook*, pp. 288-298; Michael Renner, "Assessing the Military's War on the Environment" in *State of the World 1991* (New York, W. W. Norton, 1991), pp. 132-52.
57. Jonathan Schell, *The Fate of the Earth* (New York: Avon, 1982), p. 110. Also on the ecological effects, pp. 23, 61-65, 78-96, 109-38.
58. Ibid., p. 117.

SELECTED BIBLIOGRAPHY

Writings on ecological concerns are abundant. A manageable bibliography, therefore, must be highly selective—and at least somewhat arbitrary. This one concentrates on theological and ethical perspectives on ecological concerns, supplemented by a few of my favorites among the classics and several empirical resources. Only books dealing substantially or exclusively with environmental concerns are included. Thus some fine articles are excluded. Some other valuable resources are mentioned in the notes.

Abrecht, Paul, ed. *Faith, Science and the Future: Preparatory Readings for the 1979 Conference of the World Council of Churches.* Geneva: World Council of Churches (WCC), 1979.

————, ed. *Faith and Science in an Unjust World.* vol. 2: *Reports and Recommendations.* Geneva: WCC, 1980.

Alston, Dana, ed. *We Speak for Ourselves: Social Justice, Race, and Environment.* Washington, D.C.: The Panos Institute, 1990.

Anglemyer, Mary, Eleanor R. Seagraves, and Catherine C. Le Maistre. *A Search for Environmental Ethics: An Initial Bibliography.* Washington, D.C.: Smithsonian Institution Press, 1980.

Armstrong, Edward A. *Saint Francis: Nature Mystic. The Derivation and Significance of the Nature Stories in the Franciscan Legend.* Berkeley and Los Angeles: Univ. of California, 1973.

Attfield, Robin. *The Ethics of Environmental Concern.* New York: Columbia Univ. Press, 1983.

Austin, Richard Cartwright. *Beauty of the Lord: Awakening the Senses.* Atlanta: John Knox Press, 1988.

————. *Hope for the Land: Nature in the Bible.* Atlanta: John Knox Press, 1988.

Barbour, Ian G., ed. *Western Man and Environmental Ethics: Attitudes Toward Nature and Technology.* Reading, Mass.: Addison-Wesley, 1973.

————, ed. *Earth Might Be Fair: Reflections on Ethics, Religion and Ecology.* Englewood Cliffs, N.J.: Prentice-Hall, 1972.

Barnette, Henlee H. *The Church and the Ecological Crisis.* Grand Rapids: Eerdmans, 1972.

Barney, Gerald O., Study Director. *The Global 2000 Report to the President of the U.S.: Entering the 21st Century.* vol. 1: *The Summary Report.* New York: Pergamon Press, 1980.

Berry, Thomas. *The Dream of the Earth.* Sierra Club, 1988.

Bhagat, Shantilal. *Creation in Crisis: Responding to God's Covenant.* Elgin, Ill.: Brethren Press, 1990.

Birch, Bruce C., and Larry Rasmussen. *The Predicament of the Prosperous.* Philadelphia: The Westminster Press, 1978.

Birch, Charles, and John B. Cobb, Jr. *The Liberation of Life: From the Cell to the Community.* Cambridge: Cambridge Univ. Press, 1981.

Birch, Charles, William Eakin, and Jay McDaniel, eds. *Liberating Life: Contemporary Approaches to Ecological Theology.* Maryknoll, N.Y.: Orbis Books, 1990.

Black, John. *The Dominion of Man.* Edinburgh: Univ. of Edinburgh Press, 1970.

Blackstone, William T., ed. *Philosophy and Environmental Crisis.* Athens, Ga.: Univ. of Georgia Press, 1974.

Bowman, Douglas C. *Beyond the Modern Mind: The Spiritual and Ethical Challenge of the Environmental Crisis.* New York: Pilgrim Press, 1990.

Brennan, Andrew. *Thinking About Nature: An Investigation of Nature, Value, and Ecology.* Atlanta: Univ. Georgia Press, 1988.

Brown, Lester R., et al. *State of the World 1991* [Annual since 1984]*: A Worldwatch Institute Report on Progress Toward a Sustainable Society.* New York/London: W. W. Norton.

Cahn, Robert. *Footprints on the Planet: A Search for an Environmental Ethic.* New York: Universe Books, 1978.

Callicott, J. Baird. *In Defense of the Land Ethic.* Albany: SUNY Press, 1989.

Carmody, John. *Ecology and Religion: Toward a New Christian Theology of Nature.* New York/Ramsey, N.J.: Paulist Press, 1983.

Carpenter, James A. *Nature and Grace.* New York: Crossroad, 1980.

Carson, Gerald. *Men, Beasts, and Gods: A History of Cruelty and Kindness to Animals.* New York: Charles Scribner's, 1972.

Cobb, John B., Jr. *Is It Too Late? A Theology of Ecology.* Beverly Hills, Calif.: Bruce Co., 1972.

———. *Matters of Life and Death.* Louisville: Westminster/John Knox, 1991.

——— and Herman Daly. *For the Common Good.* Boston: Beacon Press, 1989.

Cohen, Jeremy. *"Be Fertile and Increase, Fill the Earth and Master It": The Ancient and Medieval Career of a Biblical Text.* Ithaca, N.Y.: Cornell University Press, 1989.

Commoner, Barry. *The Closing Circle: Nature, Man, and Technology.* New York: Alfred A. Knopf, 1971.

Comp, T. Allan. *Blueprint for the Environment: A Plan for Federal Action.* Salt Lake City: Howe Brothers, 1989.

Derr, Thomas S. *Ecology and Human Liberation.* New York: WSCF Books, 1973.

Devall, Bill, and George Sessions. *Deep Ecology: Living As If Nature Mattered.* Salt Lake City: Peregrine Smith Books, 1985.

Dubos, Rene. *The Wooing of Earth: New Perspectives on Man's Use of Nature.* New York: Charles Scribner's, 1980.

Ehrlich, Paul R. *The Machinery of Nature: The Living World Around Us and How It Works.* New York: Simon and Schuster, 1986.

———— and Anne H. Ehrlich. *The Population Explosion.* New York: Simon and Schuster, 1990.

Eisley, Loren. *The Immense Journey.* New York: Vintage, 1957. [plus others by this same biologist who has a "spiritual" bent]

Elder, Frederick. *Crisis in Eden: A Religious Study of Man and Environment.* Nashville: Abingdon Press, 1970.

Elliot, Robert, and Arran Gare, eds. *Environmental Philosophy: A Collection of Readings.* University Park: Pennsylvania State Univ. Press, 1983.

Elsdon, Ron. *Bent World: A Christian Response to the Environmental Crisis.* Downers Grove, Ill.: Intervarsity Press, 1981.

Engel, J. Ronald, and Joan Gibb Engel, eds. *Ethics of Environment and Development: Global Challenge, International Response.* Tucson: University of Arizona Press, 1990.

Fox, Mathew. *Original Blessing: A Primer in Creation Spirituality.* Santa Fe, N.M.: Bear and Co., 1983.

Glacken, Clarence J. *Traces on the Rhodian Shore: Nature and Culture in Western Thought from Ancient Times to the End of the Eighteenth Century.* Berkeley and Los Angeles: Univ. of California Press, 1967.

Global Tomorrow Coalition. *The Global Ecology Handbook.* Boston: Beacon Press, 1990.

Goodpaster, K. E., and K. M. Sayre, eds. *Ethics and Problems in the 21st Century.* Notre Dame: Univ. of Notre Dame, 1979.

Granberg-Michaelson, Wesley. *Ecology and Life: Accepting Our Environmental Responsibility.* Waco, Tex.: Word Books, 1988.

————, ed. *Tending the Garden: Essays on the Gospel and the Earth.* Grand Rapids: Eerdmans, 1987.

————. *A Worldly Spirituality: The Call to Redeem Life on Earth.* San Francisco: Harper & Row, 1984.

Gray, Elizabeth Dodson. *Green Paradise Lost.* Wellesley, Mass.: Roundtable Press, 1981.

Gregorios, Paulos. *The Human Presence: An Orthodox View of Nature.* Geneva: WCC, 1978.

Hall, Douglas John. *Imaging God: Dominion as Stewardship.* Grand Rapids: Eerdmans, 1986.

Hamilton, Michael P., ed. *This Little Planet.* New York: Scribner's, 1970.

Hargrove, Eugene C., ed. *Religion and Environmental Crisis.* Atlanta: Univ. of Georgia, 1986.

Hendry, George S. *Theology of Nature.* Philadelphia: Westminster Press, 1980.

Hessel, Dieter T., ed. *Energy Ethics: A Christian Response.* New York: Friendship Press, 1979.

————, ed. *For Creation's Sake: Preaching Ecology and Justice.* Philadelphia: Geneva Press, 1985.

Jackson, Wes. *Altars of Unhewn Stone: Science and Nature.* San Francisco: North Point Press, 1987.

Joranson, Philip N., and Ken Butigan, eds. *Cry of the Environment: Rebuilding the Christian Creation Tradition.* Santa Fe, N.M.: Bear and Co., 1984.

Krueger, Frederick W., ed. *Christian Ecology: Building an Environmental Ethic for the Twenty-First Century.* The Proceedings of the First North American Conference on Christianity and Ecology. San Francisco: North American Conference of Christian Ecologists, 1988.

Krutch, Joseph Wood. *The Voice of the Desert: A Naturalist's Interpretation.* New York: William Sloan Associates, 1954.

Leiss, William. *The Domination of Nature.* New York: George Braziller, 1972.

Leopold, Aldo. *A Sand County Almanac.* New York: Ballantine, 1970.

Lester, James P., ed. *Environmental Politics and Policy: Theories and Evidence.* Durham, N.C.: Duke Univ. Press, 1989.

Lilburne, Geoffrey R. *A Sense of Place.* Nashville: Abingdon Press, 1989.

Limouris, Gennadios, ed. *Justice, Peace and the Integrity of Creation: Insights from Orthodoxy.* Geneva: WCC, 1990.

Linzey, Andrew. *Christianity and the Rights of Animals.* New York: Crossroad, 1987.

————, and Tom Regan, eds. *Animals and Christianity: A Book of Readings.* New York: Crossroad, 1988.

————, eds. *Love the Animals: Meditations and Prayers.* New York: Crossroad, 1989.

McDaniel, Jay B. *Earth, Sky, Gods and Mortals.* Mystic, Conn.: Twenty-Third Publications, 1990.

————. *Of God and Pelicans: A Theology of Reverence for Life.* Philadelphia: Westminster/John Knox, 1989.

McDonagh, Sean. *To Care for the Earth: A Call to a New Theology.* Santa Fe, N.M.: Bear and Co., 1986.

McFague, Sallie. *Models of God: Theology for an Ecological, Nuclear Age.* Philadelphia: Fortress, 1987.

McKibben, Bill. *The End of Nature.* New York: Random House, 1989.

Matthiessen, Peter. *Wildlife in America.* New York: Viking Press, 1959. [classic history; rev., updated ed., 1987.]

Meadows, Donella H., et al. *The Limits to Growth: A Report for the Club of Rome's Project on the Predicament of Mankind.* New York: Universe Books, 1972.

Merchant, Carolyn. *The Death of Nature: Women, Ecology and the Scientific Revolution.* San Fransisco: Harper & Row, 1980.

————. *Ecological Revolutions: Nature, Gender, and Science in New England.* Chapel Hill: Univ. of North Carolina Press, 1989.

Midgley, Mary. *Animals and Why They Matter: A Journey Around the Species Barrier.* Hammondsworth, England: Penguin Books, 1983.

Milbrath, Lester W. *Envisioning a Sustainable Society*. Albany: State Univ. of New York Press, 1989.

Miller, Hardon B., and William H. Williams, eds. *Ethics and Animals*. Clifton, N.J.: Human Press, 1983.

Mitcham, Carl, and Jim Grote, eds. *Theology and Technology: Essays in Christian Analysis and Exegesis*. Lanham, Md.: University Press of America, 1984. [extensive annotated bibliographies, including ones on theologies of creation and nature, pp. 400-14, and religious environmental ethics, pp. 441-69]

Moltmann, Jürgen. *The Future of Creation: Collected Essays*. Philadelphia: Fortress Press, 1979.

———. *God in Creation: A New Theology of Creation and the Spirit of God*. San Francisco: Harper & Row, 1985.

Moule, C. F. D. *Man and Nature in the New Testament: Some Reflections on Biblical Ecology*. Philadelphia: Fortress Press, 1967.

Murphy, Charles M. *At Home on Earth: Foundations for a Catholic Ethic of the Environment*. New York: Crossroad, 1989.

Nash, Roderick. *The Rights of Nature: A History of Environmental Ethics*. Madison: Univ. of Wisconsin, 1989.

———. *Wilderness and the American Mind*. New Haven: Yale Univ. Press, 1967 (and subsequent editions).

Norton, Brian G. *Why Preserve Natural Diversity?* Princeton, N.J.: Princeton Univ. Press, 1987.

———, ed. *On the Preservation of Species*. Princeton, N.J.: Princeton Univ. Press, 1986.

Partridge, Ernest, ed. *Responsibilities to Future Generations: Environmental Ethics*. Buffalo: Prometheus Press, 1981.

Passmore, John. *Man's Responsibility for Nature: Ecological Problems and Western Tradition*. 2nd ed. London: Duckworth, 1980.

Presbyterian Eco-Justice Task Force. *Keeping and Healing the Creation*. Louisville: Committee on Social Witness Policy, Presbyterian Church (USA), 1989.

Regan, Tom. *All That Dwell Therein: Animal Rights and Environmental Ethics*. Berkeley and Los Angeles: Univ. of California Press, 1982.

———. *The Case for Animal Rights*. Berkeley and Los Angeles: Univ. of California, 1983.

———, ed. *Matters of Life and Death: New Introductory Essays in Moral Philosophy*. New York: Random House, 1980 (First edition: William Blackstone, "The Search for an Environmental Ethic"; 2nd ed., 1986: J. Baird Callicott, "The Search for an Environmental Ethic").

———, and Peter Singer, eds. *Animal Rights and Human Obligations*. Englewood Cliffs, N.J.: Prentice-Hall, 1976.

Regenstein, Lewis G. *Replenish the Earth*. New York: Crossroad, 1991.

Robb, Carol S. and Carl J. Casebolt, eds. *Covenant for a New Creation: Ethics, Religion, and Public Policy*. Maryknoll, N.Y.: Orbis Books, 1991.

249

Rolston, Holmes, III. *Environmental Ethics: Duties to and Values in the Natural World.* Philadelphia: Temple Univ. Press, 1988.

Ruether, Rosemary Radford. *New Woman New Earth.* New York: Seabury, 1975.

Rust, Eric C. *Nature—Garden or Desert? An Essay in Environmental Theology.* Waco, Tex.: Word Books, 1971.

———. *Science and Faith: Towards a Theological Understanding of Nature.* New York: Oxford Univ. Press, 1967.

Santmire, H. Paul. *Brother Earth: Nature, God, and Ecology in Time of Crisis.* New York-Camden: Thomas Nelson, 1970.

———. *The Travail of Nature: The Ambiguous Ecological Promise of Christian Theology.* Philadelphia: Fortress Press, 1985.

Science Action Coalition with Albert J. Fritsch. *Environmental Ethics: Choices for Concerned Citizens.* Garden City, N.Y.: Anchor/Doubleday, 1980.

Shinn, Roger L., ed. *Faith and Science in an Unjust World.* vol. 1: Plenary Presentations. Geneva: WCC, 1980.

Sikora, Robert I., and Brian Barry, eds. *Obligations to Future Generations.* Philadelphia: Temple Univ. Press, 1978.

Silver, Cheryl Simon, with Ruth S. DeFries for the National Academy of Sciences. *One Earth, One Future: Our Changing Global Environment.* Washington, D.C.: National Academy Press, 1990.

Singer, Peter. *Animal Liberation: A New Ethic for Our Treatment of Animals.* New York: Avon, 1975.

Sittler, Joseph. *Essays on Nature and Grace.* Philadelphia: Fortress, 1972.

Söelle, Dorothee with Shirley A. Cloyes. *To Work and to Love: A Theology of Creation.* Philadelphia: Fortress Press, 1984.

Sorrell, Roger. *St. Francis Assisi: Tradition and Innovation in Western Christian Attitudes Toward the Environment.* New York: Oxford Univ. Press, 1988.

Spring, David, and Eileen Spring, eds. *Ecology and Religion in History.* New York: Harper & Row, 1974.

Steck, Odil Hannes. *World and Environment.* Nashville: Abingdon Press, 1978.

Stefferud, Alfred, ed. *Christians and the Good Earth.* New York: Friendship Press, 1972.

Stivers, Robert L. *Hunger, Technology, and Limits to Growth: Christian Responsibilities for Three Ethical Issues.* Minneapolis: Augsburg, 1984.

Stone, Christopher D. *Earth and Other Ethics: The Case for Moral Pluralism.* New York: Harper & Row, 1987.

Stone, Glen C., ed. *A New Ethic for a New Earth.* New York: Friendship Press, 1971.

Taylor, Paul W. *Respect for Nature: A Theory of Environmental Ethics.* Princeton: Princeton Univ. Press, 1986.

Teale, Edwin Way, ed. *The Wilderness World of John Muir.* Boston: Houghton Mifflin, 1954.

Thomas, Keith. *Man and the Natural World: A History of the Modern Sensibility.* New York: Pantheon, 1983.

Tobias, Michael, ed. *Deep Ecology*, rev. San Marcos, Calif.: Avant Books, 1988.

Turner, James. *Reckoning with the Beast: Animals, Pain and Humanity in the Victorian Mind.* Baltimore: Johns Hopkins Univ. Press, 1980.

Vischer, Lukas, ed. *Rights of Future Generations, Rights of Nature.* Geneva: World Alliance of Reformed Churches, 1990.

Wallace-Hadrill, David S. *The Greek Patristic View of Nature.* New York: Barnes and Noble, 1968.

Wenz, Peter. *Environmental Justice.* Albany, N.Y.: State Univ. of New York Press, 1988.

Wilkinson, Loren, ed. *Earthkeeping: Christian Stewardship of Natural Resources.* Grand Rapids: Eerdmans, 1980.

Williams, George H. *Wilderness and Paradise in Christian Thought.* New York: Harper & Row, 1962.

Wilson, Edward O., ed. *Biodiversity.* Washington: National Academy Press, 1988.

―――. *Biophilia: The Human Bond With Other Species.* Cambridge and London: Harvard Univ., 1984.

World Commission on Environment and Development. *Our Common Future.* New York and Oxford: Oxford Univ. Press, 1987. [Summary: Gregory G. Lebel and Hal Kane, *Sustainable Development: A Guide to Our Common Future.* Washington: Global Tomorrow Coalition, 1989.]

World Resources Institute and International Institute for Environment and Development, with United Nations Environmental Programme. *World Resources 1988-89* (and 1990-91). New York: Basic Books, 1988 (1990) [biennial].

Worster, Donald. *Nature's Economy: The Roots of Ecology.* Garden City, N.Y.: Anchor/Doubleday, 1979.

Young, John. *Sustaining the Earth: A Post-Environmentalist View.* Cambridge, Mass.: Harvard Univ. Press, 1990.

INDEX